ASCENT AND DECLINE OF NATIVE AND COLONIAL TRADING

ASCENT AND DECLINE OF NATIVE AND COLONIAL TRADING

Tale of Four Indian Cities

VIJAY K. SETH

Los Angeles | London | New Delhi
Singapore | Washington DC | Melbourne

First published in 2019 by

SAGE Publications India Pvt Ltd
B1/I-1 Mohan Cooperative Industrial Area
Mathura Road, New Delhi 110 044, India
www.sagepub.in

SAGE Publications Inc
2455 Teller Road
Thousand Oaks, California 91320, USA

SAGE Publications Ltd
1 Oliver's Yard, 55 City Road
London EC1Y 1SP, United Kingdom

SAGE Publications Asia-Pacific Pte Ltd
18 Cross Street #10-10/11/12
China Square Central
Singapore 048423

Published by Vivek Mehra for SAGE Publications India Pvt Ltd, typeset in 10.5/13 pts Berkeley by Zaza Eunice, Hosur, Tamil Nadu, India and printed at Chaman Enterprises, New Delhi.

Library of Congress Cataloging-in-Publication Data Available

ISBN: 978-93-532-8084-0 (HB)

SAGE Team: Abhijit Baroi, Vandana Gupta, Shaonli Deb and Kanika Mathur

To

My family members

Meera Seth, Arpita Seth Saxena, Vishal Saxena and Yatharth Saxena.

Thank you for choosing a SAGE product!
If you have any comment, observation or feedback,
I would like to personally hear from you.

Please write to me at **contactceo@sagepub.in**

Vivek Mehra, Managing Director and CEO, SAGE India.

Bulk Sales

SAGE India offers special discounts
for purchase of books in bulk.
We also make available special imprints
and excerpts from our books on demand.

For orders and enquiries, write to us at

Marketing Department
SAGE Publications India Pvt Ltd
B1/I-1, Mohan Cooperative Industrial Area
Mathura Road, Post Bag 7
New Delhi 110044, India

E-mail us at **marketing@sagepub.in**

Subscribe to our mailing list
Write to **marketing@sagepub.in**

This book is also available as an e-book.

CONTENTS

ACKNOWLEDGEMENTS

I have been working on this theme for the last five years, and have deep gratitude towards my family members, Meera Seth, Arpita Seth Saxena, Vishal Saxena and Yatharth Saxena, for their exemplary bonding when the family experienced an extremely difficult situation during this period.

While trying to understand its various dimensions, I have learned a great deal about my problematic from the writings of several scholars. Some of these scholars widened my perspective on the theme, some others compelled me to seek answers to new questions, and still others provided strength and support to my understanding. I am grateful to all of them. The scholars who variously impacted my understanding are Professors Daron Acemoglu, James Robinson, D. C. North, William J. Baumol, E. J. Hobsbawm, Maxine Berg, Deirdre N. McCloskey, Peter Watson, David Landes, Andre Gunder Frank, Burton Stein and Morris David Morris.

I also want to place on record my gratitude for the benefits that I received from the writings of some of the leading economic, business and maritime historians who have made significant contribution towards the understanding of the Indian historiography. These scholars have significantly influenced my writing. Their writings acted as lamp posts and milestones, which guided my intellectual journey during the writing of the book. These scholars are Professors K. N. Chaudhuri, Ashin Das Gupta, Dwijendra Tripathi, Irfan Habib, Amiya Kumar Bagchi, Sanjay Subrahmanyam, Rajat Kanta Ray, Giorgio Riello, Tirthankar Roy, Lakshmi Subramanian and Prasannan Parthasarathi.

I will also like to mention the impact of the writings and lectures of my teachers at the Delhi School of Economics, who introduced my interest in economic history. These teachers are Professors Tapan Raychaudhuri, Dharma Kumar, J. Krishnamurty and Om Prakash.

Since most of the writing of this book took place while I was working at the Faculty of Management Studies, University of Delhi, and at the International Management Institute, New Delhi, I would like to acknowledge the benefits of valuable discussions that I had with some of my colleagues, Professors H. V. Verma, Joy Mitra, Pankaj Sinha and Amit Bardhan of the Faculty of Management Studies. I am especially indebted to Professor Amit Bardhan, who helped me in procuring relevant books from amazon.com and Flipkart. I am also indebted to Professor G. K. Kapoor of the International Management Institute for long conversations over cups of tea.

I'm indebted to Mr Abdul Hamid Aboo, who remained constant in my life along with my family members. He contributed in my transformation by correcting my deficiencies and improving my capabilities. I also want to acknowledge the help that I received from my two doctoral students, Dr Bharat Singh and Dr Ritu Chikkara, while writing this book.

I am equally indebted to the librarian and library staff of the Faculty of Management Studies, University of Delhi; the International Management Institute, New Delhi; Ratan Tata Library of the Delhi School of Economic Growth, New Delhi; and Jawaharlal Nehru University, New Delhi. I also want to mention the contribution of Sarojini Rawat and Nishar Ahmed for converting the bad handwriting of my manuscript into a readable format.

Finally, I want to acknowledge the contribution made by Abhijit Baroi, Vandana Gupta and whole team of SAGE Publications who have improved the presentation of the contents of the book.

INTRODUCTION

The another surprising aspect regarding unawareness about history is that people are unaware of aspects of all the history of the cities where they live and die, how that particular city was conquered, the number of years that have elapsed since its last occupation, how the conquerors dealt with its people, how they transacted their affairs, how they lived and went about doing things, in what manner they die, and how time and society have treated them, their wives, families, followers and supporters.

—Zia-ud Din Barani (1357, 1)

Of course, ideas do not rain down from heaven. Commercial and urban societies, which could afford to sustain a substantial number of people living by their wits rather than having to toil in the fields, were necessary if intellectual ideas were to be created.... From this competitive natural selection process, changes in the intellectual environment emerged, with far-reaching consequences for the creation of 'modern' polities and economies.

—Joel Mokyr (2009, 2)

The writing of this book is inspired by the famous novel *A Tale of Two Cities* (first appeared in 1859) by Charles Dickens (1812–1870). In this novel, Dickens has told the story of experiences of people living in the capital cities of two powerful nations of Europe—London (Britain) and Paris (France)—at the same historical time. His objective was to show how people living in these two cities had divergent experiences, because they were living in cities embedded in different situations. However, unlike Dickens, I am narrating the story of four cities of the Indian subcontinent. This is because Indian subcontinent is vast and highly diversified, where experience of one region may be at variance with other regions. It is generally being said that India is a land of paradoxes, because any phenomenon which is true about one region is usually not true about other regions. To capture the impact of spatial variance in the experiences of cities, I have identified two cities—Dacca (now Dhaka) and Calcutta (now Kolkata)—from the eastern coast and two cities—Surat and Bombay (now Mumbai)—from the western coast. This choice is quite relevant, because in the absence of existence of means of transportation and communication, western and eastern regions of the Indian subcontinent existed as separate economic regions connected with each other with a fragile network created by the Mughal Empire and colonial administration.

In the present book, I have deliberately used their historical names rather than their contemporary names to put these cities in the context of their historical circumstances. I would also like to emphasize here that in both the set of cities, I have selected one *native* city and one *colonial* city. Both the native cities were centres of production of manufactured products by their *traditional flexible manufacturing*. These products had global demand. The colonial cities were established by the foreign trading company—the East India Company—as *siblings* of the native cities as trading bases to export the manufactured products produced in the native cities. The objective of telling the story of these four cities is to explore the consequences of symbiotic existences between native cities and colonial cities.

Native cities were embedded in the native economy and obtained all the elements for their sustenance from their linkages which they enjoyed with native economy. Colonial cities were generally port cities which had emerged as a consequence of the existence of a rudimentary form of globalization that had evolved after the trading links were established by European trading companies. These linkages emerged after the period of discovery, when sea route to India was discovered by Vasco da Gama in 1498. Initially, these cities were trading bases of European trading companies, but as the process of territorial occupation began by these trading companies, these cities assumed the role of colonial cities. It is because spread of colonialism began from these port cities to the inland territories. The colonial cities were used as *key devices* by colonial power to establish their political and economic hegemony on the Indian subcontinent.[1]

In this book, I am telling the story to explain to what extent colonial cities were able to use their political and economic power to impact wealth and prosperity of native cities as a consequence of their symbiotic existence. Here I am using these four cities as a proxy for understanding the impact of colonialism on pan subcontinental economy of India. People might question me for taking the experience of these four cities as a proxy for narrating the experience of the whole continent during colonial period. My belief is based on the premise that cities represent geographical spaces, which have been the birthplaces of, almost all, our more valued notions about symbols of civilization. Cities represent the microcosm of civilizations, societies and economies in which they are embedded. These are spaces where talented, rich, powerful and creative people live in greater numbers. It is due to these reasons that cities are described as a symbol of the level of development of civilization, where human experience is transformed into visible signs such as temples, markets, forts, palaces, places of learning, markets and administration.[2]

Cities emerged when societies had achieved a certain threshold level of developmental capabilities in terms of economy, knowledge base and political organization. It is because cities emerged at a culmination of a long-drawn-out process of evolution of human societies, which began with the *Neolithic revolution*.[3] The Neolithic revolution began when human beings were able to domesticate animals and plants and bring them together at a higher level, with the two earliest forms of economic activities, namely food gathering and hunting. At this level of human existence, human beings developed capability to increase, improve and control the availability of food. The integration of these two activities forced migration of human beings from dense forests and highlands through valleys to the vast alluvial plains, near river valleys. The increase in importance of fertile land led to increasing attachment to land. The attachment to land also forced them to embrace a settled life pattern and give up their nomadic existence. Women in hunter-gatherer bands, which were quite mobile in search of food and animals, could not carry more than one child at a time, unless and until the little one could walk and keep pace with the mobile band. On the contrary, settled cultivators had no such problem associated with carrying infants while moving. Therefore, women in these societies could give birth to as many children as they could feed.[4]

The settled life set in motion several kinds of forces, which completely transformed the life of human beings. Cultivation of crops got extended from food crops to crops to obtain natural fibres such as cotton, flex and hemp. The production of crops helped in domestication of animals, which further increased the supply of food items such as meat and milk, aided the obtainability of hide and wool, and the use of these animals for ploughing fields and as means of transportation. Along with surplus food, when population began to increase in size, it affected the social and political organization. The hunting band got transformed into tribe and to chiefdom. The political space which was occupied by chief became city. Cities grew based on their capacity to appropriate tribute and taxes. Human beings began to use animals like elephants and horses in war. Use of animals in war facilitated the territorial expansion of the polity.[5] The use of horses allowed Huns to attack Rome and helped Chengiz Khan to establish the vast Mongol Empire, ever witnessed by human beings, at that point in time. It was a descendant of Chengiz Khan, Babur Mirza, who founded the Mughal Empire in the Indian subcontinent.[6]

Since their origin as *Homo sapiens*, human societies have progressively replaced smaller, simpler organizations with larger and complex ones, culminating in the formation of the state. Early states had a dynastic leader with a title equivalent of a king. Every kingdom evolved its slogans which prepared its citizen for making supreme sacrifice of his life to protect its territories.[7] It was the birth of state which facilitated the origin of cities, complex social organizations, polity, language, collective learning, belief systems, crafts, trade, art, music, literature and innovations.

The earliest cities emerged on fertile river valleys such as those of the Euphrates, Tigris, Nile and Indus. These earliest cities were Eridu, Uruk, Ur, Mohenjodaro and Harappa. In Mesopotamia (Iraq), between two rivers—Tigris and Euphrates—emerged the Sumerian city of Ur. The city Ur enjoyed the reputation of having achieved several historical firsts: the first school, first historian, first pharmacopeia, first clock, first arch, first proverb and fable, first garden, first epic literature and first love song.[8] In the British Museum one can find a wooden box, inlaid with mosaic that was found at the Royal cemetery. The Wooden box is inlaid with shells, red stone, and lapisluzuli. This box amply reveals that even this earliest city, evolved by human beings, had spatial connectivity with rest of the world; for example, lapis lazuli came from Afghanistan, redstone from India and shells from the Gulf.[9] Similarly, Harappa and Mohenjo Daro were carefully planned cities with advanced drainage system. The stone seal that has been discovered from the site of Indus Valley demonstrates that these two cities were centres of trade and manufacturing which had connectivity with several distant lands.[10] These earliest cities were followed by cities for which we have recorded history. Some of these cities are Athens, Sparta, Troy, Banaras, Ujjain, Patliputra, Alexandria, Rome, Bethlehem, Jerusalem, Constantinople, Cairo and Shiraz.

Ancient Greece is one of the oldest societies, which has been studied in greater detail by the Western scholars. The knowledge about Greece is based on the most important Greece *polis* (city state), Athens. The people living in Athens enjoyed consumption of luxuries and high level of material culture. Along with this, Athens 'was [the] first democracy and fully developed money economy, where coins of various denominations including karmata (small coins) existed' (Cartledge Cohen and Foxhall 2002; Morries and Saller 2007; Trentman 2012). It is because of the character of these cities that famous historian Niall Ferguson writes, 'A civilization as etymology of the word suggests, revolves around its cities.... In many ways it is cities that are heroes' (Ferguson 2011, 2). But cities do not include only palaces, tombs, forts and other monuments; they also represent prevalent structure of governance customs, beliefs and manners of its inhabitants. Therefore, a city is more than 'the beauty of the Sistine Chapel' (Ferguson 2011, 8). This is amply revealed by the mystique of Athens—Herodotus, the first historian; Socrates, the first philosopher; Hippocrates, the first man of medicine, all lived in Athens. Plato founded his academy and Aristotle founded his Lyceum in the same city.

These cities were earliest examples of experiments of the advantages of living together of a large number of people. These advantages emerged despite the fact that these people were generally strangers to each other but lived together because of cooperation that was necessitated by their interdependence. These cities also became important places for creativity. This happened because cities provided preconditions for the flowering of creativity by giving incentives to talented people. It is due to these obvious facts that creativity among human societies has always been associated with the cities.[11] It is important to mention here that the oldest surviving work of literature, *Epic of Gilgamesh,* was written in Uruk. The important scholarly writings of Aristotle, Plato and Homer were written in Athens. Florence provided the right milieu for the creative works of Leonardo da Vinci and Michelangelo. The river banks of Banaras created a conducive environment for the creative works of Tulsidas and Kabir. All the compositions of Kalidas were written in Ujjain. The encyclopaedic works of Abul Fazal Allami—*Akbar Namah* and *Ain-i-Akbari*—were written in Agra and Lahore.

However, I would like to draw the attention of the readers to the fact that there have been scholars and thinkers who viewed cities in the context of dichotomy between city and village. These social scientists view cities as living spaces, created by social and economic parasites and leisure classes whose lives depended on exploitation of rural masses. These parasitic people survived by appropriating a large part of the surplus created by villages and by drawing manpower from villages for recruitment of soldiers, for production of crafts-based goods and for the provision of low-end services. In the writings of these scholars, cities and villages are binary opposites, where cities represent all negative features and villages represent positive elements of civilizations—namely cities have complex and hierarchical society, villages are places of simplicity; cities are inhabited by parasitical, leisure-loving and consuming classes, whereas in villages, productive people live. Similarly, they describe cities as dirty and crowded places and villages as clean and spacious. However, I want to emphasize that there exists complementarity between the city and the countryside. Moreover, it is my belief that whether you like cities or dislike them, they are interesting places to study. I also believe that cities were inhabited by people who had greater advantages in terms of power, finance and talent. If the cities experienced negative impact of the consequences of colonialism, the rest of the economy which was more vulnerable, weak and dependent on cities for their protection, might have suffered much more as a consequence of colonialism.

Having said what I have to say about my reasons for telling the story of four cities of the Indian subcontinent, I am beginning the story of these two sets of cities from an important period of the economic and political history of the Indian subcontinent, when two powerful forces of globalization simultaneously impacted the biography of these cities. These two powerful forces of globalization were (a) empire building and (b) arrival of European trading companies in the Indian subcontinent. The objective of empire builders was to unite the entire world into a single empire, and trading companies were intended to integrate fragmented markets into a single market. These two powerful influences gave birth to two different kinds of polities, which differently impacted these cities. First, the entry of European companies, through *sea route*, began with the discovery of sea route to India by Vasco da Gama in 1498. Second was the laying of the foundation of the Mughal Empire, with the entry of Mughals through *land route*, when Babur Mirza defeated the forces of Ibraham Lodhi in the First Battle of Panipat in 1526.

The impact of these two powerful forces of globalization can be appreciated if we view the process of globalization as a historical process of integration of fragmented geopolitical spaces. It is the integration of fragmented polities which facilitated the establishment of economic, cultural, political and social connectivity between them. Once connectivity between these fragmented polities was established, the individual unit of space no longer remained the same; it was transformed and reinvented. Empires provided structure of governance which was necessary to protect private property and enforcement of contract. Therefore, empires provided essential prerequisites of the process of development.[12] Empire building in this sense also played an important role in the process of globalization, by establishing connectivity between fragmented polities.

For instance, concurrent existence of four empires—namely the Roman Empire (spread around the Mediterranean), the Parthian Empire (covering landmass of two rivers along Iran), the Kushan Empire (starting from the Pamirs was spread along borders of China) and Han dynasty's China Empire—during the first century of the Christian era created connectivity between these empires. The connectivity provided favourable conditions to risk-taking merchants to engage in trade beyond the borders of their countries. To meet the needs of Rome's wealthy nobles, for their ultimate object of desire— namely silk—a trade route was established by these merchants. The route began at Venice in Rome and terminated at Chang'an, the capital of Han dynasty of China. The route has been described by historians as the *Silk Road*.[13] A similar role was played by the super empire established by Pope Gregory VII in 1075. This empire emerged as a consequence when the Roman Catholic Church founded its supremacy over European states. After the formation of this *celestial state,* merchants and entrepreneurs did not depend on the patronage of despotic and predatory rulers.[14] Unlike the contemporary process of globalization, the process of globalization which was evolved by empires emerged as a consequence of military or political events. The Mughal Empire played the same role in the Indian subcontinent. It established connectivity by unifying fragmented polities. It also integrated regional economies to create an integrated economy of continental size. The integration of fragmented economies and markets provided necessary conditions for the growth of traditional flexible manufacturing. The arrival of the European trading companies further extended the commercial integration of the economy of the subcontinent with emerging world trading networks.

The geographical space in which the two cities of the eastern coast, namely Dacca and Calcutta, are located was known as Bengal Subah (Bengal province) during the Mughal Empire. Bengal became part of the Mughal Empire during the rule of emperor Humayun, with an interregnum of seven years (1538–1545) when Sher Shah Suri ruled Bengal. During the rule of Humayun and Sher Shah Suri, Lakhnauti or Gaur was capital of Bengal Subah, which was renamed Jannatabad by emperor Humayun. Dacca became the capital of Bengal Subah in 1610.[15]

The Portuguese were the first European merchants who established direct trading link with the Indian subcontinent, after the arrival of Portuguese navigator Vasco da Gama in 1498. After occupying Goa from Sultan of Bijapur in 1510, the Portuguese also established several fortified trading settlements in Bengal at Hooghly and Chittagong. The Dutch trading company known as *Vereengide Oost-Indische Compagnie* (United East Indies Company), which was formed in 1602, also developed trading settlements at Chinsura in Bengal. The French trading company *Compagnie des Indes Orientales* (French East Indies Company) entered the Indian subcontinent in 1644 and developed its trading base at Pondicherry (now Puducherry). It also established its trading base at Chandannagar in Bengal.[16] The East India Company, the British trading company, was formed on New Year's Eve,[17] 1600, when Queen Elizabeth I signed a royal charter that granted monopoly to trade with India. The East India Company developed its trading base in Bengal when it received permission from the Mughal emperor Aurangzeb to open its offices and construct Fort Williams by occupying territories of the three villages, namely Kolikata, Gobindapur and Sutanati, located on the banks of river Hooghly in 1690. It is here that the new settlement of the East India Company grew with the name of Calcutta.[18] All these trading companies that established their trading bases in Bengal had the common purpose to take over the largest possible proportion of the market share of products produced by the traditional flexible manufacturing of Dacca.

The city of Surat was part of the Gujarat Subah of the Mughal Empire. Before it was assimilated in the Mughal Empire in 1573, it was ruled by several Hindu and Muslim dynasties.[19] The Portuguese were the first Europeans who developed direct link with Surat. They established direct contact with Surat much earlier than its integration with the Mughal Empire.[20] Thereafter Dutch trading company *Vereenigde Oost Indische Compagnie* also established trading contact with Surat in 1602.[21] The East India Company began its operation at Surat in 1608. However, it received formal permission from Mughal emperor Jahangir to conduct business at Surat after its victory over the Portuguese in 1612.[22] The last European trading company which began its operation at Surat was French trading company *Compagnie de Indes Orientales* in 1670. It was at this point in time that Bombay was formed by integrating the seven islands, namely Wadala, Muzgaon, Mahim, Parel, Mutugasion, Old Woman's Island and Colaba, when the Portuguese occupied these islands. The British King Charles II received Bombay as dowry from the Portuguese, when he married Portuguese Princess Catherine of Braganza in 1662. The East India Company acquired territorial rights over these territories from King Charles II in 1668.[23]

The historical description given about the four cities suggests why we have selected them to narrate their stories. This is quite obvious that unlike the rest of the economy of the Indian subcontinent which experienced the impact of only one force of globalization for a considerable period, namely the Mughal Empire, Surat, Bombay, Dacca and Calcutta simultaneously experienced the consequences of a second force of globalization, namely the arrival of different European trading companies. It is due to this reason that these four cities experienced intertwined impact of both the forces of globalization and thus represent important examples for the understanding of how colonialism impacted these cities. Both sets of cities shared same historical circumstances, yet they experienced different outcomes.

In both sets of cities, the native cities, namely Surat and Dacca, were important centres of traditional flexible manufacturing. Traditional flexible manufacturing was a form of organization of handicrafts. This form of organization of production became dominant during the Mughal Empire. The organizational pattern of traditional flexible manufacturing emerged as a consequence of an emerging nexus between craftsmen and merchants. Their nexus provided it capability to produce crafts-based products for mass markets. It is their capability which gave this form of organization competitive advantage to crafts-based manufacturing not only to supply its product to domestic markets but also to satisfy the demands of global markets. This form of production of handicrafts enriched these cities and also attracted the attention of European trading companies to develop trading links with them. It was through the process of their interaction with these two cities that they established Bombay and Calcutta.

In the present book, I have narrated the story of these four cities for the period 1500–1947, a time when these cities experienced different political regimes, which impacted these cities differently. I have ended the story of the four cities in 1947, because after India's Independence, distinction between colonial cities and native cities disappeared. Initially fortunes of these four cities were determined by traditional flexible manufacturing which was located in the native cities. When nature of manufacturing shifted from traditional flexible manufacturing to modern manufacturing, the growth- and prosperity-creating force shifted from native cities to colonial cities. It was the shift in the nature of manufacturing which created great divide between native cities and colonial cities in their levels of development. In changing the location of wealth and prosperity, the shifts in political regimes played a significant role. It is also worth mentioning here that colonial cities did not experience significant shifts in political regimes because they were continuously ruled by the colonial powers. It was the native cities which experienced significant impact of changes in the political regimes. All the four cities shared a long historical period from 1500 to 1947. During this long-shared history, these four cities experienced the impact of three different political regimes—the Mughal Empire (1526–1757), rule of the East India Company (1757–1857) and the British Raj (1858–1947). The shifts in political regimes had serious consequence for these cities. The main interest of telling the story of these four cities is to narrate how the forces that lead to development and prosperity keep changing their location with changes in the political regime.

The economy of each nation, region or city is embedded in political regimes. Political regimes are products of long historical processes, which give a territory rules regarding how it is going to be governed, how political power will be shared among different stakeholders and what will be its extent. Political regimes work according to their given structure which consists of institutions, regulations and their enforcement. These different constituents of political regimes work as constraints on the behaviour of different stakeholders. This is because they provide basic framework for the nature of human conduct.[24] Institutions and regulations that are formulated by political regimes also work as mechanisms through which different economic agents make their choices.[25] This is because institutions and regulations create a formal structure of incentives and disincentives, which impact choices made by different economic agents. It is when political regimes provide institutional and regulatory support to growth-promoting economic agents, which have capability to take the economy to the next level of development, that economies experience growth and prosperity.

On the contrary, if political regimes are monopolized with absolute powers, like monarchy or dictatorship, they establish regulations and institutions which enrich them and provide condition for the continuance of their political power at the cost of society. Political regimes of this type create *extractive institutions*. The political regimes that distribute political power and empower the vast majority of their members create plurality. It is plurality which facilitates the formation of *inclusive institutions*. Inclusive political institutions are based on the foundation of broad-based distribution of political power. In such polities, no single individual or group of people can take advantage. Nations fail when they are forced to work under extractive institutions.[26]

Political regimes also help in development of circumstances which may lead to economic decline and stagnation. This happens when political regimes establish incentive structure that promotes unproductive economic activities.[27] The structure of incentives and disincentives (or reward and punishment) evolved by a political regime determines the relative pay-off that it offers on different economic activities and occupations. It is when political regimes create an incentive structure which motivates their members to choose careers as innovative entrepreneurs and wealth creators that they facilitate the process of economic development and prosperity. The creation of incentive structure in favour of transformative economic agents is necessary because history gives us knowledge about several instances when political regimes were monopolized by those vested interests which obtained maximum gains from status quo. It has been the historically validated experience that when political regimes accorded dignity to wealth creators—the people living in cities who were despised by clergy, aristocrats, nobles and peasants, and for whom Marxists harboured maximum dislike and called them bourgeoisie—and gave them liberty to pursue wealth-creating activities that societies prospered. The societies progressed when these sections of the society were given liberty.[28] Here liberty stands for the liberation of wealth creators from rules and regulations that act as constraints on their behaviour. According dignity to wealth creators means that the idea of being honourable is shifted from the nobles, knights and priests to wealth creators. Bourgeoisie consisted of a new class of people which enjoyed power and influence, independent of traditional advantages of family, status and patronage. To belong to this class, a person had to establish that he has created wealth by individual effort. Since they followed professions which were new, they lived in cities.[29]

The process of providing dignity and liberty to bourgeoisie happens when political class begins to re-evaluate the city and its immense creativity. It was this important change in thinking which led to the idea of laissez-faire (make what you want) and laissez-passer (trade what you want). It is expected that an economy based on foundations established by bourgeoisie will experience not only material progress but also moral progress. This will help in creating a world of material with plenty, ever-growing enlightenment, reason and human opportunities.[30] Responding to the needs of innovators and wealth creators by political classes, who generally lived in cities, was always objected by priests, warriors, nobles and kings, who largely belonged to rent-seeking classes and enriched themselves by collecting tributes, taxes and rent from other classes. This group of people only redistributed wealth of the society in their favour without creating it. Voltaire shifted this bias against innovator and wealth creators by questioning the very basis of the existence of rent seekers, when he asked a fundamental question: 'I do not know, which is more useful to the state, a well powerful *lord* who knows precisely when king gets up in the morning, or a great *merchant*, who enriches his country sending orders from his office to Surat or Cairo, and contributes to the well-being of the society'.[31]

However, one should also remember that throughout human history there are examples when innovative entrepreneurs did not contribute to economic growth and prosperity. This happens when the same individual who has capability to organize productive economic activities redirects his capabilities to organize private army or crime syndicate. The warlords with private armies, bandits, gangsters and mafias have used their entrepreneurial skills to increase private wealth, power and prestige without creating additional wealth. Like rent-seeking classes, they only redistribute existing wealth in their favour by stealing, extortion, robbery and land grab. It is, however, not necessary that these unproductive entrepreneurs use violence.[32]

To explain this distinction between productive and unproductive entrepreneurship, we have the example of Heron, a mathematician and engineer of the Roman Empire, who lived in Alexandria during the first century AD. He created several gadgets ranging from slot machine to a working steam engine. Heron's inventions did not attract the attention of productive entrepreneurs, who would have converted his inventions into profitable innovations. This happened because at that point in time, Roman Empire did not value innovative entrepreneurs. His inventions were used by religious sects to achieve their objective of increasing numbers of their followers. Priests paid to Heron to buy his inventions to open and close the doors of the temple automatically in order to display their divine (magical) powers to innocent masses. This example illustrates how the wrong kind of incentives and institutions facilitate in squandering the talent of innovators like Heron in unproductive activities.[33]

While studying the process of economic growth and prosperity in historical perspective, one should remember the historical fact that the process of growth is in fact a 'process of creative destruction'.[34] The innovations that are created by the innovators while developing new products, processes, organizational structures and practices simultaneously destroy and replace old products, processes, organizations and practices. The process of creative destruction makes some sections of the society gainers, who use new innovations, and simultaneously some sections become losers. Fear of loss is at the root of vested interest which opposes the emergence of inclusive institutions. For a considerable period, human history witnessed existence of institutions that protected the interests of renter classes, who derived their income from privileges granted by the state. As political regimes shift in favour of new productive entrepreneurs, these groups lose the maximum. It is due to this reason that there are instances when losers have stopped the onward march of the society.[35]

The process of creative destruction also gets manifested in spatial process. It has been established by historical experience that it is due to changes in the political regimes that the locations of prosperity and poverty also keep changing. Relationship between shift in political regimes and rise and decline of cities goes back in time, since the emergence of the first cities. Rise and fall of cities also represent the shifting fortunes of regions. Two similar economies may follow different paths of development, if they are embedded in different political regimes. The process of divergence in their paths of development is similar to the outcome of the process when genes of two isolated populations of organizations drift apart.[36] In the present book, my endeavour is to unfold the historical experience of native cities when political regimes shifted from the native to colonial rule.

I have mentioned earlier that I will begin the story of these four cities from the time the Indian subcontinent experienced in tandem the consequences of two forces of globalization: the Mughal Empire, which unified the major parts of the Indian subcontinent and established a unified political regime, and the entry of European trading companies, which expanded its global contact with the rest of the world. For this purpose, the rest of the book has been organized into six chapters, where each chapter narrates the story of the four cities in the context of each political regime in order to understand how each political regime impacted these four cities. The Mughal Empire was perhaps the first empire in recorded history which ruled over a large part of Indian subcontinent. It covered the geographical space which was subsequently ruled by the East India Company, the British Raj and after Independence by different governments of Independent India. This geographical space acted as a stage which was used by different political regimes to perform their political act. To perform their part of the drama, each political regime organized this space differently in terms of institutions, regulations and biases. The reorganization of policy by different political regimes had significant influence on all the four cities.

In Chapter 1 of the book, I have described in detail how the Mughal Empire organized the given geographical space to create a particular kind of social, political and economic environment, which impacted the circumstances experienced by the three cities, namely Dacca, Surat and Calcutta, because Bombay was never a part of the Mughal Empire. In this chapter, I intend to tell the story how political and economic environment created by the Mughal Empire provided necessary conditions for the evolution of a nexus between merchants and craftsmen to evolve traditional flexible manufacturing. It also describes how traditional flexible manufacturing developed capability to manufacture a variety of products, which were produced with competitive advantage. These products were traded not only in the vast domestic market but also in global markets. It is this capability which has made the Indian subcontinent one of the most important manufacturing regions of the world. The traditional flexible manufacturing was spread over several locations during the Mughal Empire. During this time, Surat and Dacca had become important centres of traditional flexible manufacturing. It was to take the advantage of these centres of production of manufactured goods, which had a global market, that the East India Company established its trading bases at Bombay (near Surat) and Calcutta (near Dacca). The story also narrates the consequences of erosion in the authority of the Mughal state on these cities after the death of Aurangzeb in 1707. This erosion in the authority of the Mughal state led to disintegration of polity in the Indian subcontinent, when several large polities such as the Maratha Empire, Mysore, Hyderabad, Bengal and Punjab emerged, along with different small polities such as Awadh, Rohilkhand, Rajputana and in the periphery of Delhi by Jats.

Chapter 2 is devoted to narrating the consequences of the rise and decline of the Mughal Empire on Surat, Bombay, Dacca and Calcutta. Surat had emerged as an important location of traditional flexible manufacturing and trading in several products which were produced in the hinterland of the city. Presence of merchants from various countries and offices of European companies increased the volume of trade and manufacturing. Surat remained as a main centre of trading for a considerable period. However, decline in the authority of the Mughal state and the subsequent rise in authority of the Marathas impacted the prosperity of the city. The East India Company shifted its western trade from Surat to Bombay. The shifting of location of the western headquarters of the East India Company to Bombay created an initial divergence between Surat and Bombay in terms of growth and prosperity.

Dacca had become the capital of Bengal Subah during the Mughal Empire and had simultaneously also emerged as an important centre of manufacturing. The city emerged as an important centre of traditional flexible manufacturing because after its integration with the Mughal Empire, it got access to the vast domestic market. The presence of several European trading companies generated additional demand for its products in the international market. In this chapter, I have also described the consequences of the erosion of authority of the Mughal state, when the nawabs of Bengal proclaimed itself to be an autonomous region and shifted the capital of the Subah from Dacca to Murshidabad.

In Chapter 3, I have described the historical circumstances which led to political dominance of the East India Company by occupying the political space vacated by the Mughal Empire. In this chapter, I have also discussed about how the East India Company got transformed when it enjoyed twin monopoly powers, that is, monopoly of trade and monopoly of political power. The territorial occupation of the Indian subcontinent by the East India Company began with the Battle of Plassey in 1757. Having achieved political hegemony, how the East India Company transformed the sociopolitical and economic environment of the subcontinent is also part of this chapter.

In Chapter 4, I have narrated the consequences of socio-economic and political environment evolved by the East India Company on the cities of Dacca, Calcutta, Surat and Bombay. Since the rule of the East India Company began with the political occupation of Bengal, Dacca was the first city among the native cities which experienced the consequences of the rule of the company for the longest period, 1757–1857. One of the most important consequences of the rule of the East India Company was that it experienced decline in its traditional flexible manufacturing. The decline in traditional flexible manufacturing has been described by nationalist as well as Marxian historians as the process of *de-industrialization*.[37] In this chapter, I have chronicled the story of de-industrialization of Bengal in general and Dacca in particular to narrate how one of the most important manufacturing regions was transformed into an exporter of raw materials. It was the rising exports of raw materials which enriched the city of Calcutta. It has been a historical role of colonial cities to harmonize the working of colonized cities with the interests of imperial power. This role was played by Calcutta when it became an important supplier of raw materials which were required for the manufacturing enterprises of Britain.

Surat came under the influence of East India Company after the Castle Revolution of 1759.[38] The consolidation of political power in western India helped in the prosperity of Bombay by attracting migration of merchants and their wealth from Gujarat in general and from Surat in particular. In this chapter, I have also narrated the story about the impact of expansion of Bombay on Surat. It is quite obvious that Surat did not experience any significant decline as a consequence of the rule of the Company. This is because the political dominance of the East India Company in the western regions emerged quite late. The East India Company experienced resistance from the Marathas, which continued until the Third Anglo-Maratha War. The victory in the Third Anglo-Maratha War coincided with the elimination of monopoly of trade given to the East India Company by the British Crown.

In Chapter 5, I have described how the East India Company became an object of criticism by the civil society of Britain. The criticism against the East India Company was emerging as a consequence of political and economic transformation of Britain after the Industrial Revolution. This transformation created a new class of people known as manufacturers, industrialists and entrepreneurs, who were described as capitalists by Marxian scholars. The new class of people had economic and political interests, which were at variance with the interests of landed classes and merchants. The ideological premises of this new class were articulated and described by Adam Smith in his famous book *Wealth of Nations*, which appeared in 1776. The emerging accommodation of the interests of industrialists in policy-making slowly reduced the autonomy and economic relevance of the East India Company. Eventually, in 1813, the monopoly of trade given to the Company by the British Crown was abolished. In 1830, the East India Company ceased to be a commercial enterprise and became an instrument of colonial administration of the Indian subcontinent. The *Sepoy Mutiny* or First War of Independence of 1857 finally ended the rule of the East India Company and replaced it with a direct rule on the subcontinent by the British state, which gave birth to the British Raj. An important consequence of the shift in political regime from the rule of the Company to British Raj was that it led to new political and economic environment. It established Calcutta as the capital city of all the territories which were governed by the East India Company, and Bombay emerged as an important city of trade and commerce. The colonial cities left the native cities of Surat and Dacca way behind, when these cities became centres of *modern manufacturing*.

The story regarding what have been the consequences of British Raj on the four cities has been presented in Chapter 6. This chapter describes how modern manufacturing, once got consolidated in Britain, began to spread in the Indian subcontinent. The birth of modern manufacturing in Calcutta and Bombay created divide between prosperity of Bombay and Surat on the one hand and that of Calcutta and Dacca on the other. Dacca particularly became essentially a supplier of raw materials, whereas Calcutta became an important centre of export-oriented manufacturing. Moreover, for a considerable period, leadership of development of modern manufacturing remained largely with British entrepreneurs in Calcutta. The manufacturing sector that emerged in Calcutta was complementary to the requirement of British manufacturers. It was the complementarity between the British and Calcutta manufacturing which resulted in the absence of hostility between British manufacturers and those running manufacturing enterprises in Calcutta.

This chapter also narrates the story about the rise of Bombay as a centre of modern manufacturing as a consequence of the political regime created by the British Raj. As compared to the process of industrialization of Calcutta, in the western region in general and Bombay in particular, leadership to promote modern manufacturing was provided by the native entrepreneurs. These entrepreneurs promoted those manufacturing enterprises which were producing import substitutes.

It was this nature of modern manufacturing of the western regions which experienced discrimination by the British policy-makers.

NOTES

1. To know the role of colonial cities, see Horvath (1969), Balhatchet and Harrison (1980) and Norman (1989).
2. For detailed understanding about cities in historical perspective, see Mumford (1961), Hall (1978) and Spiro (1992).
3. The anthropologists describe human societies which have domesticated crops and animals as societies that have achieved Neolithic revolution; see Singer (1958) and Victor (1885).
4. See, for these facts, Heisen (1990).
5. To know about the relationship between Neolithic revolution and emergence of civilizations and politics, see Ucko and Dimbley (1969) and MacNeish (1992).
6. To understand the role of horses in human history, see Kust (1983) and Clutton-Brock (1992).
7. For the emergence of polity and state, see Dimond (2003, Chapter XIV, 239–265).
8. For details regarding earliest cities, see Hammond (1972), Leick (2002) and Watson (2006).
9. For details regarding this box, see MacGregor (2010, 63).
10. For knowing about the characteristics of Indus Valley Civilization, see Wright (2010), and for details regarding the stone seal, see MacGregor (2010, 66–70).
11. To know how creativity and innovation occurred in cities, see Jacob (1969), Hall (1978) and Landy (2008).
12. For understanding the role of empire, see Hicks (1969).
13. For knowing the history of the Silk Road, see Frank and Brownstone (1986) and Liu (1996).
14. For this fact, see Berman (1983) and Lal (2004).
15. These facts are available in Allami (1927, Vol. II, 137).
16. For details regarding different European trading companies, see Omprakash (1985), Hall (1996), Pearson (2007), Furber (2004) and Seth (2018).
17. For details regarding the East India Company, see Nick (2006), Travers (2007) and Seth (2014).
18. To know about the history of Surat before it was integrated into the Mughal empire, see Allami (1927, Vol. II, 264–266).
19. For details regarding interaction between Portuguese and Surat, see Whiteway (1899), Hall (1996) and Furber (2004).
20. To know about the history of the East India Company in Bengal, see Travers (2007).
21. For understanding the nature of contact between Surat and Dutch company, see Omprakash (1985) and Pearson (2007).
22. To know about the history of interaction between the East India Company and Surat, see Balfour (1885) and Gardner (1971).
23. For further knowledge about Bombay, see Malabari (1910), Kosambi (1980), Dossal (1991) and Dossal and Thorner (1996).
24. For knowing about the role of institutions in shaping the economy, see North (1990).

25. To know about relationship between institutions and social choices, see Acemoglu and Robinson (2008).

26. For understanding about the concepts of inclusive and extractive institutions, see Acemoglu and Robinson (2012, 78–95).

27. To know how incentive structures promote unproductive economic activities, see North (1990, 2006).

28. For ideas regarding bourgeoisie dignity and liberty, see McClosky (2006, 2010).

29. See Hobsbawm (1975, 286–287).

30. Ibid., 13.

31. The quotation of Voltaire has been taken from McCloskey (2010, 198).

32. For understanding the distinction between productive and unproductive entrepreneur, see Baumol et al. (2007).

33. This example has been used by Baumol et al. (2012) to explain the distinction between productive and unproductive entrepreneurs.

34. For details regarding the process of creative destruction, see Schumpeter (1947, 1954).

35. To understand how political losers create barrier in the process of economic development, see Acemoglu and Robinson (2000).

36. The process of drifting apart of proximate regions due to divergent political regimes has been discussed in detail in Acemoglu and Robinson (2012, 431).

37. The term 'de-industrialization' has been used by nationalist and Marxian economic historians to describe the historical process which was experienced by the Indian traditional flexible manufacturing. This process led to decline in traditional flexible manufacturing. For this, see Thorner and Thorner (1962), Morris (1969) and Chapter 4 of the book.

38. The Castle Revolution of 1759 pertains to a historical event when merchants of Surat helped in the appointment of the East India Company as the *Qiladar* (commander of the Garrison) of the castle; see Subramanian (1987) and Mir (2018).

Economic Environment During the Mughal Empire

Zahiruddin Muhammad Babur Mirza was born on 14 February 1483, as a prince of Fergana, located in Transoxiana (modern-day Uzbekistan and Tajikistan). He belonged to a dynasty that had ruled areas around Eastern Iran and Central Asia, since it was founded by Amir Timur (1336–1408). Babur Mirza was son of Umar Shaikh Mirza, who was a great grandson of Timur. Babur's mother was Qutlugh Nigar Khanum, who was daughter of Yunus Khan. Yunus Khan belonged to the lineage of Chakatai Khan, who was the second son of Genghis Khan (Babur 2003, 8). This suggests that Babur was a descendant of two important empire builders—Timur and Gengish Khan. Babur occupied the throne of Fergana at the age of 12 on 8 June 1494, due to sudden death of his father in an accident. He occupied this throne at that point in time when there were several contenders for the throne. The entire region from Arab Sea to Hindu Kush was divided into several principalities belonging to descendants of Timur and Genghis Khan. Taking advantage of his age, soon he was driven out of Fergana by Uzbek Khan. After this event, Babur became a nomadic prince striving to get back his lost empire. He spent most of his life in establishing and losing kingdom, along the way gradually moving south of Fergana. His quest for establishing his empire ended in the Indian subcontinent where he established the Mughal Empire.

His struggle to establish a kingdom of his own has been very appropriately described by Farishtha, one of the chroniclers of the Mughal Empire, 'like a king of chessboard moves from place to place and buffeted about like a pebble on a sea shore'.[1] He was able to establish his rule in Kabul in 1504, when his father's brother, Ulugh

Beg, who was ruling Kabul died leaving behind an infant son. This provided him an opportunity to become the ruler of Kabul. He was also able to regain his lost kingdom of Fergana with the help of Shah Ismail, the king of Safavid dynasty of Iran in 1511, but lost it again in 1512, when Uzbek chief Saibani Khan, descendant of Genshid Khan, captured Fergana again.

Despite ruling Kabul for a considerable period, he did not cross the Indus river till 1520. He got a god-sent opportunity, when Delawar Khan, son of Daulat Khan, governor of Punjab, a province of Lodhi empire, and Alam Khan, an uncle of Abraham Lodhi, ruler of Delhi, approached him for removing Abraham Lodhi from the throne of Delhi. Babur defeated Abraham Lodhi, the Sultan of Delhi, in the first Battle of Panipat on 21 April 1526 and occupied the throne of Delhi. He thereby laid the foundation of the Mughal Empire—the empire that continued to rule till 1858, when his last descendant Bahadur Shah Zafar was exiled by the British to Burma. The term 'Mughal' and Mughalistan has generally been used to differentiate between present-day Mongols and Mongolia, to lay emphasis on the Chagatayid Turks of Mughalistan.[2]

When Babur occupied the kingdom of Delhi, at that point in time, the polity of the Indian subcontinent was fragmented, because its different regions were ruled by different kingdoms. According to his own account, the Indian subcontinent was ruled by five Muslim and two Hindu rulers. Sultan Husayn Sharqi ruled Jaunpur, Sultan Mujaffar ruled Gujarat, Bahmani rulers ruled Deccan, Sultan Mohammed ruled the province of Malwa, which was also known as Mandu, and Nusarat Shah ruled Bengal. At that time, the Vijaynagara Empire of South India and Chittor ruled by Rana Sanga were kingdoms ruled by Hindu rulers (Babur, 2003, 331–332). The fragmented polity had given rise to several regional economies. Each regional economy contained vast tracts of fertile land, which was irrigated by several perennial rivers. These fertile tracts of land provided preconditions for growing a variety of crops, fruits and spices. These regional economies also had a long tradition of producing handicrafts, which satisfied the needs of not only common people but also the luxury needs of kings and their courtiers.

Most of these regional economies were connected through trading by land, rivers and seas with other regions and with rest of the world. The scenario of economic reality at the time was quite at variance with the general perception that Indians avoided seafaring to protect themselves from ritual impurity.[3] This perception about Indians is quite misplaced, because India is almost in the centre of the Indian Ocean and also three sides of the Indian subcontinent are surrounded by ocean and seas. The archaeological finds at the sites of Mesopotamia clearly establish the trading link of people living in the Indus Valley with other people. The existence of terms such as *mari indicum* (Indian Ocean) in Arabic, *Al Bahr al Hind* (Indian Ocean) in Persian and *Hsi hai* in Chinese clearly show the use of oceans and seas to establish connectivity between people of distant lands.[4] The Indian subcontinent had several port cities, located along the coastline of the Arabian Sea, the Indian Ocean and the Bay of Bengal. Southern part of the subcontinent was integrated through trading with economies of the Gulf and Southeast Asia including China. The coastal cities of the western and eastern parts also had a long-time trading relationship with economies of the Gulf and Southeast Asia. The northern part of the subcontinent was connected through trading by land caravan routes with the economies of Central Asia, China and Europe. The land routes existed because of the existence of contiguous land mass, which facilitated the movement of caravans of traders from Delhi, Agra, Lahore, Kandahar, Constantinople and Venice. The route was also connected with China. Most of the trade between India, Central Asia and Europe was handled by caravans. However, by this time, European merchants had arrived on the Indian coast after the discovery of sea route to India by Vasco da Gama in 1498. This was slowly helping the shift from caravan trade to sea-bound trade. This happened much before the establishment of the Mughal Empire by Babur. As the Mughal Empire was consolidating its position in the inland economy of the Indian subcontinent, several European trading companies also established their trading bases in different port cities. But most of them remained confined to the port cities due to military might of the Mughal Empire. Therefore, it was the Mughal Empire which until the Battle of Plassey (1757) determined the socio-economic and political environment experienced by the major part of the geographical area of the subcontinent.

Due to these obvious reasons, in the present chapter, an attempt has been made to understand the relationship between the economic environment created by the Mughal Empire and traditional flexible manufacturing, which was emerging as a dominant form of organization of production in manufacturing. Moreover, both the native cities, which are subject matter of my story, were also centres of traditional flexible manufacturing. Therefore, it is quite important to understand the relationship between traditional flexible manufacturing and the Mughal Empire. To understand this relationship, the rest of the chapter has been organized into three sections. In the first section, we have described the structure of governance of the Mughal Empire, which determined the economic environment it created; in the second section, we have presented the economic analysis regarding traditional flexible manufacturing. Finally, in the third section, we have presented the impact of the economic environment created by the Mughal Empire on the composition of Indian manufacturing.

STRUCTURE OF GOVERNANCE
DURING MUGHAL EMPIRE

The Mughal Empire was the first important force which established connectivity between several fragmented polities of India. Mughals ruled over quite a substantial land mass of the Indian subcontinent, which covered the geographical area subsequently ruled by the East India Company, the British Raj and governments of independent India. The Mughals were the first rulers who simultaneously ruled three out of the four cities about whom I have talked in this book. Bombay is the only city which since its inception until India's independence had been under foreign rule.

The Mughal Empire, like many other empires of Central, West and South Asia, grew as a fragment founded by descendants of Chengiz Khan. Mughal Empire in its full glory lasted till the death of Aurangzeb in 1707, after which the Mughal Empire began to decline. Its rule was confined to only Delhi when the last Mughal was sent to exile in Burma in 1858. It was said at that time 'Hukumate Shah Alam, Shuru Lal Qila, Khatam Palam', that is, the rule of Shah Alam is between the Red Fort and Palam. Palam was a village in the outskirts of Delhi.

During its glorious time, the Mughal Empire provided an important public good to a vast geographical area of the Indian subcontinent. The public good was a properly organized law and order system which is an important prerequisite of economic progress of an economy. This important role of the Mughal Empire has been aptly described by Abul Fazal Allami, a friend, philosopher and guide of the Mughal emperor Akbar. He writes:

> A king is the origin of stability and possessions. If royalty does not exist, the storm of strife would never subside nor do selfish ambitions disappear. Mankind under the burden of lawlessness and lust, would sink into pit of destruction; the world, the great market place, would lose its perspective and whole earth would become barren waste.[5]

The thinking of Abul Fazal Allami was not unique regarding the role of monarchy and empire. One of the important political thinkers of Britain, Thomas Hobbes (1558–1679) had similar views. His political philosophy got expression in his famous book *Leviathan*, which appeared in 1651. He argued in this book for the existence of a strong king to maintain order and prevent the occurrence of a state of perpetual fratricidal struggle in the society and polity. He derived the title of his book from a verse of Chapter 41 of the *Book of Job*, where Leviathan is being described as 'King of the Proud'. He defines Leviathan 'which is but an *artificial man,* though greater in structure and strength than *natural man,* for whose protection and defence it was intended, and in which the sovereignty is an artificial soul'. He also describes, in greater details, various organs of this artificial man. According to his description, judiciary and law enforcement agencies are its artificial *joints.* Rewards and punishment comprise all the *nerves,* which provide motivation to its organs to function. The strength of this artificial man depends on *material prosperity.* The notion of equity and law give it reason (Hobbes, 1651 [1974], 9).

According to Hobbes, Leviathan emerges when people appoint one man or assembly of men in such manner as if every man with every other man resolves that 'I authorize and give-up my right to governing myself to this man or to this assembly of men'. He is one person 'whose acts a great multitude by mutual covenants one with another…

to end he may use the strength and means of them all, as he shall think expedient for their peace and common defence' (Hobbes, 1651 [1974], 176–177). The person whom the people select as Leviathan is called sovereign and possesses *sovereign power.*

In Islam, after the death of the Prophet, administrative and legislative functions were performed by *Caliphs* (ar-Rashidum). Since most of the Islamic land at that time was ruled by tribal chiefs, they did not have the concept of monarchy. In the absence of the monarchy, they elected the first four caliphs: Abu Bakr (632–634), Umar-al-Khattab (634–644), Usman (644–656) and Ali (656–661). The fifth caliph, Muaawiya, established the Umayyad dynasty. In the entire Islamic world, at that point in time, only Iran had experience of monarchy. Therefore, Islamic views on king and monarchy were influenced by the Iranian scholarship, especially, the work of famous Iranian epic poet Firdausi called *Shahnama.* The Iranian concept of king views that rulers were chosen people by divine will, who were accountable only to god: 'monarchs were instruments in the execution of God's will' (Barni, 1357 [2015], 3–6; Rizvi, 1982, Vol. II, 165).

Therefore, unlike the idea of Hobbes, the Mughals believed in the divine theory of monarchy, which was based on the premise that the kings are descendants of God, and they have divine right to rule over lesser beings. To justify their divine descent, the lineage of Mughal emperors was traced to Adam, including the five Biblical prophets, and Ikhnus (also called Hermes). The lineage thereafter is followed by Joseph and his son Turk, ruler of Turkistan. It is from here that the lineage shifts from Biblical to Turko-Mongol character. After several generations, the most significant divine event occurred, when Alanquwa (Alan-quwa), a Mughal princess of Mughalistan, became a childless widow. The divine forces in the form of a ray of light miraculously entered her body and impregnated her. The progenies of this conception were triplets, three brothers, who were described as Nairum (light produced). From the eldest of the three brothers, who possessed the greatest illumination of his mother, the hidden light passed through several generations, until Shahenshah of mankind, Akbar, was born.[6] The concept of kingship as semi-divine sovereignty was not compatible with orthodox Islam; however, it found a fertile soil in India during the Mughal Empire. In its new interpretation, it is found in the writings of Abul Fazal Allami where he describes Akbar as divine light (*nur parwarda-i-izdi*).[7] The concept of *Sultan* as the *shadow* of *god* already existed in medieval Islamic political thought.[8]

In the region of Transoxiana, which was the native place of Mughals, the main source of revenue was essentially obtained by *plundering thy neighbour*. However, when the Mughals established their empire in India, the king had the right to appropriate the agricultural surplus. The right to appropriate surplus was enshrined in the Hindu world view. One of the Sanskrit words for the king is *shaspada* or the owner of one-sixth share of produce of the farmers.[9] Hence, war in India was primarily waged to acquire the right to appropriate surplus.[10] The Hindu view of social order was based on the idea of self-sufficient *autarkic villages,* organized into numerous endogamous, hierarchically ranked, occupational castes and sub-castes segmented into four broad categories (*varnas*). At the top of the social hierarchy were the Brahmins (priests), followed by the *kshatriyas* (warriors), the *vaishyas* (traders and merchants) and the *sudras* (workers and ordinary peasants). Caste system played an important role in making available a constant supply of labour for a labour-intensive agricultural system and crafts. However, these views held by the Hindus were at variance with the Mughal world view. The Mughals derived their views on social order from *Naqshbandi* and *Chishti* order of Sufism, Islam, and the then historical scenario present in Fergana.

At that point in time, when the Mughals arrived in the Indian subcontinent, the Sufi movement was segmented into various *silsilas* (sects or groups) in different parts of Central Asia and in the Indian subcontinent. Some of the prominent *silsilas* of Sufism were *Bistaniyyas, Shattariyyas, Qadiriyyas* and *Naqshbandiyas*. The Naqshbandiya order originated in Transoxiana and is also known as the *Khwaja* order. The order was named after Khwaja Beha-ud-din Naqshbandi.

In the Indian subcontinent, this *silsila* was established by Khwaja Muin-ud-din Chishti at Ajmer in Rajasthan and by Hazrat Nizam-ud-din Auliya at Delhi. Abul Fazal Allami has described this world view in *Ain-i-Akbari*. He divides social order into four broad categories; however, he does not rank them in any particular hierarchy. According to his interpretations, all societies, for the sake of work, need people belonging to these four categories. The order in which he describes them may provide an idea of the implicit social ranking of these categories.

Allami starts his account of these categories with *warriors*. He describes that the warriors have the nature of *fire*. Their flames based on their knowledge consume the straw and the rubbish, that is rebellion and strife, but kindle the lamp of rest in a world of disturbances. By giving first of all the description of the warriors, perhaps he is giving an overriding importance to this class in expanding and maintaining vast empires. This might also be due to the fact that the Mughals shared their lineage with warriors such as Genghis Khan and Amir Timur. The description of the warriors is followed by the class of *artificers* and *merchants*. This category holds a place in the society similar to *air*, because from their labour and travels, God's gift becomes available and breeze of contentment nourishes the rose tree of life. Fazal then narrates about the class of the *learned*, who, according to him, resemble *water*. From their pen and their wisdom, a river rises into the drought of the world and the garden of creation receives sustenance from their irrigation power of peculiar freshness. Finally, he mentions about the *husbandmen*, whom he symbolizes with the *earth*. It is by dint of their exertions that the staple of life is brought to perfection, and strength and happiness flow from their work.[11]

In the socio-economic order in India, before the Mughal Empire, crafts were an integral part of rural economy. The social division of labour which was based on caste lines was extended to include craftsmen also. Crafts had become caste specific and these castes were prohibited from cultivation. Instead of using a separation between craftsmen and cultivators to create market-mediated exchange relations between them, a new kind of symbiotic relationship was created between artisans and cultivators by introducing a distinct institution known as *jajmani system*. This institution was evolved by establishing a unique gift-exchange relationships amongst different occupational groups to provide the availability of different kinds of labour services needed in a village economy. The gift-exchange relationship amongst different occupational groups eliminated the market-mediated exchange and thus helped in postponement of the emergence of market in rural economy. This system also isolated village economy from the rest of the economic relations and gave birth to self-sufficient villages. The system was evolved primarily as customary systems of distribution of village produce amongst different sections of village community, performing different economic activities that were necessary in the village economy, and it was not designed as a system of production for exchange.[12]

Jajmani system as a form of organization of social and economic order was based on a symbiotic relationship between patron household and different occupational groups, such as barber, laundryman, carpenter, blacksmith, mason, watchman, folk artists, domestic servants and priests. In this system, different occupational groups received their share from the village produce, based on customary payment, in lieu of market-determined rewards. These customary payments were made on occasions such as harvest, birth, marriage, death and important festivals. This system of social organization was known as *baluta* system in Western India (especially in Maharashtra). In the baluta system, the hierarchy of functionaries in the village supplied services to all other members of the village community in exchange of specific gifts in kind, but sometimes was also accompanied by a certain amount of cash.[13] Jajmani system in Punjab was known as *Vand*.[14]

According to German scholar Hegel, jajmani system was 'the most degrading spiritual serfdom', because this system organized villages, socially and economically, in such a way that it created several kinds of rigidities based on Hindu religious beliefs. According to him, it has established a social order where the arrangement is fixed and immutable, which is subject to no one's will. All political revolutions, therefore, are a matter of indifference to the common Hindu, for his lot remains unchanged (Hegel, 1956, 154). It was Hegel's conceptualization about Hindu social order that provided basis for conceiving the idea of *Asiatic mode of production* evolved by Karl Marx.[15] This conceptualization was evolved by Marx to explain why Asian economies will remain stagnant unless and until they experience a strong exogenous force, like British colonialism, which will give it a *big-push* to come out of the stationary state. He did not realize that the premises on which he developed his concept had been significantly altered by a strong exogenous force created by the arrival of Islam and the Mughal Empire.

The Mughal India was not a purely Hindu country. The impact of the Mughal Empire had created circumstances which affected the village autonomy created by jajmani system and its various forms in different parts of India. The village autonomy registered significant decline. The decline occurred due to monetization of the village economy, created by collection of land revenue in cash. The system also became weak, because it lost grip on social order caused by migration of several craftsmen to emerging markets in urban areas to pursue their crafts trade. It has been mentioned by historians that during the Mughal Empire, the entire production of manufactured items meant for long-distance and medium-distance trade was carried out by craftsmen who were weaned away from jajmani system.[16] This suggests that weakening of the jajmani system increased the mobility of artisans, which increased the availability of craftsmen to participate in traditional flexible manufacturing.

The Mughal Empire also played an important role in establishing a pan subcontinental size of market, which was very important for the growth of the economy in general and expansion of traditional flexible manufacturing in particular. The size of the market increased due to integration of several fragmented regional markets into a single unified market. By establishing a unified polity, it also reduced inter-regional barriers to trade. The Mughal Empire also included an interregnum of seven years (1538–1545) when Sher Shah Suri ruled, while Mughal emperor Humayun was in exile in Iran. Sher Shah Suri developed a network of roads, including one major road which is now popularly known as Grand Trunk Road (National Highway No. 1). This road connected Punjab to the town of Sonargaon near Bay of Bengal (*daraya-i-shor*). Apart from this road, he constructed roads which connected Agra to Burhanpur, Agra to Jodhpur and Chittor, and Agra to Lahore. Subsequently, under Mughal rule, these roads were further extended to Cambay, Surat, Ahmedabad and Multan.[17] These roads increased connectivity between different markets.

To maintain the vast Mughal Empire, there was need for a framework of administration and organization of a large army. This was possible only by extracting a large part of agricultural surplus from the rural economy. To appropriate agricultural surplus, a military administrative hierarchy of functionaries was evolved by the Mughal state based on Mongolian system of organization of army and administration. These functionaries were called *mansabdars*. The rank of each official was described numerically, which determined pay as well as hierarchy of the rank in the overall administration. For *mansabdars*, who were also performing military function, ranks were also specified numerically into trooper (*suwars*) ranks. The hierarchy followed by the Mughals reflected the prevailing social hierarchy, similar to the ranks of officials in the Mongol Empire. In the Mughal Empire also, at the top were generally persons belonging to the royal family called *Tuman Begi* (i.e., ten thousand); followed by close relatives and nobles, *Ming Begis* (i.e., thousands); and captains *Yug Begis* (hundreds). The mansabdars with suwar ranks were required to maintain fully equipped cavalrymen equivalent to their specified numerical rank. These suwars were made available to the emperor at the time of war.[18] Along with the hierarchy of mansabdars, the Mughal Empire also created a skilled lower middle level bureaucracy to look after imperial administration, consisting of persons trained in book-keeping, auditing, correspondence, procurement and supply, record-keeping and maintenance of stores. The formation of this vast politico-military administration expanded the size of aristocracy and nobility, which generated additional demands for good and services.

To provide necessary finances, to meet the need of the vast administrative and military machine, exorbitant land revenue rates were imposed on peasantry by the Mughal Empire. These high rates of land revenue were paid by the farmers in cash. The payment of land revenue in cash needed the introduction of an official currency. For this purpose, the Mughals established centrally controlled network of imperial mints (*darl-ul-zarb*). The coins were made of gold (*muhar*), silver (*rupia*) and copper (*dam*). Most of these metals were obtained through trade of Indian products in foreign markets and also from local mines. When massive new supplies of silver and gold emerged from America and Japan, which were used by European trading companies to buy Indian goods, India emerged as the 'ultimate sink of these metals'.[19] The trimetallic currency system of gold, silver and copper was originally based on copper *dam*. However, Mughal monetary system maintained silver *rupia* as its principal coin. The Mughal silver rupee coin was 11 grams in weight and was stamped from meticulously engraved imperials dyes.[20]

According to available historical records, it is possible to obtain information regarding the treasure hoard only for the time of Akbar. This is because, apart from Akbar, no other Mughal emperor left behind information about their rule in such a detailed fashion. Calculated on the basis of information obtained from two different sources, the *Ain-i-Akbari* and *Tebaquat-i-Akbari,* Akbar's treasure consisted of slightly under 7 million gold *muhars* (weight 76 metric tons) and 7,200 million silver *rupia* (minimum 802 metric tons). Moreover, The surplus of 3.9 million silver coins was spent on three import heads: (a) salary of mansabdars, (b) military expenses and (c) expenses on the imperial household. These items of expenses also generated additional demand for goods and services.[21]

The ruling classes and nobility of the Mughal Empire lived an extravagant lifestyle, their need for luxurious goods was satisfied by artisans, who were engaged in the manufacturing of luxury handicrafts: They were manufacturing high-quality cotton (Dacca muslin), gold and silver jewellery, cutlery, decorative swords and weapons. The nobles maintained households with a large number of wives, concubines, slaves and domestic servants. The Mughal emperor's own *harem* consisted of 5,000 females divided into two categories: (a) *mahim-bano,* that is, high-ranking women, totalling 300 and (b) *parastran-i-huzur* (under the protection and service of the king). The total value of cloth consumed by the household of the emperor was valued at 1.6 million *dams*, and total value of gold pots, silverwares, dishes, cutlery, figurines, chandeliers, bedsteads, copperwares, porcelain crockery was 1.49 million *dams,* according to *Ain-i-Akbari*.[22] If we add to this amount the consumption of the thousands of nobles and mansabdars of the Mughal Empire, the total domestic demand for luxury handicrafts will be enormous.

The expenditure pattern of Mughal nobility created an urban culture and pattern of demand, which got manifested into occupation pattern, where a large proportion of working population was engaged in the manufacturing of handicrafts and providing services to the elites. It has been estimated that the village economy gave employment to 72 per cent of the total working population and contributed 45 per cent of the national income. Non-village economy employed the rest of the 18 per cent of the working population while contributing 52 per cent of the national income. The non-village economy of the Mughal Empire consisted of the Mughal emperor, courtiers, mansabdars of different ranks, *jagirdars,* native princes, merchants, bankers, shopkeepers (*baqals*), traditional professionals, soldiers, craftsmen, construction workers and domestic help.[23]

Monetization of the economy and expanding size of the market led to extensive trading which created historical premises for the formation of a class of merchants, traders, bankers and moneylenders. Each region gave birth to certain trading communities, which subsequently also developed networks of craftsmen's workshops to evolve traditional flexible manufacturing. Some of these merchants later became entrepreneurs, when the process of growth of modern manufacturing began in India. Communities of traders such as *Marwaris, Jains* and *Banias* became important in Rajasthan. Again, *Khatri, Aroras* and *Banias* in Punjab, Tamil-speaking *Chettiars* and Telugu-speaking *Komatis* in South India, and *Parsis, Gujaratis, Bohras, Khojas* and *Bhatias* dominated trading in Western India.[24]

These trading communities were involved in commodity trading, financing of working capital needs of artisans through putting out system (i.e., traditional flexible manufacturing), revenue farming and provisioning the needs of army. Some of the big traders and moneylenders formed big banking firms, which were engaged in transfer of large volumes of money from one place to another, using a wide variety of financial instruments. Such big banking firms existed in almost all of the important cities such as the firms of Jagat Seth in Bengal, Gopaldas Manohardas in Banaras, Lala Kashmiri Mal in Awadh, Virji Vohra and Abdul Gufoor in Surat, Shanti Prasad Jain (Jhaveri) in Ahmedabad and Hari Bhakti in Poona.[25] One of the important financial instruments which was extensively used by these banking firms during the Mughal Empire was *hundi* (Habib, 1964; Jain, 1929). This instrument was used by communities of merchants as a letter of credit and promissory note. This instrument helped merchants in transactions and were meant for long-distance trade and travel, when travelling carrying cash and transferring of cash was risky. The hundi was issued by reputed banking firms and its acceptability amongst its users depended on the reputation of the banking firm which issued it. The use of hundi as a financial instrument can be traced back to remote past. According to legend, it was the hundi issued by the banking firm of the *Nagarseth* of Ahmedabad to Vastupal Tejpal which helped in providing finance for the construction of Dilwara Temple, located at Mount Abu.

The widespread use of hundi as a financial instrument assumed greater importance during Mughal Empire. The hundis facilitated the transfer of revenue collected from different subahs of the Mughal Empire to the capital city of the Mughal Empire. It also helped in transferring cash required for long-distance trade. Hundis were generally of two types: (a) *Darshani Hundi*, which was treated like a bearer cheque; in their case, payments were made immediately at the time it was presented; and (b) *Muddati Hundi* or *Miadi Hundi*, which involved deferred payment after a stipulated time period, mentioned in the hundi.[26] It is quite paradoxical that during the Mughal Empire, the financial instrument which was associated with reputation and honour of the owner of the banking firm which issued the hundi is currently associated with transactions made by underworld and illegal segment of the economy. It is now popularly known as *hawala*.[27]

To facilitate the transfer of financial resources, each banking firm had branches in different parts of the Indian subcontinent. Different branches of these banking firms were either managed by different family members of the owner of the banking firm or by the same community.[28] The Mughal state depended on these banking firms for procuring their needed commodities as well as cash and credit on regular basis.[29] This happened because the main source of revenue during the Mughal Empire was land revenue. This source was seasonal and was also affected by the vagaries of nature. The monetization of the economy and system of credit in the Mughal Empire and their need for financial resources on a continuous basis made it necessary to evolve alliances with large trading and banking firms. For example, the house of Jagat Seth was involved in transferring the annual collection of the land revenue of the Nawab of Murshidabad (Bengal Subah) in advance to the Mughal emperor in Agra. The annual value of remittance from Bengal was around 10 million rupees. Similarly, the richest sheriff of Gujarat, Shantidas, received the title of Nagarseth from Jahangir. The Mughal treasury accepted all his hundis. Similar influence was exercised by merchants such as Krishn Arjunji Nathji and Laldas Vithaldas Parekh in Surat, Gopaldas Manohardas in Banaras and Lala Kashmiri Mal in Awadh.[30]

Increased reliance on networks evolved by banking firms across different regions of the Mughal Empire, to transfer revenue from provinces to the capital city, adulterated the fiscal administration. The reliance on banking firms was accompanied by direct involvement of the Mughal emperor, princes, his relatives and nobles in foreign trade. These conditions suggest that at the time of the Mughal Empire, there had emerged a sort of state mercantilism. This had emerged as a consequence of combining *imarat* and *tijarat*. By combining these characteristics, the Mughal state developed state mercantilism and was committed to increase the production from traditional flexible manufacturing by protecting employment of craftsmen.[31]

The increasing appropriation of large proportion of agricultural surplus had facilitated the growth of urban agglomerations, which could be compared in size with any big city of the world. These cities were either administrative cities such as Delhi, Agra and Lahore, or they were important centres of production of luxury handicrafts, following traditional flexible manufacturing system of organization of production, such as Patna, Banaras, Murshidabad, Dacca, Rajmahal and Surat. There were also cities during Mughal Empire which were located on trade routes evolved by imperial highways or navigable rivers. The textile manufacturing centres of Patna and Banaras had reaped immense advantages from possibilities of transporting their products through the Ganga river to European trading centres at Hugli. These network of cities and urban centres provided appropriate economic conditions for the growth of inland and overseas trade in manufactured goods and agricultural commodities. The Mughal economy was organized around a network of administrative cities, market and towns which were centres of production of manufactured goods. In this network of towns, commodities flowed from rural areas to urban centres, accompanied by a return flow of cash and currency to villages to facilitate the payment of land revenue in cash by the farmers and to buy necessary commodities that were produced in the urban centres.

Urbanization increased during the Mughal Empire due to migration of artisans from villages to cities and to urban centres of handicrafts in order to participate in the Mughal army and armies in each subah had several mansabdas maintained by rural population. Migrations to cities also took effect due to increased demand of working population for low-end service occupations, which provided employment opportunities to landless workers who migrated from villages. According to the available evidence, India at the time of Akbar consisted of 120 large and small cities, 3,200 *qasbas* (small towns) and 40,000 villages. During this time, 15 per cent of the total estimated population, somewhere between 107 and 115 million, lived in urban areas.[32]

It was a gigantic exercise to maintain regular supply of commodities and manufactured goods during the Mughal Empire amongst thousands of villages, towns and cities, in the absence of modern means of transportation and communication. It is interesting to mention that the entire supply chain was managed by the community of *Banjaras*. The banjaras were a mobile community and owned large stocks of bullock carts, wagons and packs of horses, and also had intimate knowledge about the routes to different places in the country. It is being speculated that the word *banjara* is derived from the Sanskrit word *vanij*, which again lies in the root of the Sanskrit word *vanijaya* (business).[33] Apart from the banjaras, the komatis and khojas were also performing the same function in Southern and Western India, respectively. It has been recorded that during the seventeenth century the banjaras alone transported an average 821 million ton miles a year, while in 1882 the entire network of railways transported 2,500 ton miles. There are also records regarding caravans consisting of oxen numbering 40,000, where each ox carried between 100 and 150 kilograms of merchandize. There existed caravan *sarais* (inns) at a day's distance from each other on trade routes, which had capacity to accommodate thousands of traders and their animals.[34]

Apart from a vast domestic market for commodities and manufactured goods, Mughal India emerged as a nodal centre of a dynamic world trading system with various levels of commercial interaction and interdependence between urbanized and commercial locations, spread along the Indian Ocean (China and Central Asia), the Middle East (Iran, Iraq and Afghanistan) and Europe (England, France, Dutch and Portugal). Apart from sea routes, trade also occurred through land routes. Since overland routes passing through India and Persia up to the Ottoman Empire were stable and relatively safe for trade, they provided ample opportunities for creating wealth by traders from India, Baghdad, Mosul and Damascus. A great deal of trade occurred between India and Central Asia through pastoral nomads who extensively travelled territories between the Indus and the Oxus rivers. The name for these trading nomads, known as *Powindas*, is derived from the word *Pawwel* from Pashto language, spoken in Afghanistan, or the word *puydian* from Persian spoken in Iran. These words stand for 'to graze and roam'. The Powinda traders carried with them merchandize on thousands of camels annually. Similar trade routes were also followed by the nomadic communities of *Qazags* and *Kelmuk* of south Russian steppes and the *Bhotiya* tribe of the Western Himalayas.[35]

The caravan routes remained operational during the Mughal Empire despite the fact that one *dhow* (traditional sailing boat) could cover the same distance as a caravan in one-third time, and each dhow could carry merchandize equivalent to merchandize carried by thousands of camels.[36] A dhow required manpower equal to the crew size, as compared to two men for each camel. Caravan routes remained operational because it was cheaper to take goods during early seventeenth century through land route from North India to Iran. The land route via Agra–Lahore, Kandahar, Isfahan, Constantinople and Venice was much cheaper than the maritime alternative route via Agra–Surat, Bandar Abbas and Isfahan.[37]

The vast coastline of the Indian subcontinent was dotted with several port cities. These port cities connected the subcontinent with different economies through trade and commerce. These port cities were frequented by merchants from Persia, Arabia, Egypt and the Ottoman Empire, but subsequent to the discovery of sea route by Vasco da Gama, trading links were established by Portuguese, Dutch, French and British merchants. Their activities increased the demand for the products produced by traditional flexible manufacturing. The Europeans sailed twice a year, once in September and again between January and March. This prolonged the weaving season by creating two peaks.[38] According to the estimates based on the records of only the Dutch trading company, in Bengal alone, the full-time employment opportunities increased by 10 per cent (Parthasarthi, 2001). Due to their trading and military rivalries, the Indian port cities were monopolized by different European nations. As a consequence of their rivalries, India had become a theatre of battle for market shares amongst competing European trading nations. This has been very appropriately described by scholars as 'globalization with gun boats'.[39]

The aforementioned fact about the Mughal Empire suggests that the existence of a law and order system and absence of regional trade barriers led to the establishment of integrated markets. This expanded the size of domestic economy. Integration of Indian economy with the global trading system evolved by European trading companies provided preconditions of the growth of manufacturing in the Indian subcontinent. Looking at the size of the economy of the Mughal India, it is believed that the Mughal Empire was a wealthy empire, which dwarfed the European states. In 1700, population of India was 20 times that of the United Kingdom; India's share in the total world output of manufactured goods was 24 per cent, while Britain's share was just 3 per cent.[40] This suggests that during the Mughal Empire, the increasing size of market, expansion of urbanization, emergence of class of elites and nobles and monetization of the economy helped in increasing the demand of manufactured goods and in creating a class of merchants. These are important conditions for the growth of traditional flexible manufacturing. In the section that follows, we have focused on the conceptualization of the traditional flexible manufacturing.

CONCEPTUALIZATION OF TRADITIONAL FLEXIBLE MANUFACTURING

The roots of the word *manufacture* are two Latin words—*manu* and *facers*. Here *manu* means hand and *facers* means 'to make'. This signifies that manufacturing in its initial stages was associated with handicrafts. The early form of manufacturing in India, in its embryonic stage, was carried out by craftsmen in villages since ages. The process of social and economic division of labour created separation between craftsmen and farmers. Despite separation, craftsmen remained an integral part of the agrarian economy. However, most of the economies of the world, especially of Europe, South and Southeast Asia, experienced the emergence of a peculiar form of manufacturing during the sixteenth and in some cases during the seventeenth century, which has been variously described as *protean stage* of *industrialization,*[41] *industry before industrialization,*[42] *proto-industry,* *nascent capitalis*[43] and *commercial manufacturing.*[44] Of all the terms used to describe this phenomenon, the term *proto-industry* caught the attention of a large number of scholars. Initially this term was used by Freudenbarger and Redlick.[45] However, it received the attention of scholars when it was described in the writings of Mendales.[46] The term *proto* used as a prefix to the term *proto-industry* comes from Greek and means embryonic, original, first time, earliest and primitive. In this sense, proto-industry stands for a stage of manufacturing which contained preconditions (seeds) for the emergence of modern manufacturing.

Proto-industrialization has been accepted by scholar of economic history as a stage which existed during the period between emergence of putting-out system and consolidation of factory form of production organization in manufacturing. The emergence of this stage requires the existence of craftsman and merchants in the social order. Both of these categories existed during the Mughal Empire. Some scholars view proto-industrialization as a transitional stage from *kauf system,* in which production was dominated by petty production, to *verlag system,* which was based on capital-intensive form of manufacturing.[47] Proto-industry as a form of organization of manufacturing was characterized by dominance of crafts-based methods of production, carried out in family-owned workshops. These household workshops were organized into networks by merchants through putting-out system.

The Mughal Empire had inherited a long tradition of crafts-based system of petty production, where manufacturing was organized in artisanal household workshops. This system of production was appropriate for an economy which depended on isolated autonomous village economy. This system of production had become irrelevant during the Mughal Empire. The integration of regional markets created a substantial increase in demand of products of manufacturers. The growing size of market was accompanied by a growing demand for Indian manufactured goods in foreign market. To meet the needs of such growing markets, the craftsmen were required to increase the scale of production. Since craftsmen during these periods did not have resources to expand scale of their operations, they lacked the capability to meet the growing demand of their products. The objective conditions that were prevalent at the time necessitated structural transformation in the organization of production in manufacturing. This transformation was initiated by merchants who had substantial amount of financial resources in their hand. This happened because scattered small workshops did not have sufficient resources to expand the scale of production to meet the growing need for manufactured products. Therefore, under these conditions, merchants evolved a network of artisanal household workshops through putting-out system. The putting-out system facilitated in meeting the capital requirements of craftsmen and selling their products in the market. It is, in this way, traditional flexible manufacturing emerged as a consequence of an emerging nexus between craftsmen and merchants owing to the loss of independence of craftsmen to merchants, who supplied them raw materials or working capital along with their subsistence needs to control their final output.

In this form of organization of production, there was no need to make large investments in fixed capital. Therefore, its expansion depended on *circulating capital* rather than on *fixed capital*. These characteristics of manufacturing provided it with several kinds of flexibilities. These flexibilities are now built into the modern flexible production systems.[48] These flexibilities establish similarity between proto-manufacturing and modern manufacturing. I arrived at the term *primitive flexible manufacturing* by combining a dominant characteristic of proto-industry, namely flexibility, and *primitive* which is one of the synonyms of the word *proto*.[49] However, with the realization that the word *primitive* connotes with primitive societies, here I have used the term *traditional flexible manufacturing*.

In this kind of system of production, technology and scale of production did not change. The scattered household workshops of craftsmen were made part of networks evolved by merchants. Merchants provided working capital or raw materials as well as means of subsistence to the household producers in lieu of commitment on the part of craftsmen that they will supply the final products to the merchants. In this way, large-scale marketing networks created by merchants roped in small household workshops to supply products in the mass market. Since traders purchased raw materials in bulk quantities to supply them to artisans who were part of their networks, they saved costs due to the advantages of *economies of bulk purchase*. They also sold the final products in bulk quantities in mass markets, which helped them in making substantial profits.

During the Mughal period, this system of organization of production was known as *dadni* system (system of advance). This system created a particular kind of relationship between merchants and artisans. It was based on an agreement between merchants and artisans, which specified terms regarding quantity, quality, prices and date of delivery of output and the account of advance given to the craftsmen. The agreement or contract was compatible with law of *sillim* (sales). The law of sillim derived its jurisdiction from the Quran. Here it means delivery on a stipulated date. Perhaps in the absence of law of contracts, the law of sillim provided religious legitimacy to contract between craftsman and merchant. The traders who were engaged in the dadni system were assisted by *paikars* (travelling representative of the traders), who gave advances to the craftsman, and *mukeems* (merchandizers), who helped the trader by inspecting the quality of the final output supplied by the artisans.[50]

In the dadni system, the producer (craftsman) did not sell his output directly in the market but produced it for the merchant, conforming to the specification specified by the merchant regarding quantity and quality. This suggests that merchant purchased the work effort, skills and service of equipment owned by the artisan in lieu of working capital or materials and their subsistence needs. Thus, in a way merchants provided employment to artisans. In the modern factory system, the owners of factory provide equipment, materials and wages to workers to control the selling and marketing of the output. Therefore, the difference between organization of production of putting-out system and modern factory form of production of manufacturing is that in the putting-out system craftsman still controlled the production process, and instead of working in a factory, he worked at his household production unit. This happened because the craftsman owned equipment. Tchitchirov in his study has recorded several instances of such relationships between artisans and merchants across different manufacturing industries and regions, for instance, in the production of *chintz* (block printed cloth) in Patna, in making pig iron in Bihar, in the fabric weaving industry of Coromandel Coast, Bengal and Gujarat, and in the oil pressing industry at Shahabad (Tchitechrov, 1998).

In the organization of traditional flexible manufacturing, merchants knew about market fluctuations, consumer preferences and also controlled decision regarding expansion or reduction in the capacity of the work to produce. Merchants through this process made use of supply of cheap labour from countryside. People were shifting from villages to cities because higher rates of land revenue imposed by the Mughal Empire, monetization of rural economy and weakening of gift-exchange relationships between different occupational groups. These conditions had reduced return on the small holdings. Therefore, peasants with small holdings had to make choice between *land-intensive* farming and *labour-intensive* craft production. Hence, traditional flexible manufacturing can be viewed as a first historical experience of using unlimited supply of labour for the growth of manufacturing.[51]

One of the most important advantages of traditional flexible manufacturing was the practice of division of labour and specialization. The extent of division of labour depended on the expansion of market. Perhaps after observing the practices in the traditional flexible manufacturing workshops of Kirkcaldy in Scotland, Adam Smith developed the axiom that the division of labour is limited by the size of market (see Smith, 1776, 2003). In India, for traditional manufacturing, production was organized in a manner which involved several intermediate stages. This was possible due to the existence of division of labour based on not only technology, but also on social factors like caste.

Apart from division of labour practised inside the production unit, it also provided conditions for the division of control on two important strategic managerial decisions. The decisions regarding *what to produce* were made by merchants due to their better understanding regarding markets and customer preferences. Therefore, they also influenced the decisions regarding product development, in terms of quality and design of the product. Decisions regarding *how to produce* remained with the craftsman. Since merchants had control over the final product and its marketing, accumulation occurred outside the unit of production, in the hands of merchants. The consequence of this division of decision-making was that the artisans remained poor and individual production unit remained small, whereas merchants became more resourceful (see Freudenberger and Redlick, 1964).

The separation of functions between craftsmen and merchants provided scope for several kinds of flexibilities which became inherent in the system. The merchants were divorced from risks and problems associated with the organization of production; they enjoyed flexibility of expanding and contracting the level of output in response to market conditions. This they could achieve by adjusting the size of their network according to market fluctuations, without incurring costs of lay-offs and retrenchment had these artisans been working in his factory. This system also provided to the merchant flexibility to supply variety of products customized according to the needs and requirements of different customers (*economies of scope*). This could be achieved by the merchants by employing additional craftsman to produce products with varied specifications. The system also provided opportunities to merchants to take advantage of economies of scale. The scale of operation of each merchant depended on the amount of his capital employed in stocks of raw materials, finished products and number of artisan households that were part of his network. It is an important fact to mention that the sum of capital employed by some of the merchants in their network was much larger than employed in the fixed assets by early modern factories.[52]

For instance, one of the traders Kasi Viranna of South India had created a network of around 2,200 best weavers around Jahanabad. The network of weavers and their settlements that he controlled were called Viranna villages. He along with his family controlled a substantial share of purchases made by the East India Company.[53] According to available historical records in Bayana in 1620, two local merchants, namely Mirza Sadiq and Ghazi Fazil, had established monopoly in indigo trade. Similarly, another merchant Khemchand established monopoly in textile trade in Sohroha near Balasore in Orissa. Another group of wealthy merchants led by Gurivi Setti and Kunigiri Setti had emerged as dominant merchants of textiles in Vijaynagar.[54] There must have been several other big merchants who operated their network of craftsmen in different parts of India, but their names do not appear in historical documents.

The separation of functions between merchants and craftsmen also provided scope for flexibility to the craftsmen. Because of separation of functions, household workshops of craftsmen did not have to bear the risk of market conditions. This is because they were making products according to the orders placed by merchants. The system provided scope for pace flexibility to craftsmen because they worked in their own household workshops, which provided them freedom from discipline of supervisor or foreman and also freedom to select their own pace of work. Craftsmen could follow work stoppages for rest as and when they liked. They generally followed leisurely pace during weekdays, worked harder during weekends to make deliveries of their final output, so that they could collect working capital necessary for the next cycle of production.[55]

The traditional flexible manufacturing created a household workshop economy, based on vertically disintegrated inter-industry and intra-industry, specialized and dispersed production units, localized in clusters in specific area. Each production unit produced a specific product with close networking amongst other units that formed a cluster. Such clusters had emerged in different parts of the Indian subcontinent during the Mughal Empire, which specialized in the production of specialized products. Production clusters existed in Dacca, Murshidabad, Patna, Kasimbazar, Sonargaon, Banaras, Balasore and Assam in Eastern India; Surat, Ahmedabad, Pattan, Baroda and Jaipur in Western India; Agra, Aligarh, Gwalior, Moradabad in Central India; Lahore, Amritsar, Ludhiana and Kashmir in North India; and the Malabar Coast in Southern India. These kinds of clusters of production units have been conceptualized as *flexible specialization*.[56] The cluster of manufacturing units based on traditional flexible manufacturing system achieved competitive advantage by reducing overhead and inventory costs and received *external economies* from cluster, sufficient enough to compensate for *internal economies* that give advantage to vertically integrated large production units.

The most important disadvantage of the Indian traditional flexible manufacturing was that it neither allowed any change in the size of production unit nor did it experience technological change. This happened because the traditional flexible manufacturing organized production in such a way that the craftsmen never had sufficient resources to increase the size of their household workshop or use improved technology. Accumulation in this form of organization of manufacturing occurred outside the production unit, in the hands of merchants. Merchants were not interested in bringing about technological change because they were able to expand output by increasing the size of their network. Despite the absence of technological change, Indian craftsman made good quality manufactured items with simple tools and equipment. For instance, Marx provides the example of weavers of Dacca muslin who according to him were weaving 'without capital, machinery division of labour' and states, 'It is only the special skill accumulated from generation to generation and transmitted from father to son, that gives to the Hindu, as it does to the spider, this proficiency' (Marx, 1868 [1956]).'[57] By equating skills of Indian craftsmen with those of the spider, he ignores the improvement made by each generation in improving the skills. He equates this acquired knowledge to the genetically transmitted skills of the spider which help it weave its web, or weaver bird to weave its nest. This view is also held by several scholars while describing craftsmanship of Indian craftsmen. This is because knowledge of skills remained within the community of the craftsmen, in complete isolation. Therefore, it was easily believed that 'India affords evidence for the theory of genetic transmissibility of skills amongst humans' (Dereth, 1976; Dietman, 1988, 3–11; Ray, 2010).

It is believed by some scholars that it was the absence of accumulation of capital in the hands of craftsman which discouraged the process of innovation and technological change in the traditional flexible manufacturing during the Mughal Empire. This view is expressed by the scholars who do not appreciate the historical role of capital in the process of production. Capital assumes importance when expansion in production is constrained by the supply of any of the factors of production. It is the supply side constraint which provides motivation to improve the efficiency of the limiting factor. During the Mughal Empire, 'land and labour were abundant, therefore, there was no need for capital' (see Chaudhri, 1978; Chaudhry, 1972). Some historians have attributed the absence of technological change in the traditional flexible manufacturing during the Mughal Empire to the phenomenon called *high-quality trap*. According to this view, the high-quality trap emerged in the Indian traditional manufacturing because specialization had gone to such an extent that 'it would have required great incentive to induce craftsmen to change their methods of production and habits drastically' (Ray, 2010).

It is also interesting to mention that despite the fact that in the Indian economy there was absence of institutions, such as property rights, business laws, modern banking institutions, laws regarding contracts and their enforcement, which are required for efficient working of a market economy, yet it evolved into a vibrant commercial and manufacturing economy during the Mughal Empire. The success of traditional flexible manufacturing in the Indian subcontinent depended on the pattern of organizations of two important communities which were involved in the traditional flexible manufacturing—the communities of merchants and communities of craftsmen. The merchants and big banking family firms possessed not only capital but also trade-related intellectual capital accumulated over generations. The communities of these merchants helped in protecting their capital as well as their intellectual capital. These communities developed their own rules regarding its transfer to the next generation. The membership of the community provided these merchants a code of conduct and institutional support for resolving interpersonal conflict through *community panchayats* (councils). Therefore, unlike the risk-taking entrepreneurs of the Western societies, the entrepreneurs engaged in the organization of traditional flexible manufacturing were members of *risk-reducing community* (Ray, 2010). The membership of a community provided to the Indian merchants the much needed protection of their capital, availability of cheap credit, common community-specific rules and regulations, and also protection against entry of merchants who did not belong to the community.

Similar advantages were available to craftsmen because they were members of caste-based communities. These communities of craftsmen helped in *accumulation* of skill-specific knowledge and practices. The caste-based communities also facilitated in the *transfer* of skills to the next generation by giving training in crafts to the new members of community. These communities also protected skill-specific intellectual capital by denying its spread to persons belonging to other castes. Therefore, in the Indian subcontinent, division of labour was not necessarily dependent on the size of the market as envisaged by Adam Smith, but depended on the organization of craft into specialized and dedicated caste-based communities. The system of community-based specialization of merchants and craftsmen and their community-specific rules and regulations acted as a substitute for the role of the state to legislate property rights and commercial and business laws. This happened because the Mughal state accepted the supremacy of communities forming their own laws and governing the conduct of their members. The Mughal state intervened only in instances when there emerged inter-community disputes. Due to this reason, the Mughal Empire did not evolve elaborate legal structures.

It is an important historical fact that in most of the societies, communities have played a significant role in their socio-economic structures despite the fact that the mainstream economics associates them with several kinds of distortions. Their undermining the role of communities is based on their belief that communities give rise to different kinds of market imperfections, which hinder the optimum or desirable outcome of market-mediated decisions made by different economic agents. This happens because membership of a community creates different kinds of bias in the preference of economic agents. These biases result in principal–agent problem and create a dichotomy between insider and outsider. Communities also significantly affect social mobility, occupational mobility and spatial mobility of their members. Due to these reasons, it is believed by mainstream economists that the existence of strong communities causes several types of market imperfections.[58]

On the contrary, economists have revealed preference for the existence of institutions. The economists' liking for institutions is derived from the premise that institutions define the context in which a market operates, because all economies are embedded in the institutions created by the polity. Institutions determine the rules of the game, which have to be observed by all economic agents while they participate in the market. Moreover, they also believe that good institutions insulate the individuals from the interference of communities, and make them market-efficient. Hence institutions help in establishing order as well as stability in the market.

The mainstream economists' dislike for communities is not accepted by the social scientists who have developed an understanding about *social capital*. According to these social scientists, communities are important because the bonds that emerge as a consequence of being member of a community, based on *trust* and *reciprocity*, create positive impact on development.[59] They have rehabilitated the role of communities in social sciences by evolving a concept called *communities of practice*.[60] It is being defined as 'a group of people bound together by their interest in common working practices' (Dugrid, 2008, 1). The social scientists who are conducting researches on the concept of communities of practices have identified several types of communities of practice. In this literature, task-based communications are differentiated on the bases of particular artefacts, tools and work environment. These communities are also studied in the context of awareness acquired through mastery of certain tasks in shared division of labour (Amin and Roberts, 2008, 17). These communities played important caste-based roles in addition to the tasks performed by non-caste-based communities. They have provided to their members complete exclusivity by creating strict entry barriers and by protecting their intellectual property. In the section that follows, we will focus on the repercussions of these developments in determining the composition of manufacturing in the Indian subcontinent during the Mughal Empire.

COMPOSITION OF MANUFACTURING DURING THE MUGHAL EMPIRE

As it has been described above that during Mughal rule, the economy of the Indian subcontinent emerged as an important manufacturing nation; these manufacturing industries had strong linkage with the rural economy. The most important industry which experienced a high growth rate was textile industry. Indian textiles were globally well known since they were first reported in *Perilus Maris Erytherien Sea*, written by an unknown Greek writer. There are archaeological evidences to establish that wild cotton (Arabic cotton) was harnessed by people living in the Indus Valley around 2000 BC. Since then Indians have been cultivating cotton and with time they developed skills to spin, weave, dye, print and paint textiles. These skills perfected through the centuries provided to the Indian cloth a distinct competitive advantage. Indian cotton and silk textiles were traded along most of the port cities located in the Indian Ocean, Arabian Sea and Red Sea, and also through caravan routes to Central Asia, Venice and Europe.

Due to the socio-economic and political environment created by Mughal Empire, manufacturing of textiles expanded enormously. Its production also spread to different parts of the Indian subcontinent and each region specialized in the manufacturing of distinct variety of textiles. These regional centres of textile production were interconnected through trade routes to cover domestic as well as foreign market. One of the important characteristic of the traditional flexible manufacturing during the Mughal Empire was that its extent of spatial spread, in terms of production and commercial function, was not entirely an urban phenomenon. The manufacturing was widely dispersed in cities, small town, qasbas and villages, which were dominated by craftsmen. These centres of production were like networks connected through trade routes (see Chaudhri (ed.), 1997; Omprakash, 1998; Vanina, 2004). The textile manufacturing centres in Western India were Gujarat, Sindh and Rajasthan. In South India, these centres were located around the Coromandel and Malabar Coasts. Whereas in Eastern India, textile manufacturing was prevalent in Lucknow, Banaras, Bengal, Orissa and Assam. North Indian towns such as Agra, Lahore and Amritsar were also popular for the manufacturing of textiles. Amongst the cotton textiles manufactured in India, the most important variety of textile was muslin of Dacca. The muslin of Dacca was known as *malmal khas*, which was the finest muslin in the world. An expert spinner of the muslin of Dacca could spin an even yarn upward of four miles in length from a *sicca* (*rupee*) weight of cotton. Observers have found that in comparison to muslin produced in Britain and France, Dacca muslin was of exceptional quality.[61] Muslin of similar quality was also produced by the weavers of South India, which was known as *arni muslin*.[62] Muslin was also produced in Srirampur and Bankibazar areas of Bengal. These areas were also popular centres of manufacturing cotton-stuff or *calicoe*. Lucknow and Patna were important manufacturing centres of chintz, and Ahmedabad specialized in the production of dhotis and dupattas. The towns of Nagpur, Umaer and Pooni were known for the production of silk-bordered cotton textiles, which were dyed with a popular dye stuff called *chay*.[63] Manufacturers of textile of Sindh were specialized in making embroidered quilts. The manufacturers of Coromandel and Malabar Coasts were known for the manufacturing of sailcloth, bedcovers, pillowcases, handkerchiefs and mattresses.

Traditional flexible manufacturing of silk textiles was also widespread in India. Each region specialized in the production of a specialized variety of silk textiles. Surat specialized in the production of *Patola* silk, whereas *chopphas, bandena* and *corah* varieties of silk were produced in Eastern India. Weaving of silk was done in places such as Malda, Murshidabad, Sreerampur and Bankibazar areas of Bengal. The beginning of sericulture in Bengal and in its peripheral areas began approximately around the fourteenth century. During the Mughal Empire, Bengal was the main supplier of raw silk for internal and external markets.[64] These areas also manufactured *velvet, satin, taffetas* and *tasar* varieties of silk. Assam was well known for the manufacturing of *Mugga* silk. Silk brocade work was done at Banaras and Ahmedabad. For woollen textiles, Kashmir, Ludhiana and Amritsar were quite popular.

The production of textiles involved different levels of dexterity of the craftsmen with regard to the quality of the cloth produced, depending on whether they were being produced for elites of the society or common people. The textiles which were manufactured for the royal family and nobles comprised of cloths with silver or gold brocade work, fine and expensive muslins, and hand-painted textiles with intricate designs. These fabrics had very poetic and sophisticated names such as *ab-i-ravan* (flowing water), *tanzeb* (body's beauty) and *meghavana* (cloud over forest).[65] It is generally believed that Indian weavers used simple looms to manufacture these textiles. However, historical records suggest that at this point in time Indian weavers used different kinds of looms to weave different kinds of textiles. For instance, *vertical looms* were used to manufacture carpets. Fancy patterned cloth was woven on *drawlooms,* mobile weavers used *pit-looms,* which were light in weight and could be assembled and transported easily.[66] It has been established that the loom used by poet Kabir, shown in one of the miniature paintings belonging to the Mughal period, which is presently a part of the collection of St Petersburg branch of the Institute of Oriental Studies of the Russian Academy of Sciences, is similar to the loom depicted in the painting titled *Return of Ulysses* by the sixteenth-century Italian painter Pinturicchio (Vanina, 2004, 30).

It is also important to mention that in organizing production in traditional flexible manufacturing in India, during the Mughal period, some of the processes which are integral parts of production of textiles were performed by separate specialized industries, such as printing, painting, bleaching, dying, and production of dye stuffs and indigo. Indians had mastered the art of making vegetable dyes. Each region had evolved its own variety of dye stuffs, which were prepared from local plants and flowers. These dyes remained popular in the dying of textiles in India till they were replaced by chemical dyes.[67] However, after the concern for environmental conditions affected by use of chemical dyes arose, there has been a revival of vegetable dyes. In India, indigo was produced in places such as Bayana, Sarkhej, Jaipur, Bulandshahar and Khandesh. Among these, the indigo produced at Bayana was considered to be of the best quality.

In market economies, the process of *commoditization* of products emerges, which results in alienation of products from social experience, thereby making them impersonal objects of consumption. This happens because in market economies exchange occurs between impersonal producers and consumers. In the case of the Indian subcontinent, production as well as consumption of textiles was embedded in social frameworks of the existing social order. The division of labour practised in the production of textiles was organized on caste lines, where each caste participated in the production process depending on their place in caste hierarchy. The characteristic embodied in the textiles in terms of *purity* and *pollution,* and *sacred* and *profane,* determined not only the status of persons who were involved in its production but also the status of the persons who consumed it. Therefore, ritualistic statuses of weaver, spinner, dyer, printer, tailor and washer man depended on the ritualistic quality of the cloth that each of them produced.[68] It was not only texture of the textile or type of fibre being used in the production which determined its consumption by different castes, even the colours of textiles were caste-specific. In this kind of social order, persons copied the pattern of consumption dictated by their individual caste affiliation or by their ancestors. This process of making choices regarding consumption pattern of textiles was significantly different from choices regarding consumption of textiles observed in the market economies. In market economies, consumer preferences are guided by individual preferences, imitation of strangers and are also influenced by current trends in fashion.

It is important to mention here that the Mughal emperors played an important role in reducing the caste-based consumption of textiles. This happened because the Mughal emperors began to consume the textiles as well as other products produced by their subjects to provide them royal patronage. This role of the Mughal emperors led to rise of diversity in the consumption of textiles.[69] The process of decastification with regard to consumption of textiles during the Mughal Empire made it possible that an individual need not copy the dress code dictated by his caste affiliation or by his ancestors. Now he could make individual choices regarding style of stitching, texture, type of fabric and colour of textiles.

The other major change which emerged during the Mughal Empire in the consumption of textiles was the changes in the attitude of orthodox Hindus as well as Muslims regarding choices of textiles. For instance, it altered the attitude of orthodox Hindus regarding use of stitched cloth. Since stitching of cloth could not be done without cutting textiles, it was considered ritualistically impure or profane by orthodox Hindus. Therefore, use of stitched cloth was not permitted in Hindu rituals. On the contrary, Islamic values based on the Quran required that a woman's entire body must be fully covered by cloth. To have a garment which can fully cover the body of a woman, cutting of cloth and tailoring was inevitable. Therefore, in orthodox Islam, unstitched cloth is viewed as primitive and barbaric. Due to these divergent attitudes towards stitched cloths, while Hindu women believed *sari* as the ultimate form of female garment, Muslims considered sari as an unstitched garment and relic of primitive times.[70] However, the attitude of Hindus also changed towards stitched cloth because of social necessity; even Hindu women began to cover their entire body. The use of stitched cloth led to an evolution in fashion. It is interesting to mention that till today most of the fashion designers draw inspiration from costumes of the Mughal period. These changes helped in integration of segmented markets of textiles, based on caste and religious lines, into mass market.

Similarly changes also occurred in the attitude of Muslims. Islam forbids the use of silk textiles because they are produced from the saliva of an insect. But weavers began to weave new variety of textiles, which were specifically created to satisfy the desire of Indian Muslims who wanted to consume silk textiles. These new varieties of textiles were evolved using cotton as well as silk yarn. These varieties were *mashroo* and *himroo*. These mixed fabrics were in demand amongst Muslims as well as Europeans (Ramaswamy, 2008, 277). These new varieties of textiles required new specialized skills, and this eventually created new castes and subcastes of weavers.

During the Mughal Empire, demand for textiles grew significantly in foreign markets also. It has been mentioned in the introduction of the book that India contributed 25 per cent of the world's total output of manufactured products. When British merchants introduced Indian cloths in the British markets, the consequence was described as a 'national makeover'. While describing the extent of makeover of British lifestyle by Indian textiles, Daniel Defoe wrote in 1708 that 'Indian textiles crept into our houses, our closets and our bedchambers; curtains, cushions, chairs, and at last beds themselves were nothing but calicoes or Indian stuffs'.[71] English merchants purchased huge quantities of Indian textiles that were largely used in Britain, and a proportion of this was re-exported to different European countries. At that time, British traders had nothing to offer in exchange for Indian textiles, apart from bullion earned from their trade with rest of the world, or subsequently brought from America. When massive new supplies of silver and gold emerged from America and Japan, which were used to buy Indian goods, India became the 'ultimate sink of these metals' (Reichards, 1987). English merchants were earning bullion by entering into multiple markets simultaneously by arbitrage by placing themselves as middlemen in different trading locations taking advantage of differences in the exchange rates between gold and silver in different markets (see Ramaswamy, 1980, 2008, 283).

The importance of bullion brought from America to buy Indian textiles has been very appropriately described by Andre Gunder Frank, when he mentioned that 'Europe used American bullion to buy itself a ticket to Asian train'.[72] Apart from the British, the Dutch were also exporting textiles from India, especially indigo-dyed blue colour cloth to Africa to buy slaves. This Indian cloth was used to cloth slaves. This cloth has been very aptly described as 'the cloth of sorrow'.[73]

The art of smelting iron was known to Indians since ages. The most important physical evidence of the skills of Indian iron makers is the iron pillar located near the Qutab Minar in Delhi (Bell, 1881). There are historical records to establish the fact that the best-quality steel used by Greek and Hellenistic monarchies was imported from India. Idrish-ul-Mustaq mentions that Indian iron makers were using compounds of substances while making iron.[74] Marco Polo mentions about *Ondanique* (Indian iron), which was imported in Kerman to make several metallic products such as swords, bows and quiver (Marco Polo, 1998).

During Mughal rule, due to the existence of a vast army and increase in extent of urbanization, the demand for iron for making weapons, armour, agricultural implements and household utensils increased substantially. Therefore, this industry also experienced higher growth rates. Mughal India was known for manufacturing of carbon steel (Wootz iron) (Vanina, 2004, 45).[75] Iron produced in Kutch was used to make *Koriz* swords. Iron smelting was widespread in Monghyr and Birbhum, Satghud and Rajahmundry areas in Andhra Pradesh and Gwalior in Madhya Pradesh. Chottanagpur Plateau was popularly known as *Loharmahal* (palace of iron). Here low-caste Hindus and tribal populations were involved in the production of iron. These communities were *Pharias, Santhals, Agerias* and *Kolas*.[76] Indelwai was an important centre for making swords, daggers and lances. These products were made from iron mined in Kalghat Hills. The most important innovation of metal makers during this period was the celebrated *bidri* alloy of copper, lead and zinc, perfected by the metal makers of Bidar. Later on, the manufacturing of bidri also spread to Lucknow, Purnia, Hyderabad and Murshidabad.

Along with the existence of traditional flexible manufacturing, the Mughal state had big manufacturing units which have been described by historians as royal *karkhanas* (factories). These karkhanas, like modern-day ordnance factories, were established to manufacture equipment needed by the army Abul Fazal Allami has described these royal karkhanas which were manufacturing a variety of weapons for the Mughal army. He has mentioned that guns were made in these karkhanas of such big sizes that a ball used in one of the variety of guns weighed twelve *mans* (one *man* is equal to approximately 40 kg). To transport these guns to battle ground help of several cattle and elephants was needed. These karkhanas also manufactured guns which could be taken in the form of separate components and could be easily reassembled for use. He also mentions about *gajnals* (gun which could be carried by a single elephant) and *narnals* (gun which could be carried by a single soldier) which were made in these royal karkhanas. In the royal karkhanas, matchlocks of different types were also manufactured like the one designed by ustads (master craftsman) Kabir and Husayn, which was known as *damanak*. Allami also mentions about several kinds of swords with different shapes and sizes, such as *khasa, kotal, jamdhar, yakbandi* and *khapawas*. Along with swords, different kinds of daggers, spears and lances were also manufactured in these karkhanas. Several kinds of armours were also manufactured, which were used to protect soldiers, horses and elephants. Allami records that these karkhanas also manufactured products which were consumed by the royal family and families of the nobles.[77]

Apart from weapons, traditional flexible manufacturing was also engaged in the production of several products from iron, such as household utensils, equestrian equipment (horse shoes, stirrup, curbbit, and the like) and farm equipment. Iron manufacturers were also making products which were used in the construction of houses and buildings, ship building, shoemaking, clamps, rings and needles. Along with these iron products, traditional flexible manufacturing was making products from other metals also, such as brass, copper and bell metal. Manufacturing of products from these metals was spread across different regions such as Poona, Nasik, Hyderabad, Tanjore, Moradabad and Aligarh.

Saltpetre was another important product which was required by the army and also for export. It was used for preparing gun powder. It was manufactured by processing nitrogenous organic matter and potassium nitrate found on the surface of the earth. Urban rich persons also used saltpetre for cooling of drinking water during summer months. It was manufactured at Agra, Ahmedabad, Orissa, Bihar and Bengal. Saltpetre was also purchased by the East India Company and the Dutch and French trading companies for their local use and export.[78]

Amongst the other items of mass consumption, which were manufactured by the traditional flexible manufacturing during the Mughal Empire, special mention must be made of sugar. According to Indian mythology, India is the birthplace of sugarcane. It is also quite obvious from the fact that in different languages the word used to describe sugar is quite similar to the word used in India. In India, sugar is called *shakkar* in common language; it is called *schakar* in Persian, *sukkar* in Arabic, *seachrum* in Latin and *sucre* in French.[79] Due to the availability of sugarcane, sugar manufacturing also has a long history in India. During Mughal rule, manufacturing of sugar increased due to the integration of regional markets in the Indian subcontinent and increased demand by households. Apart from domestic demand, sugar was also exported through caravan routes passing through Khyber and Bolan Passes and also through sea route to Europe. Traditional flexible manufacturing of sugar was widespread and followed the geography of cane cultivation. Manufacturing of sugar was concentrated in Gangetic India, Burdwan, Murshidabad, Gorakhpur and also in certain locations in Southern India. Sugar during the Mughal period was manufactured in the form of *gur* (jaggery).[80]

During Mughal rule, manufacturing of vegetable oils was also quite widespread across different regions of the Indian subcontinent. Regional specialization in the production of vegetable oil depended on the cultivation of oilseed crops which were available for processing. The different varieties of vegetable oil produced in the Indian subcontinent were mustard oil (produced largely in Northern India), groundnut oil (mainly produced in Western India), coconut oils (South India) and linseed oil (South India). Certain regions were also producing aromatic oils, which were used in making medicines, perfumes and *itra*. There also existed some other manufacturing industries during the Mughal Empire such as opium, which was processed in Bihar and the Malwa region. Opium became an important industry subsequently during the rule of the East India Company, when it assumed greater importance. Alcoholic drinks were also manufactured from palm and mahua plants and from the molasses in sugarcane-growing areas. Due to the abundant availability of leather, owing to the large population of domesticated animals, leather products were also manufactured in

India. Leather products were manufactured in Lahore, Sindh, Agra, Multan and Jaipur.

As it has been explained above, the socio-political and economic environment that was created by the Mughal Empire helped in sustaining and expanding the traditional flexible manufacturing. Its role increased with the production of several products in several regions. It has been suggested by some scholars that with decline in the authority of the Mughal Empire after the death of Aurangzeb, these conditions began to disappear gradually. This happened because one region after another declared autonomy from the Mughal Empire. The fragmentation of polity into new political units intensified military conflicts, plunder, banditry and quality of governance, which led to decline of trade and commerce. Again, markets got fragmented due to re-emergence of barriers in inter-regional trade. Multiple political entities led to multiple currencies issued by new political dispensations. The requirement of financial resources by local rulers increased considerably to finance frequent wars. The need for financial resources increased the significance of merchants in comparison to the historical significance of knights and warriors. The new circumstances, on the one hand, increased dependence of the local rulers on big financial firms and, on the other hand, increased the conflict between banking firms and local rulers since merchants depended on the local rulers and administrators to carry on their business and for protection of their property during the Mughal Empire. The increase in the absolute powers of the local rulers after the weakening of the Mughal Empire increased the vulnerability of business classes.

Even during Mughal rule, local governors used their absolute power to harass merchants to extract money. Historical records have recorded several instances when local administrators took away the property of merchants, which suggests that in some regions property rights were not guaranteed. When Akbar died in 1605, his death caused so much panic and insecurity amongst merchants that most of the business went underground, and it became almost impossible to distinguish between high and low, and rich and poor.[81] The biography of Banarsidas, *Ardhkathanaka*, mentions how the local governor of Jaunpur, Nawab Quilich, arrested all the rich merchants of his area to take away their wealth. It also mentions that during the rule of Jahangir one the *umraos* (aristocrats), Agha Noor, imprisoned several merchants.[82] There are also recorded accounts of travellers, who travelled during the Mughal Empire, which state that there were emerging tensions between local rulers and merchants. In one of the accounts, it is mentioned that 'since merchant's wealth consist of cash and jewels... they preserved it as closed as private as they can, lest Mughal exchequer should be made their treasury'.[83]

With the erosion of the Mughal authority, conflicts between new political dispensations were inevitable. There are several instances when properties of several big merchants were confiscated. Haider Quli Khan, the *Mutassadi* (Mayor) of Surat, confiscated the property of Mulla Mohammad Hai, an adopted son of one of the wealthy merchants of Surat, Abdul Gafoor. Property of Banarsidas, one of the important merchants of Jaunpur, was also confiscated by Nawab Quilich.[84] There is also the example of Jagat Seth, who played an important role in the battle of Plassey.[85]

It is a historical fact that when the state becomes incapable to protect private property from despotic officials, it creates circumstances which demotivate merchants, innovators and entrepreneurs to create more wealth. This is because of increasing insecurity regarding private property, falling standards of governance, rise in banditry and disruption of trade routes which put the wealth of merchants into bottomless pit. The new historical circumstances demotivated merchants to participate in financing of networks of craftsmen to organize traditional flexible manufacturing. Therefore, some scholars have evolved a fact that the emergence of disconnect between merchants and craftsmen led to disconnect between craftsmen and mass market. This established a stylized notion amongst scholars that the decline of Mughal Empire paved the way for the decline of traditional flexible manufacturing.

In Indian historiography, the decline in traditional flexible manufacturing has been described as the process of de-industrialization. De-industrializaton was experienced by the Indian manufacturing when large proportion of craftsmen who were engaged in the flexible manufacturing lost their employment, and the loss of their employment was not accompanied by the birth of modern manufacturing.[86] This stylized notion needs correction because it should be noted that the traditional flexible manufacturing is just one of the several modes of organization of handicrafts to cater to mass markets. Historical experience provides us with several other possibilities in which manufacturing of handicrafts could be organized.

In the recent past, scholars have conducted several studies of the regions which became autonomous after the decline of the Mughal Empire. They have discovered that in certain regions the conditions that were necessary for the continuity of traditional flexible manufacturing continued to exist. This happened because in some of the regions dependence of local rulers on merchants increased significantly. They even promoted trade and crafts to increase their revenue. These regional studies have established that the decline in the authority of the Mughal state led to a variety of regional experiences and repercussions on traditional flexible manufacturing. The establishment of autonomous successor states of the Mughal Empire in Awadh, Hyderabad, Mysore, Maharashtra, Punjab, Rajasthan and Kashmir continued to provide opportunities for the growth of traditional flexible manufacturing.[87] In the chapter that follows, we have narrated the stories of four cities during the Mughal Empire to understand how the rise and decline of the Mughal Empire impacted the prospects of two cities of Western India, namely Surat and Bombay, and two cities of Eastern India, namely Dacca and Calcutta, in order to see whether their prospects were impacted in similar ways or not.

NOTES

1. The statement of Faristha has been quoted in Eraly (2003, 7).
2. For details regarding the event are given in the text, see Grusset (1970) and Babur (2003).
3. See for this Thapar (2002). This is also apparent in the autobiography of Mahatma Gandhi, *My Experiment with Truth*, where he describes how his family was reluctant in letting him travel to Britain for his studies.
4. See for further details, Chaudhri (1985) and Gotthold (1987).
5. For this statement see Allami (1927), Vol. I, p.2.
6. To know about divine origin of Mughal kings, see Allami (1956) and Richard (1978), pp. 262–263.

7. For the idea of divine kingship see Mukhia (2004), pp. 45–46.
8. For the idea of kingship during the period of Delhi Sultanate, see Aquil (2008).
9. For understanding the concept of king in Hindu would view, see Walker (1968) and Bhatia (1974).
10. For details, see Shelvankar (1940), pp. 96–102 and 139–143.
11. For the knowledge about the world view of Mughals, see Allami (1927), Vol. I, p.4.
12. For understanding about Hinu *Jajmani* system, see Wiser (1969).
13. *Jajmani* system and its various regional variants have been discussed in detail in the writings of Fukazawa (1972), Commander (1983), Fuller (1989), Meyer (1993) and Guha (2004).
14. For the practice of *vand* in Punjab, see Punjab District Gazetteer (1904).
15. For the ideas of Marx on Indian social system, see Husain (ed), (2006), p. XXXI.
16. This observation has been made by Raychaudhri (1982).
17. For details regarding these roads, during Mughal empire, see Serwani (1974) and Alam and Subramanyan (eds) (1998).
18. For details regarding Mughal administration and organization of army, see Moorland (1923, 1962) and Metcalf (1993).
19. To know about Mughal monetary system in detail, see Richard (1983, 26).
20. For understanding the Trimetallic currency system followed by Mughal rulers, see Habib (1987).
21. See for more information, Mossavi (1987).
22. For these facts, see Allami (1927), Vol. I, pp. 48 and 59–100.
23. For details regarding occupational pattern of the working class and composition of national income during Mughal empire, see Maddison (1971) and (2003, p. 110).
24. To know in detail about the activities of different communities of merchants, which were important in different parts of India, see Darling (1926), Pillai (1930), Pavlov (1964), Misra (1965) and Levkovesky (1965).
25. For the historical facts regarding the house of *Jagat Seth*, see Little (1920) and (1921), Hunter (1965), and Levkovesky (1965).
26. For the uses of *Hundi*, see Jain (1929), Subramanian (1987), Siddiqi (1993) and Markovits (2000).
27. To understand the similarity between *hawala* and *hundi*, see Martin (2004).
28. For those facts, see Pavlov (1964).
29. For this aspect of the Mughal empire, see Subrahmanyam (1993).
30. To know about the role of banking firms during the period of Mughal empire, see Habib (1963). Grover (1966), Hambly (1982) Tripathi (1991), Dasgupta (1994) and Subramanian (1996, 2014).
31. See for *Imarat* and *Tijarat*, Alam and Subramanyan (1998).
32. For these important data, see Moosavi (1987).
33. The information regarding the community of *Banjaras* is given in detail in Naqvi (1986).
34. To know about the communities of *Komati* and *Khojas* in facilitating domestic trade, see Tchitchirov (1998).
35. These facts are given in Habib (1990).
36. For understanding the importance of carvan trade in the Indian subcontinent, see Bruton (1993) and Brenning (1990).
37. For details regarding the magnitude of carvan trade to different countries, see Doll (1994) and Levis (1999, 2002, 2007).
38. For these facts, see Vansanten (1991).

39. These facts have been taken from Om Prakash (1998).
40. For the idea of globalization with gun-boats, see Furguson (2004).
41. These important facts are given in Maddisan (2003) and Furguson (2004).
42. The term protean stage of industrialization was used by noted economic historian Hobsbawn (1954).
43. For this term, see Tilly and Tilly (1972).
44. The term nascent stage of capitalism was used by Levine (1964).
45. Perlin used this term to describe a transition from subsistence manufacturing to commercial manufacturing, see Perlin (1981).
46. The term proto-industry was used by Freudenberger and Redlick (1964).
47. See Mendles (1972) and (1982).
48. For appropriate meaning of *kauf* and *verlag* system Kridite, Medick and Schilumbo (1981).
49. For detailed understanding about the modern flexible manufacturing, see Kenny and Florida (1993), Knudsen (1996), William et al. (1987), Womack et al. (1990), and Womack and Jones (1996).
50. I have used these terms in my earlier paper, see Seth (2002, 2003, 2008).
51. For details regarding *dadni* system, see Chaudhry (1972) and Chaudri (1979).
52. Lewis (1954) evolved a model of economic development, which suggested, how developing economies can use excess labour for accumulation.
53. For comparing these circumstances with European economies, see Pollard (1968).
54. See for these facts, Tchitchirov (1998).
55. For these important facts, see Pelsaret (1975).
56. Similar facts have been observed by Landes (1988) regarding British experience.
57. The term flexible specialization has been evolved by Piore and Sabel (1984).
58. For understanding the attitude of economists regarding institutions, see Storper (2008).
59. For understanding the concept of *social capital*, based conceptualization of communities, see Olson (1961) and Putnam (2000). Contemporaneously, social scientists distinguish between Olson's conceptualization and Pulman's conceptualization of communities.
60. For the concept of community of practices, see Wagner (1998) and Amin and Roberts (2008).
61. This observation was made by Watson (1879).
62. For *Arni* muslin, see Parathasarthi (2001, p. 11).
63. For the use of dyriuff *chay*, see Royale (1851).
64. For this fact, see Habib (1982, p. 53) and Vanina (2004, p.2).
65. See, Allami (1927, pp. 93–101) and Vanina (2004, p.30).
66. For details regarding looms, see Pelaret (1925), Ramaswamy (2012) and Alam (2012a, 2012b).
67. For details regarding dyeing agents used in Indian textiles, see Naqvi (2012).
68. For information regarding the social context in which textiles were produced in India, see Bayly (1986).
69. For this idea, see Bayly (1987, 298).
70. This statement is attributed to writer from Lucknow Mr Abdul Halim Sherer, which is quoted in Appadurai (1986), p.296.
71. This statement is attributed to Daniel Defoe, which appeared in *Weekly Review* of 31 January 1707 and is reported in Furguson (2003), pp. 16–17.
72. To understand the business practices, which were used by British to earn foreign exchange, see Frank (1958, pp. 177, XXIV, XXV).

73. For this statement, see Chaudhri (1990).
74. For this fact, see Idrish Al-Sharif (1960).
75. For details regarding iron making, see Heath (1839) and Alam (2012a).
76. For historical account of iron mining in Chotanagpur and Birbhum, see Sanyal (1968) and Gupta (1980).
77. These facts have been reported from Allami (1927, p. 120).
78. For manufacturing of saltpetre, see Allami (1927), Gadgil (1924), Habib (1982) and Trivedi (1998).
79. For information regarding these words, see Noel (1949, 1958) and Mintz (1986).
80. About sugar manufacturing, see Khan (1929) and Gandhi (1934).
81. For this, see Banarsidas (2009, Chaupai No. 110–114, pp. 45–50).
82. See Bararsidas (2009, Chaupai No. 467–469, pp. 195–197).
83. This is mentioned in Ovington (1689, 1929, p.102) and Thevnot (1949).
84. See for this Singh (1977), Dasgupta (1967) and Lakshmi Subramanian (1987). This incident has been discussed in greater detail in the next chapter.
85. The house of Jagat Seth was wealthy business house of Murshidabad. He was transferring the annual tax collection of Bengal Subah to the Mughal empire in Delhi. For his life, see Hunter (1974, pp. 252–265), Little (1920, 1921) and Karen (1990).
86. For knowing more about the phenomenon called de-industrialization, see Thornu and Thornu (1962), Morris (1969) and Seth (2008, 2014, 2018).
87. For the regional studies of Awadh, see Alam (1986), Cole (1988) and Murad (2012); for Hyderabad, see Richard (1975) and Leonard (1979); for Bengal, see Om Prakash (1988) and Chaudhry (1998); and for Punjab, see Singh (1991) and Grewal (1995).

Tale of Four Cities During the Mughal Empire

It has been narrated in the previous chapter that during the Mughal Empire, the prevalence of law and order and absence of regional trade barriers led to the creation of a vast integrated domestic market. It also created infrastructure necessary to facilitate movement of goods and services across regions. This period also witnessed the process of advancement in urbanization leading to the growth of new towns and cities. These cities and towns were inhabited by elites and nobles, who were used to higher standards of living and lifestyle based on conspicuous consumption. These developments created demand for luxury handicrafts. The increase in the extent of monetization of the economy, on the one hand, reduced the magnitude of customary mode of exchange based on jajmani system and intensified the importance of market-mediated exchange relationship. On the other hand, it helped in the creation of a new class of traders, merchants and banking firms. These conditions provided an appropriate economic environment for the growth of traditional flexible manufacturing. The economic advantages which were created by the Mughal Empire were also available to the subahs of Gujarat and Bengal of the Mughal Empire, wherein the four cities that form the subject matter of the present narrative were located.

Surat is a port city of Gujarat which is one of the states of the Indian Union at present. Gujarat had been ruled by several dynasties before it got integrated with the Mughal Empire. From 696 to 1281, it was ruled by different clans of Rajputs: Chauhans (696–935), Solankis (635–1209) and Baghelas (1209–1281). Although Mahmud of Ghazni attacked Gujarat in 1203, his main objective was to plunder its cities and temples. The formal occupation of Gujarat by Delhi Sultanate occurred in 1281. This happened when Sultan Ala-ud-din Khilji annexed Gujarat. Thereafter Gujarat was ruled by several independent Sultans, until it was integrated by Akbar in 1573 with the Mughal Empire. During the period when Gujarat was ruled by Rajput clans, Pattan and then Champaner were the capital cities of Gujarat. However, when Gujarat came under the rule of independent sultans, they shifted the capital to Ahmedabad in 1401.[1]

Dacca city was part of the Bengal Subah when it became part of the Mughal Empire in 1536 during the rule of Mughal emperor Humayun. Bengal was earlier ruled by the Pala and Sena dynasties. During their rule, Nadiya was the capital of Bengal. Humayun's rule was affected by an interregnum of seven years (1538–1545), when Sher Shah Suri ruled Bengal while Humayun was in exile in Iran. During the rule of Sher Shah Suri and Humayun, the capital of Bengal was shifted from Nadiya to Lakhnauti or Gaur, which was renamed Jannatabad by Humayun. Dacca became the capital of Bengal in 1610.[2] It is important to mention here that both the city of Dacca and the geographical space which later on evolved as the city of Calcutta were part of the Bengal Subah during the Mughal Empire.

However, it is important to mention here that the Portuguese were the first amongst Europeans to establish direct trade link with the Indian subcontinent, much earlier than the Mughal Empire. The process of linking the Indian subcontinent with Portugal began with the discovery of sea route by Vasco da Gama, when in 1498 his ship reached Calicut, a port on the Malabar Coast. After establishing their trade links with Cochin in 1505, they also established their trading infrastructure at Surat.[3] The Portuguese also developed their settlements on the Eastern coast at places such as Chittagong, Satgaon and Hugli.[4] The arrival of the Portuguese resulted in the end of free trade, because the Portuguese were able to monopolize trade with India, especially in spices (Mathew, 1986, 1987). The monopoly of the Portuguese was challenged by a Dutch company called Vereenigde Oost-Indishe Compagnie. This company was formed in 1602 and it established its trading bases at Masulipatnam, Tegapatnam, Pulicut, Nagapatnam, Surat and Hubli.[5]

Soon the East India Company was formed in Britain when Queen Elizabeth I signed the royal charter which granted monopoly of trade with India to the company. The company began its operation from Surat in 1608. However, it received formal permission to conduct business at Surat only after it defeated the Portuguese at the Surat coast in 1612, and received permission from Mughal emperor Jahangir (1605–1627) in 1618. After establishing its foothold in Surat, it opened its factory (Office of the Factor) at Madras (now known as Chennai) in 1640 and constructed Fort St George (Balpour, 1885; Brian, 1971). The East India Company also obtained on lease from British King Charles II in 1668 territorial rights over the territory that grew into what came to be known as Bombay (Mumbai). Charles II had received this territory as a dowry from the Portuguese when he married Portuguese Princess Catherine of Braganza in 1662. The East India Company also received permission from Mughal emperor Aurangzeb Alamgir (1658–1707) to open its trading bases in three villages, Kolikata, Gobindapur and Sutanuti, located on the bank of river Hugli in 1690. It is here that a new settlement of the company sprang up with the name Calcutta. The East India Company fortified its trading base at Calcutta by constructing Fort William (Balpour, 1885).

The facts stated here clearly establish that the trading links with Europeans, which were not direct by land routes via Venice, but through sea routes, was opened by the voyage of Vasco da Gama of Indian port cities for European trading companies. This event created two important shifts in the history of the Indian subcontinent. The first important shift was that it established a direct trading link between the Europeans and the Indian subcontinent. The second shift occurred with regard to the flow of goods and services from land-based trade via Central and Middle Eastern route to maritime trade via Cape of Good Hope to Europe, which shifted the hold of Muslim merchants on the trade by increasing the dominance of the European trading companies.

This suggests that while the Mughal Empire was creating a continental sized market by integrating several fragmented polities including the native cities of Surat and Dacca, these cities were simultaneously experiencing the impact of the European trading companies.

Moreover, the East India Company had already established Bombay and Calcutta, which were their trading bases to trade in the products produced at Surat and Deccan, respectively. Therefore, native cities were simultaneously experiencing the impact of economic forces created by the Mughal Empire and the presence of another force of globalization, that is, the arrival of European trading companies. In rest of the chapter, tale of the four cities has been narrated as they were impacted by symbiotic existence of both of forces of globalization. The chapter has been divided into three sections. The first section describes the experience of Surat and Bombay during Mughal period. The second section deals with cities of Dacca and Calcutta to narrate the impact of two forces of globalization in tandem. Finally, in the third section, the experiences of cities located on the Western and Eastern Coasts are summarized and compared.

SURAT AND BOMBAY DURING THE MUGHAL EMPIRE

During the Mughal Empire, a very large number of cities existed. Some of them were ancient cities such as Ujjain and Banaras, while some others were remnants of the past. Some of the cities have emerged as a consequence of symbioses between bases of political power and administration and economic activities. Some of these cities had emerged on caravan trade routes and began to evolve at caravan sarais which provided facilities for the moving caravans which carried merchandize. Some cities such as Patna, Agra and Banaras emerged on the banks of rivers through which large numbers of boats passed carrying merchandize. Some places of market and pilgrimage got transformed in to big cities.

Native cities of Surat and Dacca were typical cities of the Mughal Empire. The cities depended on the capacity of the Mughal state to appropriate surplus. Like any other city of the Mughal Empire, these cities consisted of a fort with a palace of the local administrator like the Surat castle and palace of the Mutassadi of Surat (Mayor of Surat). Similarly, the fort and palace of the Nawab of Bengal were in Dacca, as

long as Dacca remained the capital of Bengal Subah. Certain proportions of these cities were occupied by residences of courtiers, nobles
and rich merchants. There were also areas dedicated to markets of
different products. These cities also accommodated large numbers of
clusters of households of craftsmen, who were involved in traditional
flexible manufacturing. Due to these diverse roles, cities had emerged
as centres of production, distribution and consumption.

Scholars have identified the existence of six regional economies
during the Mughal Empire, which were largely independent of each
other but with loose linkages either through land-based caravan trade
or riverine trade. Each region had its dominant cities, which were
simultaneously seats of power and places of production and trade.
These regional economies were Bengal–Bihar, with the dominant cities
Patna and Dacca; Agra, the capital of Mughal Empire; the region of
Punjab with the dominant cities Lahore, Multan and Sialkot; Gujarat,
with the dominant cities Surat and Ahmedabad; the Deccan region,
with the dominant city Burhanpur; and the Madras region, with the
dominant city Cochin.[6] Some other scholars have identified certain
cities as *primate* cities of the Mughal Empire such as Lahore, Agra,
Delhi, Patna, Burhanpur and Ahmedabad.[7] However, this list does not
include some important cities of the Mughal Empire such as Banaras,
Surat and Dacca.

Surat emerged as an important port city on the Western coast, when
it got integrated with the Mughal Empire in 1573 by Mughal emperor
Akbar. Surat became *Bab-ul-Mecca* (door to Mecca) and *Bandar
Mubarak* (blessed port) for the Mughal rulers because it was used by
Muslim pilgrims to board ships to begin their journey for *Haz* (Travers,
2007). The Western coast of India had always remained active place
for trade since Harappan times (Pearson, 1994). Before Surat, Broach
was an important centre for trade. The importance of Broach significantly declined during the rule of the independent Muslim Sultans in
Gujarat (1380–1573) and was replaced by Cambay. However, during
the Mughal Empire, Surat remained the most important port on the
Western coast of the Indian subcontinent.

At this point in time, Bombay had been formed by the Portuguese. It consisted of seven islands, namely Wadala, Mazagaon, Mahim, Parel, Matunga, Sion and Old Woman's Island. These islands were inhabited by communities such as Koli, Bhandari, Agri, Prabhu and Pachkalashis. Bombay was an important natural harbour with a vast stretch of deep waters, which was essential to anchoring big ships. Due to these characteristics of Bombay, it was described as Boon Bay by the Portuguese. It is interesting to mention here that both the port cities were described by their respective occupants as blessed ports, but the premises for recognizing their importance were different. The Mughals visualized Surat within the prism of their religion, while the Portuguese valued Bombay for its commercial potential. However, when Charles II, the emperor of Britain, married Portuguese Princess Catherine of Braganza in 1662, he received this territory as a dowry. The East India Company received territorial rights over Bombay from King Charles II in 1668. Bombay began to assume importance only after the East India Company shifted its Western headquarters from Surat to Bombay after the Maratha attack on Surat in 1680. The significance of Bombay did not emerge for a considerable period because 1640 onwards areas surrounding the city of Bombay were under Maratha occupation. Due to this reason, Bombay did not have access to the hinterland, which could have provided revenue to support the city. Due to these histori-cal reasons, Bombay remained as an isolated island during the period of the Mughal Empire. Therefore, in this section, we will focus on the consequences that were experienced by Surat owing to the working of the two forces of globalization in tandem.

It is important to mention here that Surat was already a part of global trading network before the arrival of the Portuguese and ter-ritorial occupation by the Mughals. The Muslim Sultans of Gujarat had established trading links with port cities located in the Persian Gulf and the Red Sea. Several Persian, Arab and Turkish merchants began to arrive at Surat, and some of them established their permanent residences in the port city. The maritime trade that occurred during this time was quite insignificant in comparison to the caravan trade, following the land route Delhi–Agra–Lahore–Qandhar–Isfahan–Cairo–Constantinople–Venice (Chakravarty, 2009). The most important beneficiary of the caravan trade was the Ottoman Empire when it occupied Constantinople during the rule of Mohammad II in 1453. The occupation of Constantinople by the Ottoman Empire increased the prices of Indian spices and other manufactured products. The Ottoman Empire encouraged several merchants and adventurers to establish trading links with the port cities of the Indian subcontinent. One such adventurer was Yusuf Adil Shah, who came from Constantinople and became governor in Bahmani kingdom for the Konkan region, including Bijapur and Goa. After the disintegration of the Bahmani kingdom, Yusuf Adil Shah became independent ruler of Bijapur and Goa in 1498.[8]

When Vasco da Gama discovered the sea route in 1498, it created conditions for the shift in prosperity from Asia to Europe. This happened because the caravan route which passed through the famous Silk Road and territories which were largely in the Asian region— namely South Asia, Southeast Asia, China and Central Asia—began to decline. It has been said that Europe began to prosper when trade was diverted from land route to port cities along the Atlantic via Cape of Good Hope. European monarchies that respected private property rights and provided honourable social positions to merchants motivated them to explore sea route for growing trade. This was in fact the emerging nexus between European merchants and kings which provided ideological premises for the birth of mercantilism in Europe. The Portuguese wanted to shift bulk of trade via Cape of Good Hope to Lisbon, to marginalize the trade through the route of the Persian Gulf and the Red Sea. From Lisbon, products carried from port cities of the Indian subcontinent were distributed to different European port cities. The Portuguese occupied Cochin (1505), Goa (1510), Mallaca (1511) and Harmuz (1515). The occupation of Harmuz, located on the eastern border of the Turkish Empire, posed a direct threat to the trade of the Ottoman Empire (Haellenquist (eds.), 1991).

The rulers of the Ottoman Empire did not intend to give up the fight for supremacy in trade in the Indian subcontinent to the Portuguese. They continued their struggle to corner larger proportion of trade from the Indian subcontinent during the rule of Ottoman emperors Salim I (1512–1520) and Suleiman the Magnificent (1520–1566). Ottoman armies captured Chaldiran in 1514 from the Safavid rulers of Iran.

They also occupied Aleppo in 1516, and Damascus and Cairo in 1517. This gave them hold over all the caravan routes between the Indian subcontinent and Central Asia, West Asia and Middle East. They also tried to obtain access to Surat port with the help of the Muslim rulers of Gujarat, who were recruiting several Turkish adventurers in their army. One such adventurer was Malik Ayaz. He was a Christian from Russia, who was captured and sold as a slave to a merchant in Constantinople. The merchant gifted him to Sultan Muhammad in 1484. Sultan Muhammad ruled Gujarat between 1443 and 1451. Recognizing his talent, the sultan appointed him governor of Junagarh and Diu. In response to these developments, the Portuguese fortified their trading bases at Quilon (1519), Chaul (1521), Bassein (1534), Diu (1536) and Daman (1559). For the last time under the leadership of Khawaja Safar, Ottoman soldiers were able to capture Diu in 1538. It is important to tell that at the time the Mughals occupied Surat, the city of Surat and other parts of the Western coast were still under the domination of the Portuguese; however, several merchants from Turkey also operated their businesses from Surat (Halil, 1971).[9]

The economy of Surat was significantly impacted by its integration with the Mughal Empire. The integration gave it access to all the advantages which have been described in Chapter 1 of the book. These advantages not only provided it political stability but also access to inland markets for the goods which were manufactured here, and also access to the sources of raw materials that it needed to manufacture goods. Due to the presence of the European trading companies, Surat emerged as an important port for exporting not only products manufactured in Surat and its hinterland, but also for products manufactured at several land-locked locations of traditional flexible manufacturing, such as the cities of Rajasthan, Agra, Lucknow, Lahore, Amritsar and Banaras. Surat not only enjoyed the advantages that it obtained from being a part of the Mughal Empire, it also received benefits from the existence of two empires that had been formed across the seas—the Ottoman Empire that existed since the beginning of the fifteenth century and the empire built by the Safavid dynasty in Iran. These empires provided political stability to the region and provided necessary conditions for the expansion of trade in the western seas of Surat. In these circumstances, Surat became a nodal centre of trade with ports located in the Persian Gulf and Red Sea. The trade of Surat expanded to port cities of Harmuz and Basra in the Persian Gulf, and Aden and Mocha in the Red Sea (Chaudhari, 1990; Lach, 1965; Omprakash, 1985; Pins, 2000; Richard (eds.), 1970; Subrahmanyam, 1990, 1993). Establishing links with these port cities of the Persian Gulf and Red Sea increased the demand for products of Surat in lieu of coffee from Mocha. The intertwined forces that were generated by the integration of Surat with the Mughal Empire, presence of the European trading companies and existence of the Safavid and Ottoman empires created necessary conditions for the prosperity of Surat.

To facilitate the smooth functioning of trading and manufacturing activities at Surat, the Mughals developed a separate administrative structure for the city. The administration of the city consisted of the *Mutassadi, Qiladar, Wakianavis* (recorder of events) and *harkaras* (carriers of *firman*). To maintain law and order in the city of Surat, Mughal administrators appointed the *Qazi* (Chief Justice), *Mufti* (interpreter of Islamic laws), *Kotwal* (incharge of police) and *Mir-i-Bahri* (to prevent smuggling). Mughal emperors also established an administrative framework to facilitate the commercial activities of the city. It created the office of *Daroga Furza* (customs officer) and *Daroga Kuski* (excise officer) (Dasgupta, 1994; Machado, 2009; Subramanian, 2010). To protect the Surat city from foreign aggression, the Mughal Empire developed a marine force consisting of Abyssinian slaves. This force was housed in a fort in an island called Janjira, which was located close to the Surat port. These Abyssinian soldiers were known as *Sidis* (Dasgupta, 1994; Subramanian, 2001, 2010).

Surat had access to the vast hinterland of Gujarat Subah, which had a highly diversified resource base in the river valleys of Gujarat; along the Narmada and Tapi rivers, there existed a belt of black soil, which made it an appropriate place for the cultivation of cotton. The cultivation of cotton facilitated the birth of traditional flexible manufacturing of cotton textiles of several varieties in Surat and in its peripheral areas. Cotton textiles were important items of exports to the ports of the Persian Gulf, Red Sea, East and West Africa, and Southeast Asia, and to different European markets (Dasgupta, 1994).

Surat also emerged as an important centre of supply of cotton to meet the needs of several centres of cotton textiles manufacturing, which were spread across several locations in the Indian subcontinent, especially Bengal.[10] Since Surat was also a centre of production of silk textiles, it depended on Bengal for the supply of raw silk. This complementary trade relationship helped in establishing not only a trade-related infrastructure but also a financial infrastructure which facilitated movement of financial resources along with merchandize. The movement of financial resources occurred in the form of hundis along the trade route. The trade route began at Surat and passed through Rajasthan, Agra, Banaras, Patna and terminated at Bengal (Beckert, 2014; Chaudhri, 1974; Partha Sarthi and Reillo, 2012). This trade route also created conditions which encouraged migration of several merchants to Surat.

A very large proportion of the working population of Surat and other parts of Gujarat was engaged in various stages of production of cotton textiles. Farmers were growing cotton, and a very large number of rural households was engaged in spinning of cotton yarn. There were several clusters of villages of weavers in Surat and in its hinterland, who wove a variety of textiles (Subramanian, 1996). There were communities of specialized craftsmen, organized into different castes, which were involved in dyeing, printing, painting, finishing and embroidery of textiles. According to the *Ain-i-Akbari*, Surat produced cotton textiles such as *chirah* (coloured cloth used for making turbans), *jamavars* (flowered cotton stuff) and *khares* (undilated silk) (Allami, 1929, Vol. I, 120). According to other historical accounts, other varieties of textiles which were also manufactured in Surat and in its periphery included *necanees* (low-priced striped cotton cloth, which was loom patterned), *canniker* (coarse cloth which was woven at Broach and Navsari), *tapseils* (striped cloth produced with the mix of cotton and silk yarn), *salotees, chandard madowjee, chandard turmadee, chow rangee gurum, puttch, doria, chellos, chelas* or *chillae* (cotton handkerchiefs, usually striped), *vees, bejanta pants, nega pants, turbans, dhotis, dupattas, ardians* and *baftas* (generic term used for white dyed cotton cloth from Surat). Surat was also known for coloured chintz known as *chint* in Hindi.[11]

Surat also produced a variety of cloth known as *sarasa* (painted and printed cloth with exotic motifs such as flowers, birds and human figures), but not in large volumes, despite the fact it was in great demand. This was because the production was time-consuming. This cloth was exported to Thailand, Indonesia, Japan, Philippines and China (see Guy, 1989). In Japan, *sarasa* was used in making objects which did not require large pieces of cloth. It was used in making wallet (*kamiire*), women's purses (*kinchaku*) or tobacco pouch (*tobakoire*).[12] *Sarasa* produced at Surat had assumed so much importance in the Japanese culture that it even became a part of Japanese tea ceremonies (Kyoka, 2009; Machado, 2009; Omprakash, 2007; Vardharajan 1999). Portuguese merchants also exported a variety of textiles called *mantises*[13] from Surat to different markets in Africa. Mozambique had become an important market of cotton textiles known as *vaspiece* and *barnazes* (indigo dyed cloth) produced at Surat.[14] It is quite important to mention here that these varieties of cotton textiles were used as a currency to buy slaves and import ivory (Machado, 2004). This cloth has very appropriately been described as *cloth of sorrow*.[15]

Indian cotton textiles began to reach different markets of Europe through trading operations of British, Portuguese, Dutch and French trading companies. These companies used to bring these textiles at the port cities such as London, Amsterdam and Lorient, where these textiles were sold in auction to wholesale distributors. These distributors supplied these textiles to retailors, shopkeepers, hawkers and peddlers. The existence of such an elaborate supply chain insured that the Indian textiles reached even the remotest corners of European countries (Jenkin (ed.), 2003; Lemire, 1991, 2011). Indian muslins and cotton textiles, which were popularly known as calicoes, received wide acceptability among European customers. This happened because these textiles were able to cater to preferences of diverse groups of segmented consumers due to the variety in their quality and prices. These textiles significantly affected the material culture of European consumers.

When these textiles were brought in Britain by the merchants of the East India Company, they resulted in a *national makeover*. While describing the magnitude of this makeover of the lifestyle of British customers, Daniel Defoe wrote in 1708 that 'Indian textiles crept into our houses, our closets and our bed chambers; curtains, cushions, chairs, and at last beds themselves were nothing but calicoes or Indian stuffs'.[16] The emerging acceptability of Indian calicoes by British consumers has been described by historians as *calicoe craze* (see Jenkins, 2003; Lemire, 1991, 2004, 2009). Initially European called all the textiles that were exported from India calicoes, because for the first time these textiles were exported from Calicut. As these textiles were becoming popular with British customers and were affecting their lifestyle, they were at the same time creating antagonism in British manufacturers of woollen and silk textiles, who were forcing the British government to impose restriction on the imports of Indian textiles.

The import of Indian textiles was also giving birth to another important historical process. This process was taking roots in British manufacturing. This happened because Indian textiles stood not only for products, they embodied production processes, know-how, designs and aesthetics. The imports of Indian textiles provided a learning experience to British manufacturers and motivated them to create local imitations. In the process of creating imitations, they slowly achieved import substitution of Indian textiles. In this sense, Indian cotton textiles not only affected the material culture of British society, they also provided stimulus to British manufacturers and innovators, which subsequently laid the foundation of the *Industrial Revolution*. It is a well-known historical fact that it was the inventions in the processing of cotton which began the process of the Industrial Revolution in Britain. Famous economic historian Eric Hobsbawm established that revolutionary changes in the manufacturing of cotton textiles and the Industrial Revolution were coterminous in Britain when he described in his book, 'Whoever says Industrial Revolution, says cotton'.[17]

Along with the production of a variety of cotton textiles, Surat was also famous for its silk textiles such as *patola, mussroos, hemroos* and *elacha.* Patola was double *ikat* silk fabric because while weaving patola, both warp and weft threads were separately tie-dyed. The use of this technique created magical effect on the fabric. In Southeast Asia, patola was considered as *cindai* (i.e., protective cloth from evil spirits), and was given as an important item in royal dowry (Hobsbawn, 1999, 138).

Production of cotton and silk was widespread in Surat as well as in its hinterland, in areas such as Broach, Cambay, Patan, Champaner, Navsari, Gandevi and Ahmedabad. On the main roads that connected Surat with different towns there had emerged cluster villages of crafts-men who were engaged in weaving, dyeing, printing and painting of textiles. For instance, Dabhol and Sinoor near Baroda, Nadiad and Dholka near Ahmedabad were centres of manufacturing of textiles. In the production of textiles, craftsmen belonging to various castes of Hindus, Muslims and Parsis were involved. For the production of textile, indigo was obtained from Ankleswar, Jambusarva and Surkhez. Fine quality of indigo was procured from Bayana which was located near Agra. The global demand for textiles produced at Surat depended on their attractive designs, variety of colours and use of different kinds of fabrics. The existence of traditional flexible manufacturing in the production of textiles provided to the textile manufacturers additional competitive advantage. It gave them capability to customize products according to the variety in consumer preferences located in different locations across different continents.[18]

Apart from the manufacturing of cotton and silk textiles, Surat was an important centre of production of *khapwah* and *jamdhar* variety of swords. Iron produced in Kutch was used to make famous koriz swords, which were in demand in different parts of the Indian sub-continent and Central Asia.[19] Surat had also emerged as an important centre of ship building, production of *jari* (gold thread) and jewellery. Engraving and carving of wood has been an important craft of Surat and Gujarat. Carved wooden doors and windows travelled on *dhows* to several locations in East Africa such as Zanzibar, Begamyo, Lamu, Mombasa and Mogadishu.[20] Surat being an important city during the Mughal Empire became an important port to export several products which were produced in land-locked locations of traditional flexible manufacturing such as Rajasthan, Punjab, Agra, Lucknow, Moradabad and Lahore. One such product which has been referred in historical writings is *daribadi chadars* (bedsheets) from Agra.[21]

The existence of communities of merchants was required in order to procure and distribute products produced at Surat and its hinterland to different parts of the Indian subcontinent and in foreign markets.

Merchants were also involved in bringing the products produced in other parts of the Indian subcontinent, which were then exported from Surat. Some of these merchants had developed network of craftsmen in dadni framework, from whom they procured goods for exports and for selling in different markets in the Indian subcontinent. Some other merchants worked on behalf of the European trading companies to establish networks of craftsmen in dadni system. There were some merchants who owned ships, which they rented to other merchants for carrying their merchandize. There also existed specialized banking firms owned by renowned merchants, who helped in transfer of money from one place to another through the financial instrument of hundi. There were also firms of merchants which acted as money changers. Apart from local merchants, merchants from different parts of the Indian subcontinent and other countries such as Persia, Arab, Turkey and Europe had also established their offices at Surat.

Akbar's policy of *Sulh-i-kull* (peace with all) helped in the mobility of several communities of merchants.[22] Some of these merchants also arrived at Surat to participate in different trading activities. One of the prominent Jain merchants of Rajasthan, Virji Vohra, migrated to Surat in 1619.[23] Another Jain merchant who also migrated to Surat was Shantilal Jain, who operated from Ahmedabad.[24] Similarly Bhatia merchants migrated from Multan, an area of Punjab, to Kutch and later to Surat. They were known as *Kuchi Bhatias*.[25] Since Surat had established strong trading links with Banaras during the period of the Mughal Empire, some of the families of merchants of Banaras, who were engaged in the trading of textiles, also migrated to Surat. The families of *nagar brahmins* from Banaras, Dayaram Nagar and Krishn Arjunji Nathji Travadi, became quite important trading families of Surat (Mehta, 1974). At this point in time, Gujarati merchant Laldas Vithaldas Parekh was holding the position of *nagarseth* (representative of all the merchant communities) of the city of Surat.[26]

As it has been mentioned above, Gujarat remained under the rule of Muslim Sultans for a considerable period, and several Muslim merchants of Arab, Persia and Turkey also began to live at Surat. Due to this reason, there were large numbers of Muslim merchants who were conducting their businesses at Surat. During the long rule of Muslims in Gujarat, several Hindu merchants had also embraced Islam. These Muslim merchant communities were classified into two broad categories—the *Ismailis* and the *Memons*. The Ismailis over a period of time got subdivided into two subcommunities—the *Nizaris* and the *Mutaqlis*. Subsequently, the *Nizaris* were known as *Khojas* and the Mutaqlis as *Bohras*. The *Memon* community of Muslim merchants comprised of families who accepted Islam from Lohana, located in Sindh (now in Pakistan). One part of this group migrated to a place called Halar in Gujarat, they were known as *Halari Memons;* another group migrated to Kutch and came to be known as *Kuchi Memons*, while a third group of Memons began to live in Surat. This group was known as *Surti Memons*.[27] The most important Muslim merchant of this community at Surat during this time was Abdul Gaffoor.[28] Apart from Arab, Persian and local Muslim merchants, Surat had also attracted merchants from Turkey. The Chellaby Muslim family from Turkey played an important role in the history of Surat. During the latter part of the Mughal Empire, the Chellaby family was headed by Mohammed Chellaby.

The other community which was quite active in trade at Surat was the Parsi community. The members of this community were engaged not only in trade but also in other occupations. Some of the members of the community were weavers of cotton and silk textiles. Some other members of this community were best carpenters and were occupied in shipbuilding at Surat. This community also had certain families who were engaged in brewing of liquor and with production of *itra*. Parsis were living in Surat as well as in different places in Gujarat. Parsis living in Surat were direct descendants of a group of Persians who took refuge in Gujarat after Persia was invaded by Arab Muslims. According to historical documents and Parsi folk tradition, it is believed that Parsis arrived at a place called Sanjan in Gujarat in 785, after getting permission from Raja Jed Ram. This event is recorded in the *Kissah-i-sanjan*. During the Mughal Empire, when Surat emerged as an important centre of trade, commerce and traditional flexible manufacturing, several Parsi families also migrated to Surat. The most important Parsi merchant during the Mughal period was Rustam Manock (1635–1721).[29] Apart from Manock, other Parsis whose names are recorded in historical documents of the period are Jamsetji Byramji, who was a broker of the East India Company, and Gursetji, who was given contract by the East India Company to build ships in 1672.[30] Some of the Parsi merchants were shipowners like Rustamji and Dhanji Bairamji.[31]

The details given above clearly suggest that during the period of the Mughal Empire, Surat enjoyed political stability and an organized law and order system. It was also one of the most globalized and cosmopolitan cities of the Mughal Empire. Surat was not a cosmopolitan city when considered as a geographical space, but 'cosmopolitan' in the sense where diverse people interacted with each other at all levels accepting human diversity as a way of life. In Surat, also there was *commercial cosmopolitanism*, where interaction between merchants of diverse backgrounds and faiths did occur.[32] It also emerged as a prosperous city, which was simultaneously a centre of traditional flexible manufacturing as well as a trading centre. It is also important to mention here that most of the exports of merchandize were purchased by the European trading companies with the help of bullion obtained from America. The bullion was brought in large quantities from 1600 onwards at Surat.[33] Due to the availability of bullion at Surat, Mughal emperors had imposed strict regulations which forced merchants to convert bullion into Mughal coins in a mint which was located at Surat.[34] Historians estimate that around 25 per cent of the total gold and silver coins that were in circulation during the Mughal Empire were minted at Surat (Seth, 2015, 73). It is also important to mention here that though both America and Surat were discovered around the same time by European navigators and thousands of miles of distance separated them from each other, yet it was American bullion which was helping the European trading companies to buy products produced at Surat.[35] Moreover, Surat had established strong linkages with the inland economy of the Indian subcontinent; due to these linkages, several inland locations enjoyed spillover effects of the prosperity of Surat. These spillover effects spread gains in terms of income and employment in these locations.

While Surat was at the peak of its level of prosperity, an important political force was emerging on the horizon and had begun to expand its geographical influence. This political force was the emergence of the Marathas. The Marathas were earlier working as commanders and soldiers for different political dispensations of Deccan since the fourteenth century AD. They worked under the Bahmani Sultans during 1347–1527 and for the Sultans of Bijapur and Ahmednagar during 1500–1590. Due to constant conflict between the Mughal Empire and the Sultans of Deccan, the Sultans of Bijapur and Ahmednagar were experiencing rapid decline. Taking advantage of this situation, the Marathas under the leadership of Shivaji, belonging to a family of Deshmukhs, captured territories of the Deccan Sultan and came directly in the line of fire of the Mughals. Shivaji's constant need for financial resources attracted his attention towards the city of Surat. According to folklore, Shivaji sent one of his trusted spies, Bahirji Naik, to Surat under the guise of a folk singer to collect intelligence about the city. The intelligence collected by Bahirji Naik helped him to organize a surprise raid on the city. He plundered the city twice in 1644. In 1670, the Marathas again raided the city of Surat, and plundered and occupied some of the territories in the periphery of the city. The conquest of 1670 provided to the Marathas a state route from Kalyani (Konkan) to Surat. It is mentioned that one of the rich merchants of Surat, Haji Zahid Beg, was forced to pay ₹3 lakh to Shivaji.[36] Maratha attacks on the city of Surat forced the East India Company to shift its headquarter of Western coast from Surat to Bombay in 1680. However, the Maratha raids did not significantly affect the economy of Surat. This happened because most of the merchants who were operating their businesses from Surat did not leave it. Death of Shivaji in 1680 and emergence of disputes over succession subsequently spared the city from further attacks from the Marathas until 1719, when Peshwa Baji Rao emerged as a successor of the Maratha state.[37]

The real blow to the political stability and prosperity of the city came from the death of Aurangzeb in 1707. The political instability was caused because after the death of Mughal emperor Aurangzeb, the Mughal Empire began to disintegrate into several autonomous political units. The decline in the supremacy of the centralized authority of the Mughal Empire provided opportunities to some of the *subedars* (provincial governors) of the Mughal Empire to evolve independent bases of power. The Subedar of Bengal, Murshid Quli Khan, established his own autonomous rule in Bengal, and shifted his capital from Dacca to Murshidabad. Similarly, Asaf Jah Nizam-ul-Mulk evolved his own base of political power in Southern India, with his capital at Hyderabad. Hyder Ali and Tipu Sultan assumed power in Mysore. Another subedar of the Mughal Empire, Sadat Khan Burhan-ul-Mulk, established his rule in Awadh with the capital in Lucknow. Other warrior groups who did not accept the supremacy of the Mughal Empire also established their independent kingdoms, namely Sikhs in Punjab and Jammu & Kashmir, Rajputs in Rajasthan, and Jats in Bharatpur.

Amongst all these political dispensations that emerged as a consequence of decline in the authority of the Mughal Empire, the geographical influence of the Marathas kept on increasing. The Marathas after establishing and consolidating their power in Maharashtra, under the command of Baji Rao, occupied Malwa and Dhar region in 1720, captured Gujarat in 1730, and subsequently, kept on expanding in different directions of the Indian subcontinent. At that point in time, it appeared that the political space that was vacated by the decline of the Mughal Empire will be occupied by the rising might of the Marathas. However, after their defeat in the Third Battle of Panipat, the Marathas got divided under different warlords. After 1761, the Marathas got segmented in five regional dispensations—Peshwa exercised power and domination in Western Maharashtra from its capital Nagpur, Holkar controlled Malwa region with its capital at Indore, Sindhia controlled Bundelkhand with Gwalior as its capital, Bhonsales were commanding Berar and Orissa, and finally the Gaekwads controlled Gujarat with their capital Baroda.[38] It was the occupation of Gujarat by the Marathas which significantly altered the fortunes of Surat.

The emerging political uncertainty simultaneously provided necessary conditions to the European trading companies to mobilize military and naval power at an unprecedented level. The defence mobilization of the European trading companies was also becoming necessary as a consequence of the globalization of conflict amongst European nations, especially between France and Britain.[39] The increased militarization of European countries and globalization of their conflict were preparing the foundation of a new world order, which was subsequently termed as *imperialism* by historians.[40] All these developments that were occurring in the polity of the Indian subcontinent began to adversely impact the economy of Surat.

The decline in the authority of the Mughal Empire resulted in increases in the power of the mutassadi, and he began to assert his absolute power over the city. In the new circumstances, as most parts of Gujarat surrounding the city of Surat came under the occupation of the Marathas, Maratha chief Deogi Rao, who was the local administrator of the region, began to demand *chauth,* which was 25 per cent of the revenue of the city. Similarly, *sidi* marine force, which was housed in an island called Janjira near Surat, also pressed for increased financial resources. Their representative at Surat, Masud Khan, kept on increasing his financial requirements. To meet the demands by different claimants of revenue, along with his own greed, the mutassadi of the city imposed heavy taxes on the merchants of the city. The mutassadi of Surat, Haider Quli Khan, converted the administration of the city into a form of despotic administration, and started the practice of extortion of money from the rich traders of the city. His actions were a direct attack on the right to property of the merchants. This became quite obvious when Abdul Gaffoor, the richest merchant of the city, died in 1718. His family experienced the consequences of the absolute powers of the mutassadi. He sealed and confiscated the entire property of the merchant, which was valued at that time at 8.5 million rupees. This action was taken by Haider Quli Khan under the pretext that Mulla Abdul Hai was the adopted son of Abdul Gaffoor, and therefore Gaffoor has not left behind any legal heir of his property. However, Mulla Hai was able to restore the ownership of his property through the intervention of the Mughal emperor. Abdul Hai did not live long after this incident. Therefore, his son Mulla Muhammad Ali became an important player in the political drama that continued for several years.[41]

Similarly, Mutassadi Sohrab Khan, who succeeded Haider Quli Khan, continued the practice of harassing local merchants to extort money. Therefore, to satisfy the greed of Sohrab Khan, Muhammad Ali gave him ₹18,000 per month to avoid tension between the mutassadi and local merchants. Despite the arrangement, Sohrab Khan arrested the son of Dada Parekh, a rich merchant of Surat, to extort money. However, using his contacts at high places, Muhammad Ali was able to get the release of the son of Parekh from the prison. However, in 1732, merchants of Surat under the leadership of Mulla Muhammad Ali and the nagarseth of Surat, Laldas Vithaldas Parekh, were able to replace Sohrab Khan by Teg Begh Khan as mutassadi of Surat. The merchants of Surat soon realized that by replacing one mutassadi by another is not the permanent solution from predatory character of the local administration. This happened when Teg Begh Khan declared himself as a Nawab of Surat and appointed his brothers in all important positions in the administration of the city. Soon he confiscated the property of Mohammad Ali and poisoned him in 1733. It was the decline in the quality of governance of the city which resulted in increasing insecurity of life and property of the merchants of the city.[42]

It is while the structure of governance was deteriorating at Surat, two important empires which provided stability to trade between Surat, Persian Gulf and Red Sea, also began to experience decline. The Safavid dynasty of Persia and the Ottoman Empire were getting weaker. These events further affected the conditions of conducting business in the city of Surat. The risk of conducting business with the Persian Gulf and Red Sea increased substantially. The decline of these empires had increased the power of pirates in the seas (Subramanian, 2012, 21).

Under these circumstances, leading merchants met the officials of the Surat Council of the East India Company. The situation flared up when in 1754 Ali Nawab Khan, a leading official of the Surat administration, arrested Jayaram Navaram, a merchant under the protection of the East India Company. Left with no option, he approached the Surat Council. The Council pressed for the release of Jayaram because he was serving as a contractor of the company. The attitude of the Surat Council further hardened due to the fact that Baboorjee, a merchant who was having strong ties with the East India Company, found that his treasure freight coming from Mocha had been intercepted by Munchurjee, who was acting on the behest of the local administration.

Several such incidences frequently began to occur. As a consequence, on 11 January 1759, most of the merchants of the city under the leadership of Laldas Vithaldas Parekh formally announced their support to the East India Company. Following the assurance by leading merchants of Surat, the Surat Council planned that under new arrangement Sidi Masud was to be expelled from the castle and the position of qiladar was to be taken over by the East India Company, in order to establish law and order in the city. The Maratha army did not show much resistance, which forced Teg Begh Khan to sign an instrument of treaty, which appointed the East India Company as the qiladar of the city. This incident is called by historians as *Castle Revolution* (Subramanian, 1987, 113–116). This arrangement received consent from the Mughal Darbar's firman in November 1769. For procuring consent of the Mughal emperor, two leading merchants of Surat, Laldas Vithaldas Parekh and Arjunji Nathji Travadi, played an important role. This new arrangement provided a source of financing for Bombay's growth (Allami, 1927, Vol. II, 132). This significant change in the polity of Surat provided respite to the merchants of Surat from the arbitrary use of absolute power of the nawab. However, at the same time, it increased the dependence of the merchants of Surat on the East India Company. It is quite important to mention here that the role of the East India Company in the administration of this important port city of the Western coast happened to become active just two years after the Battle of Plassey (1757), which eventually brought the East India Company at the centre stage on the Eastern coast of the Indian subcontinent.

DACCA AND CALCUTTA
DURING MUGHAL EMPIRE

The economic advantages that were created by the Mughal Empire also helped in the growth of traditional flexible manufacturing of Bengal. Dacca was part of the Mughal Empire, and the territories which subsequently became the city of Calcutta were also under the possession of the Mughal Empire. According to Abul Fazal Allami, the original name of Bengal was Bang. Even in the national anthem of India poet Rabindranath Tagore uses the word 'Bang' to refer to Bengal. According to Abul Fazal Allami, earlier rulers of Bang motivated people to build raised mounds, measuring 10 yards in height and 20 yards in breath, which were called *Al*. During long monsoon months, when the plains were submerged in water, these mounds (Als) were only the visible objects in the landscape. For this reason, Al as a suffix became popular and was added to the original name Bang and the place became popular as Bengal (Allami, 1925, Vol. II, 137).

Bengal became part of the Mughal Empire during the rule of emperor Humayun in 1538, with the interregnum of seven years (1539–1545) when Sher Shah Suri ruled Bengal, while Humayun was in exile in Iran. During the rule of Humayun and Sher Shah Suri, Lakhnauti or Gaur was capital of Bengal Subah, which was named as Jannatabad by emperor Humayun.[43] Sher Shah Suri increased the connectivity of Bengal with the rest of the Indian subcontinent, when a road was constructed during his rule, which is now popularly known as Grand Trunk Road (National Highway No. 1). This road connected Punjab to the town of Sonargaon, located near the Bay of Bengal. Although Bengal enjoyed connectivity to other parts of the Indian subcontinent through a natural inter-river transportation network, its level of integration increased substantially only after the construction of this road. Subsequently, Dacca became the capital of Bengal in 1610.

It is important to mention here that even before the occupation of Dacca by the Mughal Empire, the city was integrated into the network of trade evolved by Portuguese merchants. The Portuguese had established their base in Malacca in 1511, which was strategically located on the western side of the Malaysian Peninsula. This was an important possession of Portuguese near the Eastern coast of the Indian subcontinent. The Portuguese had already established their formidable presence on the Western coast. Malacca was an important market of spices. The importance of Malacca is quite evident from the description of Portuguese traveller Tomm Pires, who described in 1506, 'the merchants of different nations for thousand leagues on every hand must come to Malacca ... who so ever is the lord of Mallaca has his hands at the throat of Venice'.[44] It is after the occupation of Malacca that the importance of Bengal increased in the trading network developed by the Portuguese. In the Western coast, the Portuguese had followed the strategy of establishing state monopoly in the trading of spices. However, to expand trade on the Eastern coast, they followed a different strategy. On the Eastern coast, they followed the free trade policy by giving complete freedom to *casados* (Portuguese merchants married to Indian women).

This policy encouraged the casados of Cochin and Goa to undertake risk to establish trading bases on the Eastern coast. They developed their settlements in Chittagaon or Chittagong and Satgaon, located quite close to the capital of Bengal, Lakhnauti or Gaur, which was later on named by Mughal emperor Humayun as Jannatabad. The integration of Bengal in the trading network created by the casados provided global exposure to the products produced by the traditional flexible manufacturing of Dacca. In this way, the economy of Dacca began to enjoy the same advantages which were available to Surat. The integration of Dacca with the rest of the economy of the subcontinent happened by its becoming part of the Mughal Empire. At the same time, it got the advantage of getting integrated into the global economy because of the presence of Portuguese merchants (Allami, 1927, Vol. II, p. 137). According to the account given by Allami, the ports of Chittagong, Satgaon and Hugli were inhabited by Christians (i.e., by the Portuguese) (Fruber, 2004; Hall, 1996; Omprakash, 1985; Pearson, 2007; Seth, 2015, 106). In 1574, Akbar granted *firman* (permission) to Pandro Tavares to make a settlement of Portuguese on Hugli. Thus, Hugli emerged as *Porto Pageno* (prime port) of Bengal. The shift from Chittagong to Hugli also marked a shift from East Bengal to West Bengal.

The French trading company Compagnie des Indes Orientales entered into India in 1664 and developed its base at Pondicherry (Puducherry) on the Western coast and also established its trading base at Chandannagar on the Eastern coast in Bengal.[45] The East India Company developed its trading base in Bengal when it received permission from Mughal emperor Aurangzeb to open its offices and construct Fort William by occupying territories of the three villages, Kolikata, Gobindapur and Sutanati, located on the banks of river Hugli in 1690. Sutanati at that point in time was an important market of threads and fabrics. It is here that the new settlement of the company grew with the name Calcutta (Allami, 1929, Vol. II, 125). The objective of all the trading companies of Europe was to corner maximum proportion of the market share of the products produced by the traditional flexible manufacturing of Dacca.

Dacca became the capital of Bengal during the Mughal Empire and emerged as an important centre of traditional flexible manufacturing. Dacca derived its name from the Dhakeshweri Temple, which was constructed by Ballal Sen, who ruled the area around 1158–1159 (Allami, 1927, Vol. II, 132). Calcutta emerged as a consequence of expansion of trading activities of the East India Company, largely by exporting goods produced by the traditional flexible manufacturing of Dacca. Calcutta became the capital of all the territories which came under the occupation of the East India Company after the Battle of Plassey. Subsequently, Calcutta became the capital of British Raj, a status it enjoyed up to 1911. Dacca became part of Pakistan after 1947 and became the capital city of East Pakistan.

Traditional flexible manufacturing in general and particularly that located in Dacca experienced a high rate of growth during the Mughal Empire. Historical circumstances that existed at that time also established strong linkages between traditional flexible manufacturing of Dacca with Calcutta. Traditional flexible manufacturing in Dacca and in its hinterland emerged as a consequence of its climate. 'The rain begins, when sun is midway in Taurus (May) and continuous for somewhat more than six months.'[46] The climate was humid and damp, and most parts were submerged in water for almost eight months of a year. In the absence of continuous availability of land for cultivation, local population was forced to supplement its income from non-farm activities. The agrarian structure of the Mughal Empire provided ample opportunities to local functionaries for excessive exploitation of peasantry. This also forced peasants to escape from exploitation by embracing work in the flexible manufacturing to obtain their subsistence.[47] These conditions facilitated the shift of landless labourers and peasants with uneconomic size of landholdings towards traditional manufacturing. The capacity to absorb large proportions of population increased the scope of traditional flexible manufacturing of Dacca, with its spatial integration with the rest of the economy of the Indian subcontinent during the Mughal Empire. The presence of different European trading companies further increased the size of the market for the products produced by the traditional flexible manufacturing of Dacca.

Dacca is located in the Bengal delta zone and it depended largely on its traditional flexing industry. To support its manufacturing units, the peasants of the region cultivated cotton and jute and practised sericulture to provide raw materials to the traditional flexible manufacturing. The region also had availability of timber from the forests of Bengal. Forests supplied timber of trees such as *teak, sissoo, saul* and *shal*. Availability of timber provided conditions for the birth of traditional flexible manufacturing of boats and ships, which were needed to obtain raw materials from hinterland, and to distribute output of the manufactured products to different centres of consumption. This was possible because Dacca was well connected by river system with its peripheral area, as well as with important port cities and cities such as Patna, Banaras, Agra and Delhi. Dacca was well known for its production of muslin, which was called *mamal-khas*. It was the finest muslin in the world, also in comparison to the muslin produced in Britain and France. It has been observed by experts that the Dacca muslin was of extraordinary quality (Bhattacharya, 1986; Watson, 1879, 1887). In improving the quality of muslin, the dexterity of the spinners and weavers of Dacca was complemented by favourable climate. The climate of Dacca provided optimum conditions for spinning and weaving of muslin. For spinning the best yarn for muslin, the experienced women of weaver families of Dacca and its hinterland, who had acquired skills perfected over several generations, spun yarn. The best time for spinning was early morning hours or in the afternoon during monsoon months. During this time, it was less harmful for eyes and wind had high moisture. This prevented yarn from breaking. Weavers of Dacca muslin also preferred the same time for weaving. Such optimum conditions for spinning and weaving were not available at any other location.

An expert spinner of Dacca could spin thread of four miles in length from a *sicca* (rupee coin) weight of cotton. The diameter of the filament of the finest Dacca muslin thread varied from 1/1000 to 1/1500 of an inch. The Dacca muslin's fibre could receive maximum number of twists (between 120 and 110). It is also important to mention that such fine variety of fibre was woven from the cotton cultivated in the surrounding areas (Allami, 1927, Vol. II, 130). At Dacca, muslin was produced in different varieties. The most celebrated variety of Dacca muslin was *Jamdani*, which derived its name from two Persian words—*jam* (flower) and *dani* (flower pot). Apart from Jamdani, the other varieties of muslins which were produced by the weavers of Dacca were *Tanjib, Abroom, Albelee, Sarbati, Jungle, Nayansook* and *Doria*. Muslin was also produced in other towns such as Srirampur and in the Bankibazar area. It is mentioned in the *Ain-i-Akbari* that in Sonargaon a specific quality of muslin was produced, which was in great demand. In the township of Egara Sindur, there was a large reservoir of water, which gave peculiar whiteness to the clothes that were washed in it (Seth, 2015, Chapter I).

The cotton textile produced at Dacca and other centres of production were called Calicoes by British merchants. Silk was manufactured in Murshidabad, Malda, Srirampur and Bankibazar areas. The varieties of silk which were manufactured here were *Choppahas, Bhandena* and *Corah* silk. These towns around Dacca were also well known for the manufacture of *velvet, satin taffetas* and *tassar* (Gupta, 1980, 210–214). The silk industry was organized on the basis of social division of labour that gradually became occupation of different groups. These occupations consisted of *chaser* or *chasnigirs* (i.e., silkworm breeders and cocoon harvesters), *nacauds* (silk winders), *morenders* (skein makers), *tantis* (weavers), *tabekdars* or *tagadeers* (silk collectors), *paikars* and *sardars* (silk dealers and merchants).[48]

It is also important to mention here that along with the existence of traditional flexible manufacturing in Dacca, royal families of the Mughal Empire and nobles also maintained *karkhanas* (factories) for manufacturing cloth. The weavers working in these imperial karkhanas were wage workers of the royal family of the Mughal emperor. Such karkhanas were located at Dacca and its periphery such as in Sonargaon, Junglabaree and Bazetpore for manufacturing *malboos khas* (muslin for the royal family) (Athar Ali, 1978, 155–160; Verma, 1994). Nurjahan, wife of Mughal emperor Jahangir, was personally involved in the promotion of Dacca muslins such as *Jamdani* and *Abarwan*. The karkhana to manufacture muslin for the Mughal emperor Jahangir, *sudder malboos kutee*, was located in the outskirts of Dacca. Other Mughal emperors who established karkhanas at Dacca were Shah Jahan and Aurangzeb. Even some of the princes and princesses also owned their own karkhanas at Dacca, such as Dara Shikoh and Roshanara Begum (Allami, 1927, Vol. I, 363; Jahangir, (1603–1627), 2006, Vol. I, 15). Apart from the manufacturing of different varieties of textiles, Dacca also had well-developed centres of traditional manufacturing of jute products. At that point in time, manufacturing of ropes and cartage were more important jute products of Dacca. Since other parts of the Indian subcontinent did not grow jute, manufacturing of jute was a monopoly of the region.

The prosperity of Dacca and its hinterland attracted merchants from other regions of the subcontinent. These merchants purchased manufactured products of Dacca to sell in different markets of the subcontinent. It is believed that when Raja Man Singh was appointed Governor of Bengal by Akbar and subsequently by Jahangir, it motivated a large number of merchant families of Marwar to migrate to Bengal. Jahangir mentions in the *Tuzuk-i-Jahangir* that 'I made Raja Man Singh—who was one of the greatest and most trusted noblemen of my father, and had obtained alliances with this illustrious family, in as much as his aunt had been in my father's house, and I had married his sister... —as before, ruler of the province of Bengal.'[49] It was during the period of 1670–1680 that prominent Marwari merchants such as Manikchand and Fatehchand migrated to Bengal and established their banking firm. The firm was engaged in transferring annual revenue of the Nawab of Murshidabad in advance to the Mughal emperor. The annual value of the remittance was more than 10 million rupees.[50] Mughal emperor Aurangzeb had personally honoured the head of the family of the firm with the title Jagat Seth (i.e., the richest man of the world) for his timely loan of money to the emperor.[51]

The extent of demand for the products of manufactured products of Dacca originated from the vast domestic market and expanded to the size of the subcontinent. The demand for the products of traditional flexible manufacturing of Dacca had spread to several important cities of the subcontinent. Merchants of cities such as Agra, Banaras, Patna, Delhi, Bombay and Madras traded in the products produced by the craftsmen of Dacca. Merchants of Dacca had established trading links even with several business communities of Sri Lanka and Maldives, and also with Ilaput community of Muslims of the Coromandel Coast and Mappliah community of the Malabar Coast (Khan, 1927). Surat depended on the raw silk produced at Dacca for its silk manufacturing. The demand for Dacca's manufactured products originated from different maritime cities of Bengal, where trading companies of different European countries had established their trading bases. The European trading companies had established their trading bases at port cities such as Hugli, Chittagong, Calcutta, Chinsura, Chandannagar, Satgaon, Srirampur and Bankibazar. These cities worked as collection centres to export the products produced by the traditional flexible manufacturing centres of Dacca to the cities of Europe such as London, Paris and Amsterdam.[52]

Due to lack of data regarding the purchases of the products of Dacca manufacturers at different centres of consumption of the domestic economy of the India subcontinent, it is difficult to make an assessment regarding exact size of domestic markets of manufactured products of traditional flexible manufacturing of Decca. Even a very large part of the foreign trade conducted by European trading companies is not known, because it was conducted by the private merchants as well as by the employees of these companies as private trade (own account trade); it was practiced, as it has been explained in the earlier section, as an incentive for the employees of the company.[53] However, there exists data in records of the European trading companies regarding the volume of trade conducted by them officially of products produced by the traditional flexible manufacturing of Dacca. These data represent a very small part of the total demand for products manufactured at Dacca. For instance, the Dutch East Indian Company was exporting from Dacca 188,749 pieces of textiles. Out of these pieces, 49,414 pieces consisted of Dacca muslin and 5,388 pieces of silk textiles at the time of the death of Aurangzeb (1707).[54] During the same time, the East India Company of Britain exported 1.76 million pieces of textiles (Caulkins, 1970).

It is while Dacca was becoming an economically prosperous region of the Indian subcontinent and thereby contributing maximum revenue to the Mughal Empire, political forces were working quite differently. Murshid Quli Khan, who was appointed as Subedar (governor) of Bengal, shifted the capital of Bengal from Dacca to a place called Muqsadabad, which was later renamed as Murshidabad. The shifting of the capital did not significantly affect the prosperity of Dacca, because the products manufactured at Dacca still had demand from several foreign merchants such as the Armenians, Arabs, Persians, Portuguese, French and British, belonging to different nations. Moreover, demand for the products of Dacca continued to exist in different important markets spread over the Indian subcontinent. Therefore, though some scholars speculate that Dacca experienced decline after the death of Aurangzeb, historical facts contrarily suggest that due to good administration and innovative financial management by Murshid Quli Khan, the economy of Bengal had become quite stable. Murshid Quli Khan and his relationship with the house of Jagat Seth substantially increased the prosperity of Bengal.[55]

The seeds of political instability and decline of Dacca were sown by Mughal emperor Shahriyar, who gave firman to the East India Company to carry free trade in Bengal and also granted rights to buy the land of 38 villages located near the existing city of Calcutta.[56] This decision of the Mughal emperor Shahriyar in 1717 laid the foundation for the continuous rise of Calcutta and simultaneous decline of Dacca. However, at this point in time, prosperity of Calcutta depended on trading in the manufactured products produced in Dacca. The decision to give permission for free trade to the East India Company altered the situation significantly. This happened because the East India Company misused the intent of the firman. The East India Company began to issue *dastaks* (entry passes) to the officials of the East India Company for private trade, without paying any taxes to the local nawab. It also began to grant dastaks to traders of other countries by charging fees. These activities of the East India Company affected the revenue of the Nawab of Bengal. These practices therefore adversely affected the relationship between the nawab and the company.

During the rule of Alivardi Khan (1740–1756) in the 1740s, the Maratha Bhonsales of Nagpur raided Bengal every year. Many a time, they had almost reached at the gates of the capital city, Murshidabad. In order to pacify the Marathas, the Nawab of Bengal gave them Bihar. The Maratha attacks also forced the East India Company to construct ditches to protect the city of Calcutta from Maratha attacks. However, the Marathas never crossed the Hugli river. The relative security of Calcutta city motivated several wealthy merchants living on other side of river Hugli to shift to Calcutta. The ditches that were constructed by the East India Company were popularly called as *Maratha ditches*. After the death of Alivardi Khan in 1756, his grandson Siraj-ud-Daulah assumed power. During the rule of Alivardi Khan, Bengal Subah had declared its autonomy from the Mughal Empire, like many other regional rulers. Nawab Siraj-ud-Daulah attacked Calcutta and captured the city. However, after receiving enforcement from Madras under the command of Robert Clive, the army of the East India Company defeated the army of the Nawab in the Battle of Plassey in 1757. The Battle of Plassey was the most important *business deal* of the East India Company. The battle was not won by the army of the East India Company, but by a business deal which Clive had agreed upon with the commander of the forces of the Nawab of Bengal, Mir Jafar.[57] The deal that was closed between Clive and Mir Jafar was believed to have been planned by some of the wealthy merchants of Bengal, especially the house of Jagat Seth, Omichund and Khwaja Wajid. This happened because of the emerging harmonization of interests between merchants of Bengal and the East India Company.[58] Subsequently, the army of the East India Company defeated the combined armies of the Nawab of Bengal, Nawab of Awadh and Mughal emperor Shah Allam at Buxar. The war ended with the Treaty of Allahabad in 1764. This treaty granted *diwani* right (right to collect taxes) to the East India Company. The diwani right transformed the East India Company into the ruler of Subah of Bengal. This transformation converted *John Company* into *Company Bahadur*. The new circumstances provided twin monopolies to the East Indian Company—monopoly over trade and monopoly over the political power. After this event, the East India Company shifted the capital of Bengal from Murshidabad to Calcutta.

The political hegemony of Calcutta was the beginning of the prosperity of Calcutta.

One fact has to be kept in mind while telling the tale of the four cities during the Mughal Empire that cities are embedded in the political regime of the time. Their potential to develop and accumulate wealth is facilitated by the institutions, structure of governance and attitude of political elite towards wealth creators. The potential of growth of the native cities of Surat and Dacca was determined by the political regime that was evolved by the Mughal Empire. As it has been described above, the Mughal Empire provided an essential public good which is the most important determinant of growth and prosperity, namely the period of continuous political stability, peace, and law and order. The Mughal Empire also integrated several fragmented political entities into an empire and established connectivity between them. The connectivity between these fragment polities facilitated the birth of a market of continental size. Movement of goods, services and people increased the extent of urbanization, which further expanded the size of the market for the products produced by the traditional flexible manufacturing located in these cities.

However, it is important to know that the Mughals created an administrative and governance structure where the royal family along with nobles and mansabdars appropriated a significant part of economic surplus generated by the economy. Towards the end of the rule of Akbar, these sections of the society appropriated for their self-consumption around 80 per cent of the annual budget of the Mughal Empire. They spent a very large proportion of this revenue on maintaining the large Mughal army. This revenue was also spent by the royal family, nobles and mansabdars on maintaining spectacular lifestyles. Their consumption pattern got manifested in the possession of the volume of gold and silver and precious stones in the form of expensive jewellery that was matchless by any other contemporary empire. Three famous, fabled diamonds were in the possession of the royal family. These diamonds were the Koh-i-Noor (mountain of light) and the Darya-i-Noor (the sea of light) and a ruby known as Ain-al-Hur (the eye of the fairy).[59]

The Mughal emperors also spent huge amount of financial resources for creating entirely new capital cities, for example, Fatehpur Sikri near Agra by Mughal emperor Akbar and Shahjahanabad (old city of Delhi) by Shahjahan. Financial resources of the empire were also spent on the construction of forts, palaces and tombs (such as the Taj Mahal) in the cities of Delhi, Lahore and Agra. They also provided patronage to different art forms like music, painting, architecture and dance. The royal patronage to different craftsmen helped in developing several exquisite artefacts and cultural products, which are distinctly recognized around the world as a part of Pax Mughalia. Mughal aristocracy gave birth to a new kind of dress code, which became the basis of Mughal fashion. The Mughal dresses still provide inspiration to contemporary fashion designers. The Mughals also evolved distinct court manners, protocols and etiquettes (Ali, 2004; Metcalfe (ed.), 1984).

The cultural ecosystem that got evolved during the period of the Mughal Empire facilitated the concurrent existence of several faiths. The symbiotic existence of these faiths gave birth to the *Bhakti Movement*, which consisted of several shades of expression, from extreme orthodoxy to the most liberal thoughts. Sikhism evolved its distinct identity during this period and the Indian subcontinent also experienced the influence of *Sufism*. This cultural milieu evolved its own language to express its cultural ethos in the form of *Urdu*. Urdu was a hybrid language, which initially evolved in military camps of the Mughal Empire. However, while writing it people used Perso-Arabic script. Despite its richness and diversity, the cultural ecosystem that evolved during the Mughal Empire did not result in a period of enlightenment, the kind of enlightenment that was experienced by European societies during *renaissance*. Therefore, society in the Indian subcontinent did not experience a shift towards the importance of *creation of mind* over the matters of *soul*.[60]

It is quite relevant to mention here that most of the wealth accumulated by Mughal emperors was acquired through unproductive economic activities. They acquired this wealth by creating *extractive institutions* through the structure of governance which they had established. The extractive institutions helped them in redistributing existing wealth in favour of the powerful elites. This wealth was appropriated through taxation, gifts, tributes and plunder. The massive amount of wealth which the elites possessed was not spent on potential sources of wealth creation. They converted the gold and silver into unproductive artefacts like the Peacock Throne or other items of jewellery for the consumption of elites of the society. Hence wealth created during the Mughal Empire was illusory. It is due to these reasons that despite being one of the wealthiest empires during the period, the Mughal Empire did not create institutions of higher learning, mass education and improving technology. This is also an important historical fact that despite the arrival of several Europeans, since the beginning of the Mughal Empire, not a single member of the Mughal elite group travelled to any of the European countries. Had any of them made effort to visit any of the European countries, especially Britain, he would have realized that these countries were undergoing structural transformation. The transformation which the European countries were experiencing was preparing them to soon take a great leap forward to establish the age of European dominance.

The foundations for taking the European societies to a higher level of growth and prosperity were laid by the revival of the *Code of Justinian*, which was compiled during 527–565. This code consisted of institutions, principles, and the code and collection of imperial enactments. Its most important constituent was *corpus iuris civilis* (state laws affecting civil administration). The supremacy of law, even above the authority of the crown, helped in the evolution of civil society. These laws have assumed significance and were taught in the wide-spread system of schools. These schools were using a standardized curriculum. The language used to educate students was *Latin*. Since then Latin became the common language of creation and diffusion of knowledge across different countries of Europe. These developments led to the accumulation of shared knowledge which could be debated, improved and validated. This pool of knowledge became the basis for the establishment of universities, where knowledge could be simultaneously created and transferred to the next generation of students. This led to the birth of transnational groups of learned people called *scholars* (Watson, 2006). This is important to mention here that while the Mughal Empire was thriving in the Indian subcontinent, there existed several universities such as the University of Bologna in Italy, Montpellier and Paris Universities in France, and Oxford and Cambridge in Britain. There were around 70 universities which were functioning in Europe around 1500.[61] Here it is relevant to highlight that the absence of universities does not mean that in the Indian subcontinent the process of creation and dissemination of knowledge had stopped. This only suggests that there was absence of organized institutions which help in the creation and diffusion of knowledge. In India, at this point in time, knowledge was embedded in different communities. These communities created knowledge and kept it as their own intellectual property.

Europe experienced intellectual awakening after black deaths. In 1346, the plague epidemic which caused the pandemic Black Death, arrived through Silk Road in the middle of 1348. It hit Britain and killed around half of the population.[62] The Black Death resulted in a variety of responses among Europeans. Some of the Europeans became more religious, believing that the calamity has been caused as a consequence of fall of people from the grace of god. This resulted in increasing attendance of devotees in churches. It was during this period that the Pope planned to construct the Vatican City. To meet the financial needs of building the city, the Church began to sell *indulgences* (tickets to heaven). The climax of this practice occurred when in 1476 Pope Sixtus IV came with the idea that indulgences can also be purchased for dead relatives.[63]

On the contrary, the deaths of several thousands of innocent people forced some of the enlightened sections of the society to question the logic inherent in the divine will. It is while questioning the so-called divine order that they began to analyse the anatomy of the existing social order, separately and independently of divine kingdom. At this point in time, several inquisitive minds were engaged in seeking answers to questions which were agitating the minds of people. One such individual was a priest, Martin Luther, who was teaching philosophy at Wittenberg, located near Leipzig in Germany. He visited Rome in 1512 when it was experiencing *renaissance,* riding on the ideas of Leonardo da Vinci, Michelangelo and Raphael. Here he publicly challenged the idea of sale of indulgences. It was the growing tribe of such individuals which laid the foundation of a new social order.

European Enlightenment was based on the premise that material progress could be achieved by understanding of natural phenomena to evolve laws that govern nature. The process began with the influence of Francis Bacon, a British philosopher, statesman and scientist. A host of intellectuals founded the Royal Society in 1660. Even before the founding of the Royal Society, several important contributions had been made by several scholars in this direction. These scholars were René Descartes (1596–1656), Pierre de Fermat (1601–1665), Blaise Pascal (1623–1662), Galileo (1564–1642), Copernicus (1473–1543), Kepler (1571–1630), Isaac Newton (1642–1727) and Gottfried Leibniz (1646–1716), to name just a few.[64] All these scholars were contemporaries of different Mughal emperors. But due to indifference of these emperors towards Europeans, the Indian subcontinent remained outside the influence of their ideas. This isolation might have also been resulted from the fact that the Mughal emperors and Indian elites came into contact with either European missionaries or merchants. Both these sections of the European societies were embedded in old social order. However, it was the emergence of these revolutionary changes in the thinking of Europeans in general and in Britain in particular which was transforming these nations and preparing them for subsequent dominance. In the case of Britain, these new ideas were laying the foundation for transforming the small island country into the British Empire—the empire where the sun never set.

The beginning of British supremacy in the Indian subcontinent became apparent as a consequence of the emerging political dominance of the East India Company. It is interesting to mention here that the Battle of Plassey, which gave political hegemony to the East India Company in 1757 in Bengal, and two years later the Castle Revolution of Surat were the two prominent episodes in which local merchants of Surat and those of Bengal helped the company in assuming political power. This suggests that differences in nationality, religion and language do not matter in forming alliances based on common interests. However, the emerging dominance of the East India Company in the Indian polity created a paradigm shift in the history of the subcontinent. For the first time in history, the East India Company became a unique kind of ruler of the Indian subcontinent, ruling on behalf of a kingdom of a distant land. The people of that distant land were kind of extraterrestrial or alien to the Indian people. This was indeed a new paradigm. New because earlier invaders either came to plunder the wealthy places of the subcontinent and went back to their respective kingdoms with booties, or settled down in the conquered land and got assimilated by merging their identities with the identity of the people of the Indian subcontinent. In the process, their acquired identity became inseparable from their native identity. As against this, the new format in which the East India Company became an agency of the British Empire laid the foundation of colonialism. For the first time, policies regarding the governance of the Indian subcontinent were to be formulated by alien people, and the economy and the polity had to work in the interest of this alien ruler.

NOTES

1. For details, see Allami (1927, Vol. II, 264–266).
2. This information has been obtained from Allami (1927, Vol. II, 137).
3. For trade routes, see Haellenquist (ed.) (1991).
4. For details regarding Portuguese expansion on the western coast, see Whiteways (1983), Hall (1995) and Fruber (2004).
5. To know about the Dutch Company's operations in India, see Omprakash (1985) and Pearson (2007).
6. For these regional economies, see Gokhale (1960).
7. For the list of primate cities, see Chaudhri (1978).
8. For details, see Subramanian (2010, 69–75) and Roy (2013, 8).
9. For details, see Sanger (1974) and Barnes (1997).
10. For details, see Gadgil (1924), Pavlov (1978), Ray Chaudhri (1982), Subramanian (2014), Vaniana (2004), Seth (2008, 2015).
11. For these facts, see Kayoka (2009, 195).
12. For details, see Vogt (1975).
13. These facts are available in Machado (2004) and (2009).
14. For this information, see Chaudhri (1990).
15. Defoe's statement is dated 1708 and quoted in Ferguson (2003, 16–17).
16. See for this Phrase, Parthasarathi and Recllo (2013, 138).
17. For details, see Berg (2002).
18. For this fact, see Ray (2016, 146–147).
19. See for details regarding exports of door and windows having elaborate woodcarving, see Horton (2000) and Gilbert (2004).
20. For details regarding Dariabandi Chadders of Agra, see Gopal (1984, 76).

21. For details, see Divekar (1982), Riello and Parthasarathi (ed.) (2009), Riello and Ray (ed.) (2009) and Machado (2009) and Beckert (2014).
22. For details regarding the operations of Virji Vohra, see Gopal (1984, 76).
23. For details regarding the merchant Shantilal Jain, see Tripathi (1981, 25–31).
24. For knowing more about the Kuchi Bhatia community of merchants, see Mehta (2011).
25. For details, see Siddiqi (1982), Subramanian (1996), Tripathi (2011) and Kudasia (2012).
26. For details regarding different communities of muslim merchants, see Mishra (1964), Tirmizi (1984), Pearson (1997) and Goswami (2011).
27. Dasgupta (1994) has devoted one entire chapter of his book on the business group headed by Abdul Ghaffoor.
28. See for details regarding trading activities of Rustom Manock, see Modi (1929) and Blake (2008).
29. For details regarding Parsi merchants of Surat, see Guha (1984, 109–150).
30. For details regarding these Parsi merchant families, see Kulka (1978).
31. For the idea of commercial cosmopolitanism, see Nadri (2012).
32. For this fact, see Brenning (1982, 84–87).
33. To know about converting bullion into Mughal coins in Surat, see Richard (1987, 8).
34. For the magnitude of gold and silver coins minted at Surat, see Hasan (1967, 330–348).
35. For this fact, see Maloni (2015, 277).
36. To know about the Marathas and their impact on Gujarat in general and on Surat in particular, see Chandra (1973), Gordon (1977, 1993) and Ray (2013).
37. For details, see Chandra (1973) and Gordon (1977).
38. For details, see Traveres (2007).
39. For the emerging preconditions of imperialism, see Bayly (1985).
40. For details regarding the life of Mulla Muhammad Ali, see Singh (1977) and Dasgupta (1967).
41. For these changes, see Dasgupta (1994).
42. For the increases in the activities of Pirates, see Dasgupta (1994) and Subramanian (1996).
43. The quotation has been taken from Acemoglu and Robinson (2012, 246).
44. For this, see Subramanian (1990, 1993), Matekandathil (2002) and Omprakash (1985).
45. For knowing details about Calcutta, see Traveres (2007) and Seth (2014).
46. To know about the agrarian structure during Mughal empire, see Grover (1963), Hasan (1964) and Habib (1965).
47. The comparison between Dacca muslin and muslin produced on several other locations is available in Watson (1887) and (1889).
48. For knowledge regarding royal karkhanas, see Bernier (1670, 2011).
49. For details, see Pavlov (1964).
50. For details regarding the house of Jagat Seth, see Little (1920), Hunter (1974), Devera (1987); and Karen (1921).
51. For these details, see Chudhri K.N. (1979).
52. See for the consequences of own account or private trade by the employee of the East Indian Company, Seth (2012) and Seth (2015).
53. For these facts, see Omprakash (1988).
54. For the statistics reported in the text, see Chaudhri (1990, 165–166).
55. For these facts, see Sinha (ed.) (1968).

56. For details regarding the battle of Plassey, see Robins (2006, 3, 64–65).
57. For details, see Gupta (1966), Caulkins (1970) and Chaudhri (1955).
58. For this transformation, see Furber (1970).
59. The names have been mentioned in Marvi, Mohammad Kazem's Alam Ara-ye-Naderi, quoted in Dalrymple and Anand (2016, 9).
60. It is quite important to know that during the period European societies were shifting their emphasis from the matters of soul to the emphasis on creation of mind and discovery of *laws of nature*, see Watson (2005, Chapter 26, 527–549).
61. For the growth of universities in different parts of Europe, see Riddle, Seymoen (1992) and Pederson (1997).
62. For black deaths, see Diamond (2005, Chapter 11 'Lethal Gift of Livestock', 195–214, and for consequences of black death on Europe, see Acemoglu and Robinson [2012]).
63. For details regarding indulgences, see Manchester (1992) and Watson (2005, Chapter 22).
64. For details regarding these scholars, see Watson (2005, 480).

Economic Environment During the Rule of the East India Company

The emergence of multinational trading companies like the East India Company happened as a consequence of certain important socio-economic and political changes that occurred in Europe. Due to these changes, merchants were slowly gaining relative importance in their national life in comparison to the owners of land. The process began at some of the Italian cities such as Genoa, Tuscany and Venice. Venice had emerged as a terminal point of land-bound trade that was taking place between Europe and economies of Asia, such as India and China, through the famous Silk Road and through other caravan routes, which originated from Indian subcontinent, such as Agra–Lahore, Peshawar–Khyber Pass, and Kandahar–Isfahan–Constantinople–Venice. The Silk Road had emerged as a consequence of cooperation between several contiguous empires, such as the Roman, Parthian and Kushan Empires, and the empire established by the Han dynasty of China. Cooperation between these empires established connectivity and interdependence between them. This connectivity provided opportunity to merchants to engage in trade beyond their national borders. These merchants procured luxury and exotic products for nobles, royals and the rich of their countries. Subsequently, the Silk Road came into prominence when Genghis Khan's Mongol Empire restored peace and tranquillity along this road.

The Silk Road covered a distance of 7,000 miles and established link between the East and the West. Its Eastern terminal was at the old Chinese capital city Chang'an (present-day Xian) and the Western terminal was at Byzantium or Constantinople (present-day Istanbul, a city of Turkey). From Constantinople, merchandize travelled to Venice. From here the products were transported to different port cities of Europe. In this trade, the port city of Venice assumed centrality. It is due to this reason that Shakespeare wrote his famous play called *The Merchant of Venice* rather than *The Merchant of London*.

The Silk Road was not a well-developed highway; it in fact consisted of several interconnected caravan routes, trails, oases and market towns. The vast trading route had several branches, which established connectivity with other cities and towns (Frank, 1990). For instance, one of its branches left the southern route and connected it with the desert of Taklamakan. 'Taklamakan' literally means a place where 'You go in, you don't come out'.[1] This branch of the Silk Road terminated at Balkh (in today's northern Afghanistan). Another branch left the southern road at Yarkand and connected Karakorum with the cities of Leh and Srinagar. It touched the northwestern parts of the Indian subcontinent and established trading links between different land routes spread over the vast subcontinent. Thus, India occupied the central place in the Silk Road with China in the East and Rome in the West.[2]

The Silk Road provided to the European economies spices and luxury handicrafts such as cotton and silk textiles produced by the traditional flexible manufacturing of India and China. This pattern of trade continued to exist for centuries. This trade was dominated by Asian merchants, while European merchants played a peripheral role by occupying operations at the lowest end of supply chain. The occupation of Constantinople by the Ottoman Empire under Muhammad II in 1453 changed the flow of trade significantly. By achieving dominance over terrestrial routes, the Ottoman Empire denied Europeans access of trade in spices and luxury products of the East. The use of pepper was necessary for Europeans to make preserved meat edible. Therefore, it became an essential part of the life of Europeans.

The new circumstances forced Europeans out into the Atlantic to search for sea routes, because land routes were under the dominance of Islamic states. Discovery of sea routes was essential to get access to spices such as pepper, cinnamon, nutmeg, clove and mace.[3] The necessity to buy spices also increased pressure to search for gold and silver. These twin needs of Europeans provided preconditions for the beginning of the age of discovery. These needs converted European monarchs into venture capitalists, because they began to finance very risky voyages for discovering sea routes to Asian sources of spices. The competition to discover new sea routes amongst European monarchs was as intense as the competition between the USA and USSR to reach moon during the period of Cold War.

Supported by the king of Spain, Christopher Columbus began his journey to discover the Indian subcontinent by going west across the Atlantic and discovered America in 1492. Discovery of the American continent provided Europeans with ample supply of bullion. Portuguese sailor Vasco da Gama planned his voyage towards south along the coast of Africa and Cape of Good Hope, and succeeded in reaching Milindi. The folklore suggests that here Vasco da Gama met an Indian merchant and sea pilot Kanji, who guided him to reach Calicut, which was the source of spices in 1498. The Portuguese were able to occupy *Ticuari* (means 36 villages) which was named Goa in 1510 under the command of Alfonso de Albuquerque. The entire maritime empire established by the Portuguese in the Indian subcontinent was known as Estado da India (Lach, 1965; Omprakash, 1985; Pearson, 2007). The Portuguese kept the discovery of the sea route to India as a national secret for a considerable period, because the rulers of Portugal, King John II and King Manuel, imposed heavy penalties, including death penalty for leaking the information to nationals of other countries. This discovery remained a secret until 1550. The secret could not be kept forever, because of the arrival of Jesuit priests in Goa. These priests converted Goa into a headquarters of missionary activities of Jesuits. When Francis Xavier reached Goa in 1543, he wrote a letter to Rome, in which he mentioned that Goa has already become an 'entirely Christian City' (Watson, 2006, 60). Jesuit missionaries were in regular contact and were exchanging information with Rome. It was from these exchanges of information that the knowledge about sea route of India spread to other European countries. Subsequently, according to the permission granted by the Pope, trade with America was granted to Spain, which gave them monopoly over yellow metal, and for trade with Asia to Portugal, which gave them monopoly over sugar, spices and slaves. This division of world trade laid the foundation of the Spanish Empire, which was spread from Madrid to Manila, including Peru and Mexico. It also created the Portuguese Empire which spread from Madeira and Sao Tome to Brazil, West Africa, Indonesia and India.

It is quite important to tell here that despite the fact America and the Indian subcontinent were separated from each other by vast geographical space, they sustained each other for a considerable period. It happened because the bullion which Europeans obtained from America helped them to buy spices and products produced by the traditional flexible manufacturing of the India subcontinent. Discovery of sea route by Vasco da Gama encouraged other Europeans to participate in the trade with the Indian subcontinent. Slowly, Europeans connected several port cities located in the Arabian Sea, Indian Ocean and Bay of Bengal with the port cities of Southeast Asia, China and Africa. These connected port cities gave birth to a network of global trade. The establishment of the linkages with these port cities shifted the trade from *terrestrial trade*, occurring through caravan routes, into *maritime trade* conducted via port cities. This shift in pattern of trade resulted in the beginning of the decline of Asia and the rise of Europe. This paradigm shift in the global trade laid the foundation of European supremacy.[4]

Contemporaneously, as economies of India and China are again experiencing high rates of growth, while economies of Europe and America are showing relative stagnation, the Chinese President Xi Jinping is trying to revive the old Silk Road. In 2013, he issued the first series of announcements, unveiling his plan for the new Silk Road. If the plan succeeds, a substantial volume of global trade will shift from maritime trade to terrestrial trade, which may harm the interests of Europe and America. The new route intends to connect Central China to its border provinces, and the border provinces to sea ports of China and to other ports including ports of Gwadar (which the Chinese are building) and Karachi in Pakistan to Chittagong in Bangladesh, Kaukpyu in Myanmar, and Colombo and Hobota in Sri Lanka. The Chinese believe that when this new trading network will be complete, it will correct the historical injustice of the past, which resulted in the supremacy of the West (Aneja, 2016; Bhardwaj, 2016; *Economist*, 2006).

The supremacy of European merchants in international trade emerged as a consequence of nexus between European monarchs, merchants and native producers. The emerging supremacy of European merchants was not possible without the involvement of European monarchs. Monarchs supported them to get access to new markets by financing voyages to discover new routes and new lands. They also gave diplomatic support to facilitate establishment of trading bases in different countries by entering into treaties with different kingdoms. They also provided military support to merchants to subjugate hostile rulers of distant lands. Support of monarchs was also necessary to manipulate tariffs to protect interests of domestic producers and merchants. Monarchs also provided privileges to merchants in terms of granting monopolies of trade in some markets. In this way, European monarchs created a large *rent-seeking class*, which enriched itself and in turn also enriched the Crown. The riches given to monarchs gave them resources to increase their military strength. It was the military strength of the monarch which determined the extent of their market share in the global trade. The emerging nexus between European kings and different rent-seeking classes led to the birth of an ideology, which has been described as *mercantilism*.[5] This ideology was highly nationalistic, which jealously protected the interests of home market and home producers.

The followers of mercantilist school of thought believed that it is the stock of gold in the possession of an economy which determines the extent of real wealth of a nation. Since gold stock can be increased by foreign trade alone in countries that do not have gold mines, it can be carried out through manipulations of tariff structure in favour of home market. For them, trade was zero-sum game, where gains of one caused losses to the other. Therefore, gain from trade was only possible by making terms of trade unfavourable for the others. Because of this ideological obsession, gold became a European obsession during this period.[6] It is a well-known historical fact that the main objective of discovering new lands was primarily to get access to gold. Their attempts for discovering new routes were largely targeted and motivated by the stories regarding possession of large volumes of gold by certain peoples (Wright, 2000, 11). Christopher Columbus, who opened the American continent for Europeans, writes that 'Gold is a wonderful thing. Whosoever own it, is the lord of all he wants. With gold it is even possible to open soul of the way to paradise' (Wright, 2000). There is also the incident of Atawallpa, the ruler of Peru, who was made hostage by Spaniard conquistador Castilian Francisco Pizarro, and was killed by him despite paying the amount of ransom never ever paid by any other hostage in human history. The ransom that was paid included a roomful of gold and two rooms full of silver (Presscott, 1847; Wright, 2000). The obsession with gold amongst Europeans was quite surprising to natives of Peru, where gold had only ritualistic or iconic value. For Peruvians, 'Gold was sweat of sun, and silver, moon's tears.'[7]

It was in these historical circumstances—after defeating Spanish Armada, when Britain had proven its naval supremacy in Europe, during the rule of Queen Elizabeth I—British merchants were provided opportunity to expand their trading links with other nations of the world. The process of expansion of trade began with granting of royal charter to several trading companies, such as Levant, Muscovy, Royal African Company and Hudson's Bay Company, floated by British merchants (Bowen, 2006; Carlos and Nicholas, 1988; Robins, 2006). The East India Company was formed through a royal charter granted by Queen Elizabeth I, on New Year's Eve of 1600. The royal charter gave to the East India Company monopoly right to trade with the East. The East India Company was the first joint-stock multinational company of the world. It had continuous existence as a commercial corporation from 1600 to 1833, and from 1833 to 1857, primarily as an agency of the British Empire.

After getting patronage and privileges from the British Crown, the company was formed with the help of three different stakeholders of the British society, who hardly interacted with each other in the normal course of their life. These stakeholders were bound together to satisfy their private interests. The East India Company was financially supported by the rich merchants of London. It received logistic support for transporting its merchandize across different oceans from navigators and sailors. Protection of its merchandize from pirates in the sea and from hostile rulers of different ports was provided by the soldiers. Therefore, its organization structure had to evolve in such a way that it could harmonize the interests of all the stakeholders of the Company. The East India Company was a classic example of conducting business with sword in your hand. Subsequently, the East India Company emerged as a large multinational enterprise; its size and operations may put to shame some of the contemporary big corporations that are listed in the Fortune 500, in terms of volume of merchandize traded, number of people employed and extent of market power enjoyed by them. Most of the consequences that were experienced by the four cities of the Indian subcontinent during the Company's rule between 1757 and 1857 can be attributed to the nature of its organization and the kind of historical role it was designed to perform during the prevailing historical circumstances.

For the purpose of understanding the role of the East India Company in determining the condition of the Indian subcontinent in general and in the tale of the four cities in particular, the rest of the chapter has been organized in three sections. In the first section, the process of evolution of the East India Company has been described. The second section narrates the process of transformation of the East India Company into the ruler of Indian subcontinent and, finally, in the third section, consequences that were experienced by the traditional flexible manufacturing during the rule of the Company have been described.

EVOLUTION OF THE EAST INDIA COMPANY

As has been described above, the East India Company was a company which was granted the status of a royal chartered company by the British Crown as a specific privilege. The status was given to a company which was able to establish harmony between private profit motive, public interest and the interest of the Crown. This status empowered the company with quasi-sovereign rights such as right to mint its own coins, exercise law and order, and arbitrate in its own overseas settlements.[8] The chartered status did not provide any additional advantage to the managers who were operating in Britain. However, this status provided more scope for opportunistic behaviour by the overseas managers. This is because the chartered status provided them freedom to bribe, enter into treaty or fight war with local rulers. Therefore, overseas operations of the company necessitated the empowerment of overseas managers of the company. These additional powers given to overseas branches helped them to evolve their own strategies for conducting their businesses.

The Crown used to grant royal charter to certain selected enterprises. However, granting of royal charter created intellectual divide amongst the contemporary scholars. Some of them accepted the granting of royal charter to the East India Company, while some of them were against it. The scholars who were antagonistic to the granting of royal charter to the Company argued that such companies are established primarily to obtain privilege from the Crown, which bestows on them monopoly power which facilitates the companies to enjoy monopoly profits.[9] However, the scholars who justified the practice of granting royal charter to selected companies believed that the granting of royal charter to a company was similar to protecting the intellectual capital of the company. This is because it amounts to giving monopoly to an inventor by granting of patent right, or copyright to an author. The similarity emerges because it is granted only to those companies which either collected new information or created new knowledge about new overseas markets, new products and new routes to reach new lands. By empowering such companies with royal charter, the Crown was minimizing their risk in conducting their business (Jones and Ville 1996). However, scholars who were against granting of royal charter argued that though it protects intellectual capital of the company, at the same time, it encourages the chances of following opportunistic behaviour for rent seeking amongst the promoters of chartered companies.[10] The supporters of granting of royal charter to the companies, like the East India Company, stated that chartered status did not *pari pasu* result in rent. To earn rent such companies had to either minimize costs or maximize mark-up from the transactions.[11]

The contemporary scholars generally accepted the logic provided by the protagonists of the granting of royal charter. These scholars accepted the appropriateness of the practice of the Crown based on the premise that discovering new markets, products and locations amounts to development of intellectual capital; therefore, such companies be permitted to enjoy monopoly status for a certain period of time. This is because granting of royal charter is equivalent to protection of intellectual capital developed by the company.[12] Adam Smith, who was an important antagonist of the East India Company, also accepted the premise for granting the royal charter to the East India Company. He describes:

> When a company of merchants undertakes at their own risk and expense to establish a new trade with some remote and barbarous nation... it is easiest and most natural way in which the state can recompense them.... A temporary monopoly of this kind may be vindicated upon the same principles on which monopoly of a new machine is granted to its inventor and that of new book to its scholar. Baendel (1982, 436)

The East India Company also used a new innovation in its organizational structures. The Company was organized as a joint-stock company. It was a new innovation, which was at variance with the organizational structure of similar trading companies. For instance, though the Portuguese company and the Dutch company were owned by their respective governments, they accepted investments from individuals. These individuals could only share profits, but did not enjoy voting rights. The concept of joint stock is based on the Italian word *compagnia*, which is similar to the Latin term *cum panis*, which means 'sharing of bread'.[13] In the beginning, the East India Company invited dedicated joint stocks for each voyage separately. The process of raising such stocks began in 1603. Each investor in the stocks of the company invested for each voyage separately and profits earned by the company from each voyage were shared amongst the stockholders after the termination of each voyage. To finance the first fleet of four ships, 218 investors collectively raised a total capital of £68,373. The system of voyage by raising stock for individual voyage was given up in 1613, and was replaced by annual investment in stock. The first annual stocks raised by the East India Company amounted to £420,436, which financed the shipment of merchandize for four consecutive years (1613–1616). Through its second annual stocks, the Company collected a total capital of £1.6 million, which financed its annual shipment of merchandize between 1616 and 1622 (Lawson, 1993, 21). Thereafter, such annual stocks were raised by the Company until 1653, because after 1653 joint stock got converted into a permanent joint stock.[14] Initially, the stocks of the Company were traded at the head office of the East India Company, which was located at Leanon Hall Street in London. Soon the trading of company stocks was held at the Royal Exchange of London. However, after the establishment of London Stock Exchange, its stocks were traded there from 1773. The stocks of the Company were held by people belonging to diverse backgrounds and were geographically spread over each and every part of Britain. The pattern of stockholding of the East India Company, as described by some historians, suggests that there were 3,084 individuals who owned stocks of the Company in 2,826 separate holdings. These shares were owned by corporations, in partnerships, jointly as well as individually.[15]

Since the East India Company was a joint-stock company operating through the grant of royal charter, it did not enjoy permanence like modern join-stock companies. Modern joint-stock companies have longer permanent life than the promoters of such companies. The peculiar charter of the East India Company necessitated its periodic approval by the British Crown. This is because Royal charter was given for limited period. Its permanence depended on the patronage of the British Crown. To receive patronage of the Crown on a continuous basis, the East India Company was required to establish good relationship with the British Crown. To guarantee its continuous existence, the East India Company used the strategy of bribing important persons, including the Crown itself. During the period in which Sir Josiah Child was a member of the Board of Directors of the Company (1674–1699), he followed the practice of bribing important persons. He strictly accepted the ideology of mercantilism and believed royal patronage can be obtained by following the policy of reciprocity. To justify the premise of mercantilism, he wrote several articles and pamphlets. His important pamphlet *A New Discourse on Trade* was identified by Adam

Smith to attack mercantilist ideas in his book *The Wealth of Nations*. In 1681, when the Company needed to revive its royal charter, Josiah Child paid 10,000 guineas to the British king Charles II. This amount became annual payment to Charles II while he ruled Britain. However, payment of this annual sum established a cordial relationship between the Company and the Crown. This relationship was reciprocated by Charles II when he granted occupation of Bombay to the East India Company (Bowen, 2006; Robins, 2006).

In the summer of 1688, British aristocrats and merchants staged a bloodless coup against the British king, James II, and invited the Dutch, under the leadership of William of Orange, to Britain. This event has been described in British history as the Bloodless Revolution or Glorious Revolution. This event led to Anglo-Dutch merger, which removed the competition between the East India Company and the Dutch Company in the Indian subcontinent. This happened because the Anglo-Dutch merger was based on the understanding that the British trading company will have freedom to trade in the Indian sub-continent and the Dutch company will be free to trade with Indonesia and engage in spice trade. This was an important achievement for the East India Company. However, subsequently, when the charter of the Company was renewed in 1693, bribes were also paid by the Company. However, this time the British Parliament was vigilant and appointed an enquiry committee to investigate the charges of corruption. The enquiries by the committee revealed several acts of bribing by the Company to receive renewal of the charter. In each incidence of bribing, Thomas Cook, governor of the Company, who was also the son-in-law of Josiah Child, was involved. This enquiry clearly established that the East India Company was buying the patronage of the Crown through bribes.[16]

The details regarding the administrative structure of the East India Company were made available for the first time in 1785 by one of the secretaries of the company. This provides description of the organizational structure of the Company. This organizational structure has been reproduced in a recent book written by Bowen.[17] The overall administration of the Company was looked after by the Board of Directors. The Board consisted of 24 directors. The Board of Directors performed their duties with the help of several committees. Each committee was headed by a director of the Company. Actual operations of the Company were looked after by the governors of three presidencies, namely Bombay (Western), Calcutta (Eastern) and Madras (Southern), which were located in three different corners of the Indian subcontinent. The committees that were formed by the Board of Directors consisted of three different classes. The first type of committees was classified as first-class committees and consisted of correspondence committee, legal committee, committee for resources for the military of the company, and treasury committee. In the category of second-class committees, warehouse committee and committees dealing with accounts, buying and housing were included. Finally, in the third-class committees were included committees which looked after shipping, troops, private trade and its prevention, and stores. In this organizational structure, for the first time in 1776, a separate new position of examiner was included, in addition to the office of secretary of the Company. The position of examiner subsequently assumed greater significance because it established administrative connectivity between the head office of the company in London and different presidency head offices located in the Indian subcontinent. It is also important to mention that the office of examiner was graced by some of the leading persons who had contributed towards greater understanding about India. These persons were Nathaniel Brassey, the scholar who compiled the *Code of Gentoo Laws*, which appeared in 1776; Halhead, who had written *Grammar of Bengali Language*, which appeared in 1778; and James Mill, the famous classical political economist, whose book *British India* attracted attention of the policymakers. Even famous poet Thomas Love Peacock also worked as the examiner at one time.[18]

In addition to the administrative structure of the Company, it also had formed a separate organizational structure in the offices of the three presidencies in the Indian subcontinent. A new employee in the Company began his career as a writer in company office. After serving for a period of five years, he was promoted as a *factor* of the company. His office was known as a *factory*. A factor was promoted after three years as a junior merchant. As and when the position fell vacant, he was elevated to the position of senior merchant. Some of its employees, those who were meritorious, were included in the presidency councils and some of them were also promoted as governors of the presidency. Clive was one of the employees of the Company who entered as a writer and retired as governor of the Bengal Presidency.

The East India Company functioned like a modern corporation because it was managed by a hierarchy of professional managers. These managers were engaged in performing diverse operations of the Company, both at the head office of the Company at London and at different offices located at different places in the Indian subcontinent, and other port cities where the East India Company had its operation. The organization of operations of the Company, which were spread across different geographies, provided possibilities of opportunistic behaviour to the managers whose works were geographically separated from the head office. These possibilities necessitated to rely on *managerially coordinated transaction* rather than *market-mediated transactions*.[19]

In the modern theory of firm, a firm is viewed as an entity formed by entering into several contracts. The nature of the contract determines the relationship that will emerge or evolve between different contracting economic agents. The East India Company was also based on several contracts with different stakeholders to achieve efficiency in its operations. Its initial contract was with the British Crown and Parliament, which was implicit in the charter granted to the Company. Its second stakeholders were thousands of stockholders of the company, who made investments in the company stocks. Another group of stakeholders of the Company were managers and employees working at distant locations. Therefore, to obtain expected behaviour from each stakeholder, there was an organizational need to evolve appropriate contracts with different stakeholders and to design an appropriate mechanism for their enforcement. For proper enforcement of contract, there was also need to establish third-party institutions.[20]

The possibilities for the opportunistic behaviour on the part of management out of the Company were embedded in the organization of the East India Company as a joint-stock company. The joint-stock format of organization of a company creates separation between *ownership* and *control*. Although formation of a company as joint-stock company provides several kinds of benefits to the company, such as arranging large volumes of investment by pooling investments made by thousands of investors and dependence on paid talented professionals rather on hereditary owners, this form of organization also results in several kinds of disadvantages. The limited liability of stockholders and promoters provides them freedom from bearing the consequences of their decisions, because consequences for each investor are limited to the magnitude of their investment in the stocks of the company. The most important disadvantage is that the separation between ownership and control can give rise to opportunistic behaviour by the managers, when they begin to maximize their own objective function, which may be at variance with the objectives of the stock owners. In economic theory, the possibilities of opportunistic behaviour on the part of the management has been studied with the help of *principal* (owners of stocks) *agent* (management) problem.[21]

The principal–agent problem arises in the case of joint-stock companies because once owners of the company (stockholders) appoint managers (agents) to work for their benefit, do not have any say in the day-to-day running of a joint-stock company. They get chance to evaluate the performance of the management only in the general body meetings. The absence of stockholders in the running of the company provides scope for the existence of opportunistic behaviour on the part of management. In economic analysis, the principal–agent problem has been discussed since the inception of economics as a separate subject. Adam Smith, who is considered as a father of economics, also explained the presence of principal–agent problem in the joint-stock companies. It is also interesting to mention that he analysed the principal–agent problem in the context of the East India Company. This is because when he was writing his book, the famous *Wealth of Nations*, the East India Company was the most important joint-stock company which was in operation. Adam Smith identified the problem of principal–agent when he stated that joint-stock companies suffer from 'negligence, profusion and malversation of their own servants' (Bearle and Means, 1972).

However, quite an enormous amount of water has passed through the Thames since the days of Adam Smith. Contemporaneously, the problem of principal–agent has been elaborated by several scholars with the help of different models that have been evolved to analyse this problem. This is because, now, joint-stock form of enterprises are dominant in most of the economies. The joint-stock form of business organization had become a dominant form of organization in America as early as 1930.[22] Since then attempts have been made by the scholars to evolve different theoretical constructs which can establish harmony between the self-interest of different stakeholders. To establish harmonization between interest of owners and agents requires the minimization of *incentive conflict* between them. To minimize the *incentive conflict* there is a need to evolve appropriate criterion for hiring agents to avoid *adverse selection*. This also requires that once the agents have been hired, appropriate incentive structure should put in place to avoid *moral hazard*.[23]

The organization structure of the East India Company also provided scope for the opportunistic behaviour to its management, because like all other joint-stock companies, the East India Company also suffered from principal–agent problem. It has been explained above that the East India Company was formed by entering into contracts with several stake holders; these multiple contracts provided scope of multiple principal–agent problems. In comparison to other joint-stock companies, which are nation bound, the multinational joint stock company, like the East India Company, experienced most serious principal–agent problems that existed between the management functioning in the London office and managements working in the different presidency towns located in the Indian subcontinent. The seriousness of the problem originated from the fact that geographical distances separated them, which caused the non-availability of complete information about the managements operating businesses in the Indian subcontinent. The problem associated with incomplete information is described as the problem of information *asymmetry*. The problem information asymmetry was difficult to overcome due to existence of poor means of transportation and communication.[24] Another reason which has caused principal–agent problem between the management of London office and managements of presidency offices was the status of royal charter given to the East India Company.

This status endowed the managements working at the presidency offices with quasi-sovereign rights. This quasi-sovereign status of the branch offices of the Company in foreign locations, which gave the managers of the branch offices additional advantages to follow their self-interest, may be at variance with the objectives of the stockholders of the company. The most important scope for such managers existed in the form of annexing local territories, entering into treaties with local rulers and conducting private businesses to maximize their individual wealth. This suggests that the organizational structure of the East India Company provided scope for opportunistic behaviour to not only its managers but also to its private army, which acted like Spanish conquistadores who acted as agents of colonization of South America.

Several scholars have studied the contents of the contract and capacity of the Company to enforce the contract between the East India Company and its overseas employees to understand how far the Company was able to harmonize the interests of both the stakeholders. They have also studied the nature of incentive structure that was developed by the Company to minimize the consequences of principal–agent problem. The study of the contract which was signed by the employees of the East India Company shows that the contract consisted of two segments. The first segment was called *covenant of indenture*, and the second segment was in the form of a *bond*. The covenant of indenture was a long document which was mandatory for the overseas employees of the company. This document also had clause regarding dismissal of an employee. The bond required guarantee of two persons. The minimum eligibility for entering into the service of the Company was 17 years of age. The duly signed contract was valid for only five years; however, it was generally extended for the next five years. To overcome the problems associated with principal–agent problem, employees of the Company received a fixed income, which was of course quite low. Employees were promoted to higher ranks on the basis of seniority. The low salary which was given to the employees was compensated for by giving them permission to conduct own-account business also. The income from private trade compensated their low salaries. The East India Company had also evolved a mechanism so that these overseas employees could remit their earnings to their relatives in Britain. The remittance was conducted through a bill of exchange. The employees submitted the amount of money they wanted to transfer to their relatives. This was sent to Britain in the form of bill of exchange. The Company's London office paid to their relatives the amount of sterling that their money could get in exchange.[25]

In the beginning, the East India Company had no option but to give permission to its overseas employees to conduct private business, because the Company did not have administrative capability to prohibit private trade. However, officially private trade by the employees of the Company was permitted when new contracts were formalized in 1675. This form of private trade was described as *privileged trade*. Since the Company was not able to stop the practice of private trade by its overseas employees, it used it to minimize cost to the Company. They did this by paying them lower wages. This practice provided opportunity to the middle- and senior-level employees of the Company to accumulate private wealth before their retirement from the Company. Some of these employees used to enjoy comparable standards of living when they went back to London after completing their term. However, this practice increased the greed of its employees for accumulating private wealth. The private greed made roguery necessary. The British civil society used the term *Nabab* for the wealthy ex-employees of the company who returned from India. The first such Nabab was Edward Stephen, who returned after completing his services in Bengal in 1730. The wealth of such employees became the cause of envy amongst the British landed gentry.[26]

The employees of the East India Company were able to increase their private wealth considerably after the East India Company received firman to carry on free trade in Bengal Subah in 1717 by Mughal emperor Shaharyar. The officials of the company earned money by selling *dastaks* (entry passes) to merchants of other European trading companies. This practice increased the private income of the officials of the company and at the same time reduced the income of the Nawab of Bengal.[27] Even the employees of the East India working at Madras also got opportunity to make private wealth when the East India Company implanted Prince Mohammed Ali Wallajah as Nawab of Arcot in 1752. In supporting this prince to become the Nawab of Arcot, Robert Clive made quite a fortune, along with Paul Befield. Some of the officials of the Company also made private earnings by giving personal loans to the Nawab of Arcot and Rajah of Tanjore at very high rates of interest. Subsequently, this practice took the dimensions of a scandal, and the East India Company was forced to frequently change the governors of the Madras Presidency.[28]

The opportunistic behaviour of the employees of the company assumed serious consequences, when the East India Company got the diwani right in Bengal after the Battle of Plassey. This event gave to the East India Company monopoly of trade and monopoly of political power in Bengal. The opportunity for making private wealth by the officials of the company came when monsoon in Bengal failed to arrive for two consecutive years 1769 and 1770. The draught resulted in famine in Bengal. It was observed that the Bengal famine was caused by the malpractices in the trading of rice by the officials of the East India Company (Smith, 1776 [2003], 664). It was the opportunistic behaviour of the employees of the East India Company which had converted food shortages into famine. Adam Smith described the causes of Bengal famine in his book *Wealth of Nations*, which appeared in 1776, that is, six years after the Bengal famine. He writes, 'The drought of Bengal a few years ago might have occasioned a great *dearth*. Some improper regulations, some injudicious restraints imposed by the servants of the East India Company, upon rice trade, contributed, perhaps to turn that *dearth into famine*.[29]

TRANSFORMATION OF THE EAST INDIA COMPANY INTO COMPANY BAHADUR

It has been already described in the earlier chapter that after the death of Aurangzeb, Indian polity got fragmented into several large and small political entities. These segmented polities were engaged in conflict to carve out maximum space from the available political space vacated by the centralized authority of the Mughal Empire. Apart from conflict amongst these political entities, there were also issues regarding succession of local rulers. The rival claimants to the seat of power needed help from different local rulers including the East India Company. This gave opportunity to the East India Company to become party to the disputes.

As it is evident from the earlier section of this chapter, that the East India Company was a chartered company, which had been empowered by the British Crown with semi-sovereign powers. These powers always provided possibilities to the East India Company to acquire territories and govern them. Therefore, transformation of a commercial enterprise into a ruler of a territory was in the DNA of the East India Company. The changed circumstances in the Indian subcontinent after the death of Aurangzeb provided it the necessary preconditions to transform its character from a purely commercial enterprise into an agency of an empire. The acquisition of diwani right in the one of the richest subahs of the Mughal Empire also provided it with necessary financial resources to raise an army as well as conduct its commercial operation.

It is also worth mentioning here that there existed serious conflict of interests amongst different European trading companies, because each one of them wanted to appropriate largest share of the market of the Indian subcontinent. So long the Mughal Empire was strong, their conflict remained confined to coastal regions. These companies were conducting their businesses in the subcontinent largely through goodwill and patronage of the Mughal Empire. Therefore, these companies remained primarily trading companies till the decline of the Mughal Empire began. After the death of Aurangzeb in 1707, the Mughal Empire began to disintegrate. Emerging political uncertainty provided objective conditions to European companies to mobilize military and naval power at unprecedented levels. The defence mobilization of the European companies was also becoming necessary as a consequence of globalization of conflict amongst European countries, especially between France and Britain.[30] The increased militarization of European countries and globalization of their conflict for possession of territories and markets were laying the foundation of an epochal transition to a new world order, which has been termed by historians and political analysts as 'imperialism'.[31] In the present section, we are narrating the story of how the East India Company exploited these circumstances in the Indian subcontinent to emerge as a Company Bahadur.

The decline in the centralized authority of the Mughal Empire, after the death of Aurangzeb, created opportunities for some of the provincial rulers to carve out independent regional bases of power. The autonomous kingdom in Awadh was established by Sadat Khan Burhan-ul-Mulk, with its capital at Lucknow. Similarly, Asaf Jah Nizam-ul-Mulk declared the establishment of an autonomous kingdom in Hyderabad in 1724. Murshid Quli Khan was appointed governor of Bengal by Aurangzeb to make it a financially viable province. His policies had helped in increasing the revenue of the province with the help of a few big landlords and banking firm of Jagat Seth. But in 1739–1740, his successor Sarfraz Khan was replaced by Alivardi Khan due to influence of the banking firm of Jagat Seth. Alivardi Khan declared Bengal as an autonomous province. This happened after the attack of Nadir Shah, which exposed the weakness of the Mughal Empire in terms of defending its territories against foreign aggression. In 1739, Nadir Shah plundered and massacred the inhabitants of Delhi during the rule of Mughal emperor Muhammad Shah (1719–1748). This date is quite significant in the history of the Indian subcontinent because after this date most of the European trading companies realized that for their operations regional powers are more relevant than the Mughal Empire.

Taking opportunity of the situation, some of the warrior groups who were earlier subdued due to the might of the Mughal Empire also established their regional power bases in different parts of the Indian subcontinent. The Marathas formed their empire in Western India, which has already been described in the earlier chapter. The 10th Guru of Sikhs, Guru Gobind Singh, had already transformed Sikh Panth into soldiers. Militarization of Sikhs had already created tension between Sikhs and Mughals. In 1765, the Sikhs were able to form a small independent kingdom in the Bari Doab area of Punjab. For a considerable period, several Sikh leaders occupied different territories and ruled independently, organized into misls (which were constituents of the Sikh confederacy). These misls were united under the leadership of Ranjit Singh in 1765. He established his kingdom which covered the Punjab (undivided) and Jammu & Kashmir. Rajputs had established their rule in Rajasthan. The Jats had also established a small kingdom around Delhi, at Bharatpur. Hyder Ali and then Tipu Sultan had emerged as rulers of Mysore with their capital at Srirangapatnam near Bangalore.

This new reality also provided opportunities to different European trading companies to expand their sphere of influence. As has been already explained in an earlier chapter, the East India Company had already spread its political sphere apart from its earlier possessions of Madras, Bombay and Calcutta to the entire province of Bengal after the Battle of Plassey (1757) and Surat after the Castle Revolution of 1759. The possession of these territories had provided advantage to the East India Company in terms of resources in comparison to other European trading companies. It nevertheless experienced stiff competition from the French company which had been able to make inroads in territories such as Tipu's Mysore and the Marathas' Malwa and Puna.

The East India Company followed three different strategies to expand its territorial occupations. In the first case, they took sides with different parties during the dispute on successions, which had become quite frequent. While helping one claimant to the dispute, they entered into a business through a treaty, which gave them access to revenue as well as economically important territories. Following the second strategy, they waged wars with these provincial rulers, who either did not accept their terms or were constraints in their economic objectives. The third strategy or game plan that they followed with weaker regional powers was to enter into a *subsidiary alliance*. The strategy was evolved by Lord Wellesley, when he was Governor-General of the East India Company-occupied territories between 1797 and 1805. In this form of treaty, the East India Company gave protection to regional rules against rival rulers. To protect their territories, they imposed the condition that a part of the army of the East India Company will be located in their province. The ruler had to pay the cost of its maintenance and the Company was also to appoint a *Resident*, who would coordinate with local rules and the office of the East India Company. The new Governor-General Lord Dalhousie, who replaced Wellesley, developed an ingenious way to annex the territories of provincial rulers, who were already dependent on the East India Company. He developed the *Doctrine of Lapse* (1848). According to this doctrine, any territory which was under the protection of the East India Company, if its ruler died without leaving behind a biological heir, it sovereignty will lapse and it will become the territory of the East India Company.

The first strategy, which has been referred to above, was used by the East India Company in Hyderabad. When Nizam-ul-Mulk, the ruler of Hyderabad, died in 1748, it led to war of succession amongst his sons. A similar war of succession occurred after the death of Nawab of Arcot. In both the wars of succession, the French and the British trading companies supported rival claimants. When successions were finally settled after the wars, it so happened that the French company supported prince became the ruler of Hyderabad, and the British company backed Prince Muhammad Ali Wallahjah became the ruler of Arcot. These two incidences increased the participation of the forces of European trading companies in the conflict amongst local rulers.[32] We have already discussed about the occupation of Bengal and port city of Surat by the East India Company in the earlier chapter.

Amongst all political dispensations that emerged after the decline of the Mughal Empire, the Marathas were emerging as a strong contender to replace the centralized authority of the Mughal state. Their formidable presence in the Western region affected the economic interests of the East India Company. The Marathas had been working as commanders and qiladars of several Sultans of Deccan. They worked under the Bahmani Sultans (1347–1527) and the Sultans of Bijapur and Ahmednagar (1500–1690). These kingdoms had to fight constant wars with the Mughal emperors. Due to these continuous attacks by Mughal forces, these Deccan kingdoms were experiencing decline. To take advantage of this situation, the Marathas under the leadership of Shivaji Bhonsale captured territories of Deccan sultans. However, after the death of Shivaji in 1680, owing to emergence of dispute over succession, the Marathas did not expand their territories. In 1719, Peshwa Baji Rao emerged as a successor of the Marathas.[33] The Marathas, after forming their kingdom in Maharashtra under the command of Baji Rao, occupied Malwa and Dhar region in 1720 and occupied Gujarat in the 1730s. Subsequently, they occupied territories in Berar and in the 1740s attacked Bengal several times, which forced the East India Company to dig the Maratha ditch to protect the city of Calcutta.

The occupation of Malwa and Ujjain by the Marathas was harming the interest of the East India Company in trading opium with China. The presence of the Marathas in Gujarat was denying them access to cotton-growing areas. However, after 1751, the Maratha power was segmented in five regional dispensations under the *Maratha confederacy*. Under this arrangement, the Peshwas exercised power and dominance in Western Maharashtra from its capital at Poona, the Holkars controlled Malwa region from its capital Indore, the Sindhias ruled Bundelkhand with Gwalior as its capital, the Bhonsales were commanding Berar and Orissa with Nagpur as the capital, and the Gaekwads controlled Gujarat with their capital in Baroda.[34] Maratha expansion virtually stopped in 1761, when combined force of the Marathas was defeated in the Third Battle of Panipat by the forces of Ahmed Shah Abdali.

The death of Peshwa Madhav Rao in 1772 created an opportunity for the East India Company to intervene in the affairs of the Marathas. After the death of Madhav Rao, Raghunath Rao became Peshwa and planned the assassination of Narayan Rao. These events forced Raghunath Rao to leave Poona and to seek the support of the East India Company. The East India Company supported Raghunath Rao which led to the First Anglo-Maratha War which began in 1775 and continued till 1802. This war provided to the East India Company two other ports near Bombay, namely the ports of Salsette and Bassein. This increased the presence of the East India Company on the Western coast. In the meantime, to protect their territories, the Marathas employed French mercenaries under the leadership of De Baogne, who trained the Maratha army between 1751 and 1830, and after him Perron was appointed in his place. This was the time when the epicentre of Maratha power had shifted from the Peshwas to the Sindhias.

However, after the death of Mahadji Sindhia in 1794, Jaswant Rao Holkar decided to take the supremacy of the Marathas. This resulted in a civil war between different Maratha warlords. The civil war provided an opportunity to the East India Company, when Peshwa Baji Rao II approached the Company for help. The new situation became the cause of the Second Anglo-Maratha War (1803–1805). After the conclusion of this war, the Sindhias and the Bhonsales had to accept conditions of the treaty imposed by the East India Company. The Company received the cotton-growing areas of Gujarat and Orissa. Since the war had come quite close to the borders of Delhi, the Mughal emperor also requested the East India Company for protection. In the new circumstances, the merchants as well as the Mughal emperor accepted that they will accept the office of Residence of the East India Company. The final blow to the remaining power of the Marathas was inflicted in the Third Anglo-Maratha War (1817–1818). This resulted in the breakdown of the Maratha confederacy, and in its place small princely states were carved out which had to accept the Subsidiary Alliance.[35]

For a long period, Awadh was used as a buffer province between expanding armies of Marathas and their possession Bengal, through an understanding with Nawab of Awadh Shuja-ud-Daulah (1753–1775) that East India Company's forces will provide protection to Awadh. To provide protection to Awadh, the army of the Company was posted in the capital city. The agreement, which was signed in 1765 provided scope for the company to slowly expand the size of the company's army contingent in the province, and force the nawab to keep on reducing the size of his army. This method provided a new revenue model to finance its army. The model was to outsource a part of the army of the company to a provincial ruler. The ruler will finance the maintenance of the force. Therefore, the East India Company could maintain a large army without spending large financial resources. As the size of the army contingent kept on increasing in the province, the local ruler did not have resources to finance it. At that stage, the Resident of the Company would accuse the local ruler of mismanagement of the province. The same strategy was followed by the East India Company in annexing the province of Awadh. In the meantime most of the economy was monopolized by British private traders and their *gomastas* (agents), especially in sugar and cotton grading areas. Awadh was also converted into some kind of colonial relationship, where its important raw material was taken to Calcutta and from here they were exported to Britain. Finally, in 1856, Awadh was annexed by the East India Company by sending its Nawab Wazid Ali Shah (1829–1857) in exile to Calcutta. However, his Begum Hazrat Mahal participated in the Sepoy Mutiny or First War of Indian Independence in 1857 (Robinson, 1912, 70; Sinha (ed.), 1968, Vol. III).

Sikhs had enjoyed the status of autonomous kingdom under Maharaja Ranjit Singh. However, his death in 1839 led to dispute of succession between different Sikh warriors that controlled the Sikh state. The rival claimants requested company to support their claim. This led to two Anglo-Sikh wars—between 1845 and 1846, and 1848 and 1849. By the end of the Second Anglo-Sikh War in 1849, the minor Maharaja Dalip Singh had signed the instrument of annexation of Punjab (Mukerjee, 1982). The minor Maharaja was kept in the care of a Christian priest, who converted him to Christianity and took him over to Britain. He lived like a hostage of the British till his end.[36]

The East India Company also evoked the Doctrine of Lapse, which affected imminent annexation of several provinces because their rulers did not have natural heir to succeed them. For instance, Rani Luxmi Bai of Jhansi had adopted a son after the death of her husband. Therefore, Jhansi faced annexation after Rani Luxmi Bai. Similarly, Nana Saheb was adopted son of the Peshwa, therefore, he could not assume the power of Peshwas. Following all the strategies that have been mentioned above, the East India Company had occupied substantial part of the territories of the Indian subcontinent. According to the details given by Fisher regarding the annexation of territories by the East India Company in 1856, it had annexed 62 per cent (98,000 square miles) of the total geographical area of the India subcontinent (157,000 square miles). The remaining 38 per cent of the area was occupied by several small princely states which entirely depended on the goodwill of the East India Company (Fisher, 1993). The organizational transformation of the East India Company into an agency of the British Empire became so paramount for the British Crown that it continued to control territories in India on behalf of the Crown up to 1857. This happened despite the fact that the East India Company ceased to be a trading company in 1833, when the British Parliament stripped the Company of its commercial functions. This suggests that the East India Company performed the *Business of Empire*[37] from 1757 to 1857. During this period, the dictates of the East India Company were enforceable in a vast geographical area. The Company had its own army and administrative set-up, which had developed capability to impact the destiny of millions of people living in the Indian subcontinent and influence its economy.

After annexation of Awadh, the East India Company employed 500 gomastas in Awadh. Under the new circumstances, the private British merchants, who were related to the top officials of the Company, like the Resident of Awadh, were able to gain maximum. One of the British merchants, Job Scott, was able to establish his commercial dominance in trading of cotton piece goods in the *aurang* (cluster of handicrafts manufactures with a market) of Tanda under the patronage of the Resident of Awadh, Nathaniel Middleton. Here he enjoyed near monopoly power which he used to appropriate large part of the output of the weavers of the *aurang*, without experiencing any competition. He continued to get patronage of the new Resident of Awadh, John Hyde (Bhatacharaya, 1982, 288). Similar types of nexus between British free merchants and local important functionaries of the East India Company emerged wherever the Company established its political hegemony. Such nexuses were prevailing rampantly in most of the centres of traditional flexible manufacturing. British private merchants also used the political hegemony of the East India Company to impose several kinds of regulations to reduce the bargaining power of the Company as well as with regard to increasing their dependence on the company agents (gomastas).

The East India Company formulated rules regarding *khatbandi* (indenture) in 1770, which made weavers almost like bonded labourers of the Company. This regulation made craftsmen akin to bonded labour who were bound to sell their output to the gomastas of the Company, and they lost the right to sell their products in the open market. By imposing these restrictions, Company agents had full control over the production of weavers along with power to determine the price of cloth. The company also imposed *motarfa* tax. It was tax on weavers, fixed according to the number of looms a weaver operated in his household workshop (Dodwell, 1922, 2). Looking at the negative consequences of this tax, the Company abolished this tax in the Bengal Presidency in 1793 and in the Bombay Presidency in 1844. However, it continued be in operation in the Madras Presidency. Due to the imposition of motarfa tax, according to the estimates of Dodwell, employment in the manufacturing of textiles declined by almost 50 per cent (Parthasarthi, 2001, 84).

The East India Company also used its political supremacy to force craftsmen to work in the centres of production organized by the Company in different locations. The Company established these cen-tres of production to manufacture different varieties of manufactured goods in each of the important centres of production of manufactured goods. For instance, it set up a factory in the Madras Presidency to meet its requirements of muslin, and to meet its requirement for calicoes, it established factories at Cuddalore, Ingram and adapollam (Hunter, 1888 (1974), Vol. IX, 252–268; Seth, 1987, 25–26; Sinha (ed.), 1968, Vol. I, 360). In these factories, workers were forced to work for longer hours and at low wages. Working conditions in these centres of production organized by the East India Company were much worse than the conditions of work in the Mughal karkhanas, which were established by Mughal emperors, members of the royal families (price and princess) and subedars of different provinces during the Mughal Empire (Bown, 2006).

On the one hand, different practices of the East India Company which marginalized the role of Indian merchants in the traditional flex-ible manufacturing, and on the other hand, the regulations it imposed on the craftsmen resulted in the preconditions which were necessary for the existence and continuance of traditional flexible manufactur-ing. The decline in the patronage of royalty and nobility also caused decline in the traditional flexible manufacturing because they were important consumers of luxury handicraft. Moreover, the increasing power of local rulers, due to decline in the authority of the Mughal rulers, caused large scale migration of Indian merchants to the colo-nial cities such as Bombay, Calcutta and Madras. Bombay became an important attractive destination for Gujaratis, Parsis, Khojas, Kuchi

Bhatias, Ismailis and Bohras. It provided them protection from the Marathas and protected their wealth and property. Similarly, the Marwaris migrated to Calcutta. The East India Company provided the same public good, the protection of their property and rule of law which was provided by the Mughal Empire before the death of Aurangzeb. The process of migration of merchants from port cities such as Surat and Calicut, and the Coromandel Coast to the colonial cities led to decline of trade in the native cities (Travers, 2007, 145). These native port cities experienced isolation and disruption in the sources of supply because of political instability which had weakened the networks of supply chain. The migration of merchants to colonial cities transformed them from being part of the organization of production of manufactured products to traders of commodities. The East India Company needed their services in procuring commodities from villages to bring them up to the colonial port cities for export.

It is important to inform that while the East India Company was occupied in expanding its economic supremacy and political hegemony in the Indian subcontinent, British society, polity and economy were undergoing the process of transformation. The newly transformed circumstances were slowly digging the very roots of the premises on which the existence of companies like the East India Company depended. The existence of companies like the East India Company depended on mercantilist ideology; the new changes were seriously shaking the foundation which had facilitated the birth of the East India Company. After the glorious revolution of 1688, one of the most important pillars on which mercantilism was based, that is, the power of the king, who was the most powerful rent seeker of a country, began to erode. The declining powers of the monarchy were increasing the power of the British Parliament and the rule of law. Therefore, slowly, it was becoming quite difficult by the Crown to provide continuous patronage to companies like the East India Company.

This happened because of shift in the ideological supremacy of the classical political economy in comparison to the mercantilist ideology. The shift in the dominant ideology occurred because for the first time a new class of people had emerged in Britain as a consequence of the Industrial Revolution—the class of manufacturers or industrialists.

This new class had better potential to create wealth and employment for the economy. The interests of this new class were at variance with the interests of merchants. Even landed gentry of Britain became antagonistic to the East India Company. The landed gentry were also losing social and economic space to the wealth of employees of the Company, who were returning to Britain after completing their overseas services with the East India Company. These employees had enough wealth to buy their estates, which were giving less return. These employees were also able to enter the British Parliament. Their entry into the British Parliament had altered the composition of the membership of the British Parliament. Due to these changes in the society, polity and economy of Britain, the attitude of British civil society towards the East India Company was also changing significantly. The changes in the perspective of the civil society towards the East India Company were forcing the policymakers to effectively regulate the activities of the East India Company. In the following section, the response of the civil society of Britain towards the acts of omission and commission of the East India Company has been described. It also narrates the processes which slowly eroded the power of the Company.

TAMING THE EAST INDIA COMPANY

It is important to mention that when the East India Company was emerging as an important institution in the British society, foreign trade was emerging as an important economic activity. Its importance was manifested in its linkages with the economy, polity and society of Britain. It provided necessary financial resources to the Crown, earnings for the economic growth of the economy, jobs for several thousands of British citizens and paid dividend to its stockholders. Therefore, it contributed in the prosperity of the nation on which the basic economic structure of the British economy was build. The East India Company enriched the Crown, and the Crown, as a return gift, provided to the Company patronage as well as protection through its military strength. Hence, the interests of the East India Company and the dominant groups of the British society were coterminous. The nexus between the Crown, the Company and the dominant groups of the British society gave rise to mercantilist ideology. This ideology served the interest of not only merchants and other stakeholders but also established the social relevance of the East India Company. However, after the Industrial Revolution which gave birth to modern manufacturing, the importance of a new group of people was established, whose interests were at variance with the stakeholders who depended on the East India Company. This new group of people was manufacturers, who were also creating wealth and jobs for British citizens. The emergence of these new wealth creators gave birth to a new ideology and a new thinking, which was articulated by Adam Smith.

Under the influence of the enlightened political economy, when ideas of free trade, freedom to enterprise and free markets were replacing the mercantilist ideology in Britain, the attitude of the British civil society about the most important manifestation of the mercantilist ideas, namely the East India Company, was also changing. This happened because during this time, the East India Company was not only engaged in trade but also got involved in the business of empire.[38] The civil society was debating how a company whose stocks were being traded in the London stock market could establish an empire. The attitude of the civil society was also affected by the acts of omission and commission of Robert Clive and Warren Hastings, which were known in the public domain. The news about the famine in Bengal in 1770, which found its echo in Adam Smith's *Wealth of Nations*, also impacted the understanding of the British civil society about the East India Company. These events led to debate amongst British citizens, intellectuals, policymakers and parliamentarians on some basic issues pertaining to the East India Company. These issues were how come a commercial enterprise can wage wars, enter into treaties and follow a foreign policy, independent of the Parliament and the Crown, with other sovereign powers. It was generally accepted by the civil society that the Company cannot be given complete freedom to formulate its own foreign policy, which enjoyed autonomy from the British Crown and the Parliament.

Another issue which was drawing the attention of British policymakers and intellectuals was regarding how to control the opportunistic behaviour of the employees and officials of the East India Company, which has also been discussed in detail earlier in the chapter. The

British civil society wanted that regulations should be imposed on the East India Company which could minimize the chances of the opportunistic behaviour of the company executives. However, some members of the civil society of Britain were against regulating the working of the East India Company because they believed that the status of a chartered company given by the British Crown empowered the Company against any parliamentary intervention. They also argued that giving powers to the British Parliament to interfere in the working of the East India Company amounts to undermining the private property rights of the Company. These ideas were not held by a large number of people. The weakening of the mercantilist ideas had affected the opinion of large numbers of British civil society members against monopolies created by the Crown.

Under the influence of the public opinion prevailing at that time, initially the Parliament initiated reforms regarding the mode of election to the positions in the Board of Directors of the Company. Two Acts were passed by the Parliament in quick succession in 1765 and 1767. In the Act passed in 1765 (7 Geo IIIc48), the Parliament changed the composition of the Electoral College which participated in the election of members of the Board of Directors. This Act gave voting right and the right to participate in the election to elect the members of the Board of Directors to only those stockholders who owned company stocks of worth £500 for a period of at least six months. In 1767 Act, a complementary regulation was passed (7 Geo IIIc49) which prohibited the owners of stocks from stock splitting. These regulations proved to be ineffective to impact the election process because cartels of stockholders were able to practise splitting of stocks six months prior to the annual elections. These cartels could do so by changing the ownership of stocks during the months of September and October because annual elections of the Board members were held in April.

Following the Bengal famine of 1770, there was a sharp fall in the stocks prices of the East India Company, which has been described as the *Bengal Bubble*. This fall in the prices of the Company stocks caused significant financial losses to a large number of people of Britain, who had invested their savings in the company stock. Amongst the individuals who lost their savings in the Company stocks were Edmund and William Burke, who were important antagonists of the East India Company. Under the pressure of public opinion, British government passed the Regulation Act of 1773, which was introduced in the Parliament by Lord North. The Regulation Act altered the voting qualifications and extended the term of the Board of Directors. According to the conditions mentioned in the Act, only those stockholders were considered eligible to participate in the election for electing the Board members who owned stocks worth £1,000 and kept them for a period of at least 12 months. The Act also introduced for the first time the method of proportionate voting, that is, voting in proportion to the value of the stocks. The stockholders who were in the possession of stocks exactly worth £1,000 were given right to cast only one vote (minimum vote), and those who owned shares worth equal to or more than £10,000 were given right to cast four votes (maximum). It also fixed the term of elected directors to four years, with a condition that every year only quarter of the directors will retire. This Act marginalized the role of small stockholders in the process of election of the Board members. The small stockholders were 55.4 per cent of total stockholders of the Company in 1773. Through these reforms, the Regulation Act provided stability to the Board of Directors. It also increased the role of big stockholders in influencing the decision made by the Company. Here the intention was to provide bigger role to persons with larger stakes in the Company. This Act also put a ceiling on the dividend which can be paid by any joint-stock company at 10 per cent.

The Regulation Act also introduced changes in the structure of governance of the East India Company in the Indian subcontinent. The Act introduced the position of Governor-General of India. The office of Governor-General was senior to the existing governors of the Calcutta, Bombay and Madras Presidencies. The office of Governor-General would be based in Calcutta. Moreover, to make the governance structure more effective, a Supreme Council was constituted consisting of five members. It was included in the Act that out of these five members, two members will be nominated by the Company and three members will be appointed by the British Parliament. Moreover, to reduce the chances of opportunistic behaviour of the Company officials, it provided monopoly in trading salt and opium to the East India Company. This was introduced to minimize the chances of private trade in these commodities by the officials of the Company. The main objective of the Regulation Act was to control the opportunistic behaviour of the officials of the Company. This was quite obvious from the selection of the members of Supreme Council. The governor of the Company Warren Hastings was elevated to the position of Governor-General and another person who was associated with the Company, namely Richard Borwell, was appointed as a member of the Supreme Council. The government of Britain appointed General John Clavering, Colonel George Monson and Philip Francis as three other members of the Council. Since in the committee, representative appointed by the government enjoyed majority, it led to hostility between them and the Company-appointed members. This happened because Warren Hastings systematically undermined the three members appointed by the government in the Supreme Council. However, out of these three members, Philip Francis, emerged as an important critic of the affairs of the Company in general and of Warren Hastings in particular.

Through their actions the officials of the Company were making several members of the civil society as their enemies. William Bolt wrote a book entitled *Consideration on India Affairs*, which he published in 1772, to highlight the conduct of Harry Verelst, who was Governor of Bengal after Robert Clive. Through this book Bolt drew the attention of British civil society towards the malpractices of the officials of the Company. Following the publication of this book, the Governor of Bengal made it difficult for Bolt to live in India and he was deported to London. He pursued a legal case against Harry Verelst in the British courts. The British courts finally provided judgement on this case in 1774, in which Verelst was found guilty.

Similarly, Edmund Burke and William Burke, who lost substantial amount of their financial resources in the Bengal Bubble, informed Philip Francis about several malpractices committed by the officials of the East India Company. Philips Francis, who was a member of the Supreme Council and undermined by Warren Hastings, was emerging as an important critic of the East India Company. William Burke was working with the Rajah of Tanjore, who had provided information about the scandal in which several officials of the East India Company were involved in providing personal loans to Nawab of Arcot and Rajah of Tanjore. The financial consideration in this scandal amounted to £3 million in 1779. Edmund Burke also received information regarding activities of the officials of the Company from Philip Francis, who published the 8th Report of the Select Committee in 1783. He mentioned in the report that since the territorial occupation of India by the East India Company 'trade ceased to be exchange, and has been transformed into plunder'. He further added that 'company factors have turned in one stroke, the whole trade of the company in their own hands, on their own capital, at their own risque (risk) and the company has become factor for them' (Marx, 1881).

The information available from different sources forced Edmund Burke to rethink about his basic understanding about the Company. He was personally against the idea of government intervention in the internal affairs of the Company, so long the Company did not violate the provisions and mandate contained in the royal charter. Therefore, he was against the formulation of the Regulation Act of 1773 by Prime Minister Lord North. However, after receiving information on malpractices by the officials of the East India Company from William Bolt and Philip Francis, his idea about the Company significantly changed and he became an important member of the civil society, who wanted to regulate the conduct of the East India Company. At this point in time, the coalition government of Lord North and Charles James Fox was occupying the position of power in the British Parliament. Edmund Burke actively participated and lobbied for the formulation of East India Bill, which became popular as Fox India Bill. This Bill was placed in the British Parliament in 1783 in the House of Commons. It was approved by the House with a very large number of members of the Parliament supporting it. The Bill wanted to replace the Board of Directors of the Company by seven commissioners, who will be appointed by the British Parliament. Once it was approved in the House of Commons, the directors of the Company feared that Fox India Act may also get approval from the House of Lords.

In these circumstances, the East India Company used the existing ambiguity between the powers of the Crown and powers of the

Parliament to maintain status quo. They did so by provoking the British Crown that the Fox India Bill will provide more powers to the prime minister and the Parliament on the affairs of the East India Company in comparison to the powers of the Crown. This explanation appealed to the vested interest of the British king, George III. He issued a kind of whip to the members of the House of Lords by arguing that any member of the House who supports the Fox India Bill will be considered as a person against the British Crown. The consequences of this whip were quite obvious. The Bill did not get approved from the House of Lords. The defeat of this Bill in the House of Lords led to the fall of the coalition government led by North and Fox in 1783. In 1784, when elections were held for the British Parliament, the East India Company supported and financed the opposition party in the elections. As a consequence, William Pitt the Younger formed the new government.

The East India Company supported the government formed by William Pitt to protect its interest. However, even the new government could not protect the interest of the Company against mounting pressure created by the British civil society. The government headed by William Pitt was compelled to introduce Government of India Act in July 1784, drafted by Henry Dundas, in the Parliament. The Bill did not challenge the status of chartered company given to the East India Company by the British Crown. Instead supporting the appointment of seven commissioners by the Parliament to replace the Board of Directors of the Company, the new Bill incorporated the provision of a five-member board of control appointed by the king. In the new Act, the king was also given right to recall any company executive. Through this new Act the government of William Pitt on the one hand pacified the civil society by showing that it intends to regulate the Company. However, at the same time, through another hand it provided powers to the king in the appointment of five members of the Board of Control instead of the Parliament. This way the East India Company used the fluidity of the situation where powers of the king and the Parliament were undefined (Bowen, 2006, 161). These tricks used by the East India Company to safeguard its interest left Burke a dejected and depressed person. After these incidences, he stated that 'all the tyranny, robbery, destruction of mankind practiced by the company in the East are popularized and pleasing to the country' (Desai, 2009, 48).

Burke did not give up his fight against the East India Company. He waited for the right moment to strike back. The moment came in 1788, four years after the East India Act was passed in the Parliament, when Hastings arrived in Britain after completing his term as the Governor General of Bengal. On his arrival, Burke initiated impeachment trial against Warren Hastings because at that time, the British judicial system did not have legal provisions to try the acts of omission and commission of a company executive. Therefore, he appealed to the British Parliament for impeachment of Hastings. As an intelligent person, he knew from the very beginning of the trial that he was going to lose the case. Despite this knowledge, he asked for the impeachment because the hearings of the proceeding in the Parliament may force the average citizen of the country to debate about the verdict. The impeachment trial continued for seven years, and as it was expected, Warren Hastings was acquitted after trial in 1795 by the British Parliament.

The outcome of the impeachment trial and the debates that it generated inside and outside the Parliament by the members of civil society and parliamentarians established in the minds of the British citizens that the East India Company enjoyed impunity from all its misdeeds, unethical behaviour and inhuman practices, because at that point in time, the necessary legal framework did not exist in Britain to regulate activities of corporations and its executives. In the absence of a regulatory framework, courts were not competent enough to punish them and to bring their deeds on books. A similar weakness still exists amongst legal systems of different countries to try the practices of multinational companies which are inhuman, unethical and criminal in nature. This has happened despite the fact that the businesses are becoming globalized, but the globalization of businesses has not been accompanied by commensurate efforts to globalize institutions of corporate governance. However, in the case of the East India Company, what a toothless legal system could not achieve, even the Parliament could not achieve, was achieved by the rise of classical political economy and fall of mercantilism. The shift in the ideology resulted in the birth of a new socio-economic and political transformation in Britain, which removed all the rent-seeking institutions including the East India Company. The British Parliament also made several attempts to regulate the behaviour of the executives of the Company and to improve the quality of governance of the Company by passing several legislations such as the Regulation Act, Fox India Act and Pitt's India Act. These attempts were not effective due to the continuing struggle between the British Crown and the Parliament to arrive at a stable division of power amongst them. The tussle between the Crown and the Parliament also revealed the level of penetration of the institutions of democracy in the British society. This was the period when British democracy was at a crossroads, when 'the electorate was narrow and consisted of scores of rotten borough' (Desai, 2009, 48). In the chapter that follows, we have presented the consequences of the rule of the East India Company on the economies of the four cities that we have identified for the purposes of our study.

NOTES

1. For details regarding Silk Road, see Hopkirk (1980), Frank (1990), Folz (1999) and Bauman (2000).
2. For the facts regarding Silk Road, see Frank and Bowstone (1986), and Frank (1990).
3. To know about the historical importance of different spices, see Hobhouse (1999).
4. To know how prosperity shifted from Asia to Europe, see Frank (1998) and Maddison (2003).
5. To know more about mercantilism, see Hecksher (1931), Ekelund and Tollison (1981) and Ekelund and Roberts (1997).
6. For the historical importance of gold, see Bernstein (2012).
7. This is available in Wright (2000, 81).
8. For details regarding quasi-sovereign rights of the Chartered companies, see Robins (2006, 25).
9. For the views regarding the scholars who opposed the granting of chartered status to the company, see Jones and Ville (1996).
10. For explanations regarding this idea, see Jones and Ville (1996).
11. The scholars who believed that granting of Royal charter was amounting to granting of intellectual property right, see Scott (1912), and Carlos and Nicholas (1993).
12. For the fact, see Adam Smith (1776 [2003]), Book IV chapter I, 957.
13. For these facts, see Mukerjee (1974, 393) and Keay (1993).
14. To know about the pattern of stock holding of the East India company, see Bowen (1987, 1989).
15. These facts are given in Robins (2006, 11).

16. To know about the administrative structure of the East India company, see Bowen (2006), Chapter VII, 185–186.
17. These details are given in Bowen (2006).
18. To understand the difference between managerially coordinated transactions and market coordinated transactions, see Chander (1977).
19. For these ideas, see Alchian and Damsetz (1972), Grief (1993) and Hajeebu (2008).
20. To know about the opportunistic behaviour of the managers, see Alchien and Demsetz (1972), Fama (1980) and Arrow (1985).
21. This quotation has been taken from Smith (1776 [2003], 937).
22. For the understanding of economic role of incentives in influencing the behaviour of economic agents in greater details, see Shavell (1979), Holmstorm (1979, 1982) and Grassmann and Hart (1983).
23. Information asymmetry that existed between employees of the East India Company working in the Indian subcontinent and London office, see Anderson (1983), Carlos and Nicholas (1990), and Carlo (1991, 1992).
24. For the process of sending remittance of earnings of overseas employees of the East India company to their relatives in Britain, see Hajeebu (2005).
25. To know how employees of the company working in India became wealthy after completing their services in India, see Holzman (1926) and Marshall 1970, 229).
26. To know what were the consequences of the use of *Dastak* by the East India company on the relationship between *nawab* of Bengal and the company, see Robins (2006).
27. For installing the Prince Mohammad Ali Wallajah at Arcot by the East India Company, see Bayly (1958).
28. For inside trading in the stocks of the company by Robert Clive, see Robins (2006, 85–86).
29. For understanding about the process of globalization and conflict amongst differences in European countries, see Travers (2007).
30. For knowledge regarding the transformation of the World order towards imperialism, see Bayly (1989).
31. For knowing details about the wars of successions, see Bayly (1988b).
32. The reason which led to participation of European trading companies in the local conflicts between native rulers, see Stein (1998).
33. To know about the Marathas and their impact on the India polity during the period of the East India company, see Chandra (1973) and Gordon (1973, 1977).
34. For details, see Chandra (1973) and Gordon (1977).
35. For details regarding Anglo-Maratha wars, see Cooper (2003) and Gordon (1993).
36. For the history of Sikhs, see Grewal (1990) and Singh (1956).
37. For this term, see Robinson (2006, 76).
38. The quotation has been taken from Robins (2006, 120).

Tale of Four Cities and the East India Company

The political supremacy of the East India Company in the four cities which are the subject of the present narrative emerged much earlier than the rest of the Indian subcontinent. Bombay and Calcutta were always under the control of the Company, because these cities were respectively the headquarters of its business operations in the Western and Eastern coasts and were governed by the East India Company. The city of Surat came under the direct control of the East India Company after the Castle Revolution of 1759, in which the merchants of Surat facilitated the transfer of the office of Qiladar of Surat to the East India Company. This episode has already been described in detail in the earlier chapter. Similarly, the whole of Bengal, including the city of Dacca, also came under the dominance of the East India Company, after the famous business deal of the Company, which is erroneously described as the Battle of Plassey (1757). However, there was marked difference between the political dominance of Dacca and Surat.

The East India Company received right only to administer the city of Surat. This shift solved the micro-level problem of the city, that is, it saved the merchants of the city from predatory and despotic local nawabs. However, the macro-level political reality that emerged after the decline of the Mughal Empire was beyond the control of merchants of Bombay and Surat, and was also beyond the control of the East India Company. This happened because both the cities were surrounded by Maratha territories, especially most of the peripheral areas of the cities were under Maratha occupation. The existence of hinterland is an essential precondition for the growth and prosperity of the cities. In the case of Dacca and Calcutta, not only both the cities were under political dominance of the East India Company, but also the entire Bengal Subah was under political hegemony of the East India Company. This provided substantial hinterland to the Company to tax, appropriate agricultural surplus for the growth of the city of Calcutta and finance wars in which the East India Company participated. Bengal was the richest province of the Mughal Empire. The access to this financial muscle provided strength to the East India Company. While at the same time, it made the Mughal Empire poorer by the equal extent. This was the most important difference between the occupation of Surat and occupation of Dacca by the East India Company.

To achieve complete control over the cities of Bombay and Surat and their respective hinterlands, the East India Company had to wage three successive Anglo-Maratha wars, during 1775–1802 (First Anglo-Maratha War), 1803–1805 (Second Anglo-Maratha War) and 1817–1818 (Third Anglo-Maratha War). These wars established political hegemony of the East India Company on the Western coast. The East India Company kept on annexing several important regions of the Indian subcontinent. Its political ascendency was established over the Carnatic (1765), Northern Sarkars (1766), Banaras (1775), Malabar and Canara (1792–1799), Northeastern region and Burma (1825–1826), Sind (1843), Satara (1848), Punjab (1849), and Jhansi, Nagpur and Berar (1856). The last territory which the East India Company annexed was Awadh (1856).[1]

These annexations of territories by the East India Company transformed it into an agency of the British Empire. This transformation of the East India Company has been variously conceptualized by scholars. Some described it as *imperium in imperio*,[2] while some as *the East India Company state*.[3] Some other scholars conceptualized it as *sovereign merchant*[4] or *corporate state*.[5] The government of the Company was powerful in Asia, as it was a government whose revenues were larger than the government that had given it charter status. This was a peculiar kind of government, which was owned by a trading company, whose shares were traded daily in the London Stock Exchange. Despite its territorial occupations, political control of the East India Company was not complete in the territories located near Surat and Bombay.

There were several territories which were still ruled by local princes such as the Maharaja of Baroda, the Nizam of Hyderabad, the Maharaja of Mysore and the Portuguese territories of Goa and Diu. It is due to these obvious differences in the circumstances in which the cities of Eastern and Western coasts were placed that they experienced different consequences of the rule of the Company. As it has been described in the earlier chapter, both the native cities (Dacca and Surat) were centres of traditional flexible manufacturing during the Mughal Empire. It was the strength of their traditional flexible manufacturing which determined their prosperity. Therefore, in the rest of the chapter, we have analysed how the rule of the East India Company impacted their traditional flexible manufacturing.

The chapter has been organized into three sections, where each section is dedicated to narrating the experience of these cities. In the first section, the consequences of the rule of the East India Company on the cities of Surat and Bombay have been analysed. The second section, the impact of the rule of the East India Company on Dacca and Calcutta has been described. In the third section, debate on de-industrialization (decline of traditional flexible manufacturing) has been narrated. This debate has occupied an important place in the writings of historians.

SURAT, BOMBAY AND THE RULE OF THE EAST INDIA COMPANY

The Castle Revolution enlarged the role of the East India Company in the administration of the city of Surat. Bombay was already governed by the East India Company. However, both the cities were surrounded by Maratha territories. In fact, most of the hinterland of Surat, which provided it connectivity with the rest of the economy of the Mughal Empire, was now under Maratha control. Fragmentation of polity in the Indian subcontinent disrupted the free flow of merchandize and finances to Surat, which had helped in increasing its prosperity during the Mughal Empire. Disconnect between Surat and the rest of the economy affected economic linkages that the city had established with other parts of the economy of the Mughal Empire. Trade routes passed through several political units, which increased the insecurity in the transportation of merchandize and transfer of finances. It, at the same time, increased the transaction costs of conducting business, because taxes had to be paid at several locations. This had emerged as a consequence of creating entry barriers by each political dispensation. These entry barriers affected inter-regional trade. The most important adverse impact on the economy of Surat was caused by the disruption of caravan trade between Surat and Bengal, because Bengal depended on the cotton from Surat and Surat received raw silk from Bengal. This problem was partly solved by the fact that during this time both Bengal and Surat were under the control of the East India Company. Therefore, to overcome the risk and insecurity of caravan trade, the East India Company introduced littoral trade between Surat and Bengal.[6]

Around the same time, two intertwined events occurred in the global economy, which altered the course of economic prosperity of Surat and Bombay. Repeated crop failure of cotton in China in the 1770s and near-famine conditions in the cotton-growing southern provinces of China forced Chinese farmers to cultivate grains in place of cotton. These conditions increased the dependence of Chinese cotton textile industry on Indian cotton. From 1774 onwards, exports of cotton to China increased substantially.[7] The second event was that in the 1780s, with the promulgation of the Commutation Act of Pitt, the import duties on Chinese tea in Britain were drastically reduced. As price of the tea declined in Britain, British citizens became more addicted to Chinese tea. During the same period, large numbers of Chinese became slaves of Indian opium.

This new development gave birth to a tripartite trade relationship between Britain, China and India, in which commodities produced in the Indian subcontinent were used to finance the consumption of tea by the British. In this trade relationship, the Indian subcontinent occupied central stage. In the new circumstances, Indian cotton and opium were exported to China in exchange of imports of Chinese tea by Britain. This trading pattern assumed greater importance over time. In the new trading triangle, Bombay emerged as a nodal centre. This shift in the directions of trade and commodity composition affected the significance of trade between Surat, the Persian Gulf and the Red Sea. This trade was already showing decline because of decline of the Safavid dynasty of Persia and the Ottoman Empire. This structural change in the direction of trade reduced the importance of Surat and replaced it with the increasing importance of Bombay on the Western coast.

After the 1730s, a very large part of the shipbuilding industry of Surat had shifted its base to Bombay, when the East India Company invited master shipbuilder Lowji Nessarwanji Wadia to establish Bombay Dockyard. His family kept occupying the position of master shipbuilder of the Bombay Dockyard for more than three generations.[8] The shifting of the shipbuilding industry also attracted other ship-builders of Surat to migrate to Bombay, such as Nouroji Jamsetji, Jahangir Naaroji, Rustomji Ardeshir and Hirji Bhai Merwani.[9] This happened because Bombay was more suitable for shipbuilding, as it had access to better quality timber from the Malabar Coast.

As it has been described in the earlier chapter, the imports of Indian textiles were providing learning experience to British manufacturers to develop import substitutes for Indian textiles. The process of import substitution began with the invention of *flying shuttle* by John Kay in 1733, which revolutionized the weaving of cloth. The mismatch that had emerged between the speed of weaving and speed of spinning was bridged by the invention of *spinning frame* by Richard Arkwright in 1764. However, after the invention of *spinning jenny* by Hargreaves in 1769, cotton textile manufacturing of Britain became more competitive than traditional flexible manufacturing of cotton textile of Surat, and also than those centres located in different parts of the Indian subcontinent. These technological changes that occurred in the manufacturing of textiles in Britain were collectively described as the Industrial Revolution. This revolution shifted the location of cotton textile manufacturing from Surat and other parts of the Indian subcontinent to Britain. The process of relocation of textile manufacturing also created conditions for relocation of prosperity from Surat to other parts of the country.[10] The process of import substitution of cotton textile manufacturing was further facilitated by the availability of raw cotton from cotton plantations, which were established by British expatriate planters in the Caribbean, Virginia, Georgia and the Carolinas. These plantations used slave labour, which produced cotton quite cheaper than the cotton cultivated by Indian farmers using family labour on small holdings.[11]

These developments give impressions that the economy of Surat was adversely affected. However, due to the existence of demand of cotton in China and its manufactured products in the Persian Gulf, the Red Sea, Southeast Asia and Africa, its immediate decline was arrested. Since 1757, the East India Company had acquired monopoly of trade as well as political power in Bengal. As a consequence, it also had monopoly on export of cotton produced in Bengal and opium produced in Bihar to China. However, cotton-growing areas of Gujarat were under the occupation of the Gaekwads of Gujarat, and opium produced in Malwa, particularly in the districts of Mandsaur, Ujjain and Ratlam, was under the control of the Holkars. For a considerable period, Indian merchants of Surat and other areas of Gujarat remained involved in the trading of Malwa opium, which provided very high return. Traders such as Motichand, Amichand, Hatheesing, Kesareesing and Karmchand Premchand were quite important in the trading of Malwa opium. This was possible because the East India Company could not monopolize the trade in opium in the Western region owing to the fact that it did not enjoy political control over the region. As a consequence of the prevailing position of the East India Company, Jardine Matheson & Co. had to depend on several Parsi merchants such as Jamsetjee Jeejeebhoy, the Banajee families and Harmusjee Wadia to procure Malwa opium. These merchants played a significant role in the opium trade of Malwa. In Malwa opium trade, the Baghdadi Jews also participated, who owned China Merchants' Steam Navigation Company.[12] The lack of control over Malwa opium motivated the East India Company to wage wars with the Marathas. The incidence of the three successive Anglo-Maratha wars has been already described.[13]

The facts given above give an impression that these developments adversely affected the economy of Surat and that like the economy of Bengal, Surat also experienced de-industrialization during the rule of the East India Company. De-industrialization is understood as a process of decline of traditional flexible manufacturing of the Indian subcontinent as a consequence of the Industrial Revolution, which provided capability to British manufacturing to produce better substitutes. This phenomenon has been discussed in greater detail in the last section of this chapter. However, it should be noted that despite the fact that the East India Company had achieved control over the administration of Surat, its economy did not become subservient to the needs of the East India Company. This happened because the East India Company was not able to manipulate the economy of Surat in the same way as it did in the case of Bengal's economy. Bengal experienced de-industrialization because the East India Company was able to break the nexus between craftsmen and merchants, which was the basis of the organization of production of traditional flexible manufacturing (Seth, 2014, 2015). Surat began to export cotton to China to fulfil the needs of the East India Company to buy Chinese tea, but did not completely depend on the exports of raw cotton. The value of textile exports from Surat far exceeded the value of export of cotton (Janaki, 1974). Surat kept exporting cotton and silk textiles to Arabia, Persia, Burma, Southeast Asia and Africa. The possibilities to export manufactured goods continued to exist despite large-scale migration of merchants from Surat to Bombay. The migration of merchants of Surat happened because they wanted to take the advantage of emerging business opportunities and the existence of better governance in Bombay. However, large-scale migration of merchants from Surat was more than compensated by the immigration of craftsmen to Surat from other centres of traditional flexible manufacturing of Gujarat. The craftsmen were pushed from other centres of manufacturing of Gujarat as a consequence of disruption of inland routes (Heynes and Roy, 1999). These intertwined processes transformed Surat from being a city only of trade and commerce into a centre of manufacturing as well.[14]

In the new circumstances, traditional flexible manufacturing of Surat focused on the production of certain specialized varieties of textiles for which the British mills had not developed any substitute. Moreover, these products were customized to serve *niche* markets of Zanzibar, Arab and Persia, Burma and Mauritius. The traditional flexible manufacturing of Surat was engaged in the production *jari* thread (gold thread, wire and tinsel) and cloths which were embroidered with jari thread and pearls (See Heynes, 2012). The exclusive textiles which were exported from Surat were *gazi* (silk and silk satin cloth), *himro* and *mashroo* (mixed cotton and silk cloth), *lungis* (especially for Burma), *kinkhab* (rich with jari) and cloth which was embroidered with jari thread and pearls.[15] By manufacturing these exclusive textiles, by transforming its manufacturing to produce these specialized products for niche markets, Surat was able to arrest the process of de-industrialization (Heynes, 2015, 35–37). This suggests that despite the birth of modern textile manufacturing in Britain, the traditional flexible manufacturing of Surat, although weakened, did not decline (Heynes, 2015, 40). It is also important to mention here that whatever losses the merchants of Surat incurred due to decline in the export of textiles, they compensated it by shifting their capital to finance ivory trade of Zanzibar. They stayed during winter at Zanzibar to sell the goods they shipped from Surat, such as textiles, sugar, iron bars and rice, and while coming back they purchased ivory from Zanzibar.[16] While Surat was struggling to maintain its economy, Bombay was slowly emerging as an important centre of commerce and trade. Bombay had developed significant advantages in terms of shipping and shipbuilding capacity. It had become a Presidency town, which had developed administrative infrastructure to maintain law and order and court of mayor. This court helped in the enforcement of contracts amongst merchants across communities. Establishment of the court created conditions where merchants belonging to different communities could enter into business relationships. In the absence of such a court, during the Mughal Empire, merchants in Surat usually established business relationship with the merchants belonging to the same community to minimize risk. This is because in the absence of modern legal institutions, the community's code of conduct and community-based panchayats helped in the enforcement of contracts. The establishment of modern legal institutions provided opportunities to the merchants for pooling financial resources across different communities. The Bombay Presidency had also developed a marine force called Bombay Marine, which had capability to protect the port city from aggression and ships from pirates. Moreover, after the opening of trade with China for commodities such as cotton and opium, Bombay was emerging as a prosperous city and land of opportunities. These advantages of the city attracted merchants of several communities of Gujarat in general and from Surat in particular. These merchants were the Parsis, the Jains, the Marwaris, the Kuchi Bhatias, the Khojas, the Memons and the Bohras.

As it has been described above that until the end of the Third Anglo-Maratha War (1818), the East India Company could not establish its complete control over the cotton-producing areas of Gujarat and the opium-producing areas of Malwa and Central India. Due to this reason, the East India Company's profits from cotton and opium depended on the cooperation between local merchants, bankers and brokers. These native merchants procured cotton and opium for the Company. Moreover, native merchants also had opportunity to redirect these commodities for exports through ports under the occupation of the Portuguese. The dependence of the East Indian Company on native merchants gave them scope to have share from the profits of China trade. Several native merchants made substantial amount of financial gains from being part of the supply chain of opium and cotton. Some of the merchants who made large sums of financial gains from opium trade were Lakshmichand Panray, Bhaidas Gopaldas and Jadonjee Chabeelchand. In this trade was also involved persons such as Tatya Jog Kibe, who was a minister at the court of the Holkars.[17] He was operating in the business through a partnership with Bahadur Mal Seth, who has been described by historians as the Rothschild of Malwa. Hirji Jivanji and his brother Maneckji Jivanji were the first Parsi merchants who were able to develop direct business contact with China. Their operations in China had made them so rich that they always had ready money to provide financial help to different merchants. Because of the possession of large amounts of ready money, this family adopted the surname of Readymoney.[18]

The economy of Bombay in particular and economy of the Indian subcontinent in general experienced an important structural break from the past as a consequence of the Industrial Revolution that occurred in Britain. This happened because the polity, society and economy of Britain underwent a transformation after the Revolution.

The transformation occurred because of the emerging importance of manufacturers in the British society, polity and economy as creators of wealth and opportunities of employment for masses. The Industrial Revolution created this new class whose interests were at variance with the interests of landed classes and merchants. This new class of manufacturers recognized that the privilege of monopoly of trade given to the East India Company was arresting the expansion of manufacturing and gains from trade. They began to propagate the idea that the British economy will immensely benefit if British manufacturers are given open access to the large Indian market for selling their products and for buying important raw materials at cheaper prices. The new power elite was demanding the removal of the monopoly of trade given to the East India Company by the royal charter.

The ideological premises of a new social order were articulated by Adam Smith in his famous book *The Wealth of Nations*, which appeared in 1776. The most fundamental criticism of the East India Company is given in this book.[19] This book paved the way for an ideological shift in policymaking from mercantilist ideas to classical political economy. The new ideology epitomized the virtues of free trade, freedom to enterprise and free market. In the new circumstances, the list of antagonists of the East India Company also included the landed gentry of Britain, who were slowly losing economic and social space to the wealthy ex-employees of the East India Company. These employees who had made substantial wealth in India were buying their estates on returning and were also competing for the women belonging to same strata of the society for marriage. These ex-employees were also entering the British Parliament, which had altered the social and economic composition of members of the Parliament. This in turn was altering the nature of debates and issues which were being debated in the Parliament. As a consequence of the new ideology articulated by classical political economy and pressure of several strata of the British society, which were antagonist to the East India Company, the British Parliament passed the Pitt's Act of 1784, which increased parliamentary control over the East India Company. Subsequently, the Charter Act of 1813 ended the trading monopoly of the East India Company. Finally, in 1833, the East India Company was stripped of its commercial function, but was allowed to remain as the agency of the British Empire in India until 1857.[20] This suggests that by the time the East India Company had established its political hegemony in the Western regions, in 1818 after the Third Anglo-Maratha War, its monopoly of trade was lost.

The elimination of trading monopoly of the East India Company by the British Parliament gave access to cheap machine-made goods produced by the British modern manufacturing. These products were slowly replacing the products produced by the traditional flexible manufacturing of the Indian subcontinent. As a consequence, Indian merchants from whom British merchants were procuring the products of traditional flexible manufacturing of the Indian subcontinent for exports now became importers and distributors of British manufactured products. In the changed circumstances, several officials of the East India Company became free merchants by giving up their employment of the company. These free merchants pooled their resources and formed *agency houses*. Some of the agency houses were also formed by pooling the resources of native as well as British merchants. These agency houses worked not only as exporters and importers of products, they also acted as bankers who accepted deposits from British officials of the East India Company and helped in transfer of remittance of the employees of the East Indian Company to Britain. The first agency house was formed in 1767 by John Forbes in Bombay, called Forbes & Company. The second agency house which was established in 1790 at Bombay was Bruce Fawcett & Company.

James Matheson of Calcutta and William Jardine of Bombay formed Jardine Matheson & Co. This company achieved near-monopoly status in the export of opium to China. Famous Indian merchant Jamsetjee Jeejeebhoy, associated with this agency house, accumulated immense wealth. He also spent a very large proportion of his wealth on charities. He founded JJ Hospital and JJ School of Arts Bombay.[21] In order to protect British interest in opium trade with China, the British administration waged war with China which is popularly described by historians as the Opium War (1839–1842).[22] The other agency houses which were active in Bombay during this period were Blay Mackintosh & Company founded in 1805, Ritchie Stewart & Company (1816) and Lecki & Company (1818). It is being described that around this time there existed, apart from these agency houses, 18 agency houses formed by Parsi merchants, 15 by Hindu and 4 by Bohra Muslim merchants (Tripathi, 2004).

From the above description, it is quite evident that the prosperity of the Bombay city largely depended on the exports of cotton and opium to China. Bombay emerged as a typical colonial port city. It specialized in the export of primary goods. This also indicates that during the rule of the East India Company, slowly the Indian subcontinent was being transformed into a supplier of raw materials and importer of manufactured goods. Despite being a typical colonial city, Bombay provided scope to native merchants to participate in trade and accumulate financial resources. It was this accumulation of wealth, earned both by Indian and British merchants, which subsequently gave them advantage to invest in modern manufacturing. (This is subject matter of the next chapter.) Unlike Bombay, in Surat, exports of manufactured goods such as cotton and silk had higher percentage in total exports.

RULE OF THE EAST INDIA COMPANY AND ITS CONSEQUENCES ON DACCA AND CALCUTTA

After the Battle of Plassey and the Treaty of Allahabad, the entire province of Bengal came under the control of the East India Company. The capital of Bengal was shifted from Murshidabad to Calcutta. In 1773, Calcutta became the administrative capital of all the territories occupied by the East India Company in the Indian subcontinent. In the early years, the East India Company depended on the administrative structure evolved by the nawabs. When Warren Hastings was appointed as the Governor-General of the Company in 1772, the East India Company appropriated revenue of Bengal as well as its civil administration. As a consequence, *diwani adalats* (district courts) were established in each district headed by district collectors.[23] The metamorphosis of the East India Company into an agency of the British Empire transformed the relationship between the Company and the economy of the Bengal Subah in general and of Dacca in particular. This new relationship changed the economic environment of the region and caused significant impact on the formation of Dacca and Calcutta. Political hegemony of the East India Company resulted in reduction in participation by the trading companies of other European countries in the trade in Dacca as well as in Calcutta. The decline in the participation of other trading companies reduced the level of competition amongst the buyers of the products produced by the traditional flexible manufacturing of Dacca. These manufacturers for the first time experienced the consequences of trading monopoly of the East India Company.

The most important macro-level change was that the East India Company began to use substantial part of the revenue it earned from its diwani right on financing its purchases of Indian merchandize for exports. It began to buy Indian cotton textiles, silk and muslin without making payment in bullion. The new arrangement reversed the historical pattern in which Britain had nothing to offer apart from bullion to buy manufactured items produced in Dacca and other parts of Bengal. In the new circumstances, the directors of the East India Company decided that the revenue earned from land revenue of Bengal will be used to finance the purchases of merchandize in India for exports, and whatever surplus remained would be spent on buying tea at Canton in China. Moreover, revenue from Bengal was also used to finance different wars that the East India Company had to fight with different political dispensations that emerged in the Indian subcontinent after the fragmentation of polity with the decline of authority of the Mughal Empire. These wars have been already described in the earlier chapter.

The arrangement that helped the East India Company to finance its exports through land revenue earned in India without paying bullion or any other product in exchange has been described as *unrequited trade*.[24] The new trading arrangement brought to an end the advantage which the Indian subcontinent had enjoyed since the days of the Roman Empire—to receive bullion in exchange of products. The economic consequences of this arrangement were described by Burke, who was the author of the Ninth Report of Select Committee, which appeared on 25 June 1783. He called the new arrangement as *drain of wealth* from India to Britain.[25] According to Burke, the drain of wealth from India took place under different heads: (a) through the use of land revenue to buy Indian manufactured goods for exports, which was described by the East India Company as *investments* and (b) £400,000 was paid annually to the British Crown, which was described by Burke as *tribute* (Burke, 1783, 1981, Vol. V, 224). While describing the drain of wealth, Burke wrote:

> Numerous fleets of large ships, loaded with most valuable commodities of the east annually arriving in England gave rise to opinion of happy conditions and growing opulence of a country, whose surplus production occupied so vast space in the commercial world. This export, from India, seemed to imply reciprocal supply, by which the trading capital employed in the production was continuously strengthened and enlarged. But a payment of tribute, and not beneficial commerce to that country, wore this spacious and divulsive appearance.

The understanding of Burke regarding the extent of drain of wealth from India were based on calculations made by Philip Francis. Similar opinions were also expressed by William Bolt, Alexander Dow and Harry Verelst.[26] The idea of drain of wealth was also highlighted by Dadabhai Naoroji and nationalist historians like R. C. Dutt, who held the drain of wealth to be a reason for deteriorating state of the Indian economy (Dutt, 1906, 29–31; Naroji, 1901 [1962]). Noted historian Irfan Habib has also calculated the magnitude of drain of wealth from India to Britain. According to his estimates, the amount of drain was 2 million pounds during 1789–1790 and over 4.7 million pounds during 1790–1801. This amount, according to Habib, was 9 per cent of the GNP of India at that time.[27] The Indian economy always suffered from shortages of bullion; it was the bullion earned from trade that performed an important function in the economy of the Indian subcontinent. It provided metal for minting coins, which were necessary for the smooth functioning of the economy. The East India Company created shortages of bullion by taking over the treasury of the Nawab of Bengal and by financing trade from India with the land revenue earned from Bengal. These practices of the East India Company created shortages of currency which caused virtual stagnation of business activities in Bengal. A group of merchants of Calcutta submitted a petition to the Calcutta Council, complaining how the shortages of currency had brought virtually all businesses to halt (Chaudhari, 1971).

In order to increase the supply of silver for coinage, the East India Company imposed Regulation XXXV of 1793 to encourage imports of silver in Bengal. It also introduced *seigniorage* of 2.5 per cent on coinage along with import duties on gold. The duty on imports of gold were introduced irrespective of the purpose of import, for example, for ornaments, for re-export or for coinage. It increased the price of gold and encouraged its holding by public. Government of the Company also earned gold through land revenue. It is calculated that between 1796 and 1803, a substantial part of the land revenue was paid in gold. Despite the shortage of bullion, it was shipped to Britain when markets were depressed. During the period between 1821 and 1832, around 190 million worth of rupees were shipped to Britain (Chaudhri, 1971). The East India Company also extracted gold from local princes as indemnity. Tipu Sultan alone paid 3.3 million gold coins to the East India Company (Siddiqi, 1987).

As exports of textiles declined, it was substituted by the exports of indigo and opium from Bengal. Since Bengal was under political hegemony of the East India Company, its territories were used to force farmers to cultivate new crops. The opium-producing territories of Malwa and Central India were under the occupation of the Marathas, therefore, the East India Company did not have control over those regions. Indigo was emerging as the main dye, which was gaining importance in Britain with the birth of modern textile mills in Lancashire and Manchester. Since Bengal was endowed with all the conditions for the cultivation of indigo, British merchants followed the dadni system which was prevalent during the Mughal Empire as a mode of organization of cultivation of indigo (Roy, 2006, 63). The East India Company also established its monopoly over opium trade. Farmers who cultivated opium had to sell it to the East India Company only.

The twin monopolies enjoyed by the East India Company, namely the monopoly of trade and monopoly of political power, also resulted in several micro-level changes. One of the important micro-level changes was decline in the dependence of the East India Company on native traders. Before the territorial occupation of Bengal, company officials depended on local merchants for purchasing products produced by the traditional flexible manufacturing of Dacca and its periphery. For this purpose, local merchants had organized networks of artisanal household workshops, based on dadni system, to procure products for the East India Company. The trading houses of merchants of Bengal such as the houses of Jagat Seth and Omichund were far bigger in size. Due to this reason, employees of the East India Company who were engaged in private trade were dependent on local merchants for procurement of products and for meeting their credit needs. The phenomenon of interdependence between the local merchants and British merchants has been described as mutual *mercantilism.*[28] The East India Company depended on the cooperation of native merchants, like the famous Bengali merchant Naba Krishna Deb, for their businesses. In 1776, Clive awarded him the title of Maharaja with a salary of ₹2,000 and subsequently Warren Hastings appointed him the *Talukdar* of Sutanuti. Mutual mercantilism prevailed because 'company's rise to prominence came about with the help of collaborations collision, coexistence and symbiosis' with local merchant elites (Robins, 2006, Chapter IV, 60). The East India Company had to share the existing business opportunities in Bengal with several other European companies. Along the river Hugli, north of Calcutta, the first place was Srirampur which was occupied by the Dutch company, Chandannagar was occupied by the French and Chinsura by Dutch company. However, after the elimination of competition with Dutch company, following the Glorious Revolution of 1688, French company remained as the main rival. Through its newly acquired political power, it tried to marginalize the role of local traders by following strategies to develop its own monopoly over production and exports of manufactured goods of Bengal.

To begin with, the East India Company declared its direct monopoly of trade in certain products. In these products, the East India Company became the sole buyer or monopsonist. In 1750, it acquired monopoly of trade of saltpetre from Mir Jafar. Subsequently, it monopolized the trade in salt and opium in 1793. The appropriation of monopoly right to trade in these products eliminated the role of Indian merchants. Once the East India Company gained political power, it imposed duties on inter-regional trade. The East India

Company altered the circumstances of trading in Dacca. Through the newly acquired political power, it began to marginalize the role of Indian merchants, and merchants of other nationalities in market of products which it was buying for exports. This was done to break the nexus that existed between merchants and craftsmen, which was basis of the dadni system. It was the nexus between merchants and craftsmen which had provided competitive advantage to Indian flexible manufacturing to supply crafts-based products in the mass markets. The East India Company used its political power to deliberately create conditions to break this nexus. To break this nexus, the East India Company made policies to isolate native merchants from organizing the production networks.

To isolate the native merchants from traditional flexible manufacturing, the East India Company curtailed the role of Indian merchants in the procurement of products. For this purpose, the Company developed its own independent supply chain for the procurement of products of traditional flexible manufacturing directly from the Indian craftsmen through Company-appointed gomastas (agents). Between 1757 and 1772, the Company servants along with Company-appointed gomastas had completely deterred the Indian merchants to do business in Dacca. To facilitate the process of procurement, the East India Company divided markets of each product into *aurangs* (a place where household workshop of craftsmen exist in clusters), consisting of important centres of production, where the household workshops of craftsmen existed in clusters. Each *aurang* was working under the supervision of a gomasta appointed by the Company. The gomasta then appointed deputy gomasta and *paiker* (the person who gave advances to the craftsmen). Under each gomasta, the Company also appointed *muquim* (supervisor of looms), *muhri* (clerk) and *tagadeer* (village-level officials). The office of gomasta was also assisted by *jassendars* (classifiers of textiles).[29] These functionaries controlled the supply chain of procurement of textiles for the Company and virtually eliminated the role of Indian merchants from traditional flexible manufacturing.

In the administration of collection of textiles, the Company provided excessive powers to the Company gomastas, who had to enforce contract on the craftsmen. These Company agents used these powers to extract rents from the craftsmen in different forms. Their rent-seeking opportunism got manifested in charging *dasturi* (commission), *salami* (tribute) and *kharcha* (expenses).[30] Gomasta also made additional money by false appraisal of the quality of textile that weavers used to bring. They even began to cheat the Company by showing they have paid higher price for better quality cloth but actually paid to the weaver price of inferior-quality cloth. The opportunistic behaviour of gomastas depended on the geographical distribution of villagers as to what distance they were away from the office of the Commercial Resident, who used to supervise the gomastas (Hussain, 1958).

The final action which completely eliminated the role of India merchants in the traditional flexible manufacturing was that the Company banned the dadni system in Bengal in 1770. The association between craftsmen and merchants was the basis of existence of traditional flexible manufacturing, which led to the growth of manufacturing at Dacca. The disassociation between Indian merchants and craftsmen increased the vulnerability of craftsmen and resulted in excessive dependence of craftsmen on the agents of the East India Company. As dependence of household workshops of craftsmen on the agents of the company increased, it gave the agents of the Company power to redesign the contract between the East India Company and craftsmen. Since the East India Company had become the sole buyer of their products, in the new format of contract, the Company took away the power from the craftsmen to break the contract and gave itself the right to cancel the contract. The Company also removed from the contract the obligation of the East India Company to buy the entire volume of output specified in the contract. Apart from these advantages in the new contract, the East India Company also empowered itself by keeping the right to reject cloth which did not meet the quality standards specified in the contract (Sinha (ed.), 1968, Vol. II).

After eliminating the participation of Indian merchants in the traditional flexible manufacturing, the Company also imposed several kinds of regulations on the vulnerable craftsmen. The regulations were introduced to reduce bargaining power of the craftsmen by increasing their dependence on the agents of the East India Company. These regulations gave it monopolistic power to determine the pricing, procurement and availability of largest proportion of total quantity of products produced by the craftsmen. They increased their power by preventing craftsmen to produce products for either other European trading companies or even for Indian merchants. For this purpose, the Company introduced *khatbandi* (indenture) regulations, which remained in operation in Dacca during 1770–1786. The khatbandi regulations converted weavers of Dacca into some kind of bonded labour, as under this regulation craftsmen were bound to work and produce their products exclusively for the agents of the East India Company. The khatbandi regulations denied to the craftsmen the right to produce and sell their products in the open market. This regulation had serious adverse effects on the life of several craftsmen, such as *tantis* (weavers), *mulungis* (salt workers), *nunias* (producers of saltpetre) and *nacauds* (silk reelers) of Dacca.[31]

The East India Company also used its political power to compel craftsmen to work in the production centres organized by the Company in certain important areas. In these centres of production, craftsmen were forced to work under the company-appointed supervisors for much longer hours. In these centres, craftsmen were given lower wages. The conditions of working in these company-managed centres of production were quite inferior to the karkhanas run by Mughal princes and nobles in Dacca.[32] In all other centres of production, where independent craftsmen were running their household workshops, the Company imposed *motarfa* tax on weavers. The motarfa tax was payable by the craftsmen according to the number of looms that were operative in his workshop. This tax seriously affected the cost of producing textiles. In order to reduce the burden of motarfa tax, weavers reduced the number of looms in their workshops. According to Dodwell, due to the imposition of motarfa tax, during the period 1800–1857, employment in the manufacturing of textiles declined by almost 50 per cent.[33]

Bolt is perhaps the only historian who has provided detailed account of the excesses of the East India Company on the weavers in Dacca. He writes the Company used all possible methods to exploit weavers such as fines, imprisonment, flogging and forcing bonds on them. He writes, 'Roguery practiced in this department is beyond imagination, but all terminate in defrauding the poor weaver' (Bolt, 1772 [1998], 74). He further writes that the prices which the Company gomastas and, in confederacy with them, the jassendars fix upon the goods are in all places at least 15 per cent and in some 40 per cent less than the goods so manufactured would sell in the public bazar or market upon free sale. The impact of the tyranny of the Company was so devastating for the weavers of Dacca that they began the practice of self-mutilation by cutting their thumbs to avoid exploitation by the officials of the East India Company. This practice, according to Dodwell, slowly eclipsed the whole industry which was known to produce the best quality muslin or *malmal khas*.[34] In 1848, while delivering a speech before the Democratic Club at Belgium, Marx said:

> At the moment Dacca district is crammed with English yarn and calicoes. The Dacca muslin renowned all over the world … has been eclipsed by the competition from English machine-made goods. In the whole history, it would perhaps be difficult to find suffering equal to what this whole class of India had to submit to. (Marx, 1853)

Spinning and weaving of silk around Dacca was organized into three separate independent processes: (a) Cocoon rearing and harvesting, that is, sericulture, (b) reeling of silk, that is, making of raw silk, and (c) weaving of silk. Sericulture was spatially highly localized in areas where mulberry trees were found. Due to the reason that cocoons need processing within a period of four to five days after harvest, spinning and reeling of silk was also localized near the places where cocoons were harvested. Once the reeling of silk is complete, weaving of silk can take place anywhere. This characteristic of silk weaving made it footloose and made it possible to weave silk in all the corners of the Indian subcontinent, from Bengal, Assam, Banaras in the east to Surat in the west and Malabar Coast in the south. The main interests of the East India Company were focused on procurement of raw silk only. The East India Company was exporting raw silk to provide raw material to British silk weavers. The demand of Dacca's raw silk industry expanded with the birth of silk-weaving industry in Britain at places like Spitalfields, Manchester and Paisley.[35] Since raw silk produced by nacauds using traditional method of reeling produced raw silk of poor quality, it needed significant improvements. Therefore, to safeguard the interest of workers employed in the British silk weaving, the first thing that the East India Company ensured after it assumed political power in Bengal was improvement in the quality of raw silk.[36]

To improve the quality of raw silk, the East India Company introduced *filature silk* in the areas around Dacca and other parts of Bengal, where cocoons were harvested. The method used the mechanism of double crossing and twisting of silk thread, which gave the silk thread roundness and even thickness. During the period 1790–1823, the quantity of silk yarn wound on filature machines mostly replaced the silk yarn wounded by traditional methods used by local nacauds. Soon the production of filature silk became quite widespread in the areas such as Jangipur, Kamarhati, Malda, Ganutia and Purulia (Bhatacharya, 1966; Sanger, 1974). The filature silk-making equipment necessitated investment in fixed assets. The magnitude of investment needed to install a unit to manufacture filature silk was beyond the means of Indian craftsmen. These units were generally owned by the East India Company or by the employees of the Company, who were using investments for private profits. The widespread use of filature silk reeling led to decline in the silk reeled by nacauds.

The East India Company also reduced the dependence on Indian merchants for meeting its credit needs and the financial needs of private British traders. To achieve this objective, the East India Company established the Bank of Bengal. This bank provided cheaper credit to the East India Company and its employees, who were engaged in private trade. This happened because the bank was able to mobilize public deposits by public borrowing. As a consequence of the formation of this bank, the Indian investors had larger share in the non-remittable portion of the government debt in Bengal, in the public borrowing raised by the Company in 1814–1815.[37] As a consequence of following different strategies as mentioned above, the East India Company was able to marginalize the role of Indian merchants by reducing their participation in the economy of Bengal in general and in financing traditional flexible manufacturing of Dacca in particular. It was now possible for the East Indian Company to break the nexus between local merchants and craftsmen's household workshops. This nexus was the precondition for the existence of traditional flexible manufacturing. The changing disconnect between merchants and craftsmen led to disconnect between craftsmen and mass markets. This is because it is the merchants who had established the connection between isolated workshops of craftsmen and the market. This disassociation of merchants from dadni system paved the way towards the slow and systematic decline of traditional flexible manufacturing in Decca. The prosperity of Dacca was intimately linked with the growth of traditional flexible manufacturing. The process of decline in the traditional flexible manufacturing has been described as the beginning of the process of de-industrialization of Dacca. The process of de-industrialization received additional strength from another powerful force. At that point in time, while political power of the East India Company was expanding in the Indian subcontinent, Britain was experiencing the Industrial Revolution. Manufacturing of textiles was the leading sector of the Industrial Revolution (Chaudhri (ed.), 1971; Siddiqi, 1982). The machine-based manufacturing of textiles reduced the competitive advantage of crafts-based manufacturing of Dacca. The increasing importance of manufacturers in British economy also impacted the policymaking in Britain. British manufacturers, on the one hand, forced the government to impose tariffs on imports of Indian textiles, and on the other hand, wanted free access to the markets of the Indian subcontinent. The interest of the British manufacturers forced the East India Company to allow entry of free merchants, who acted as agents of the British manufacturers to sell their products in the Indian market. These agents formed *agency houses* in the same way they had formed agency houses in Bombay.

These agency houses were generally partnership companies formed by some of the ex-employees of the Company under the patronage of the administrators of the East India Company. These agency houses became the instruments of selling cheaper British machine-made goods to Indian consumers. The supply of cheaper machine-made goods reduced the demand of Indian manufactured goods in the domestic market. The first agency house which was founded in the Calcutta Presidency in 1767 was Alexandra Company, followed by Palmer & Company formed in 1810. This agency house became the largest agency house of Calcutta. Subsequently, Calcutta became the location of several agency houses, such as Ferguson & Company, Colvin & Company and Pickard & Company.[38]

It was at the same time that certain events were occurring in the distant land, which had in their womb consequences for the economy of Bengal. In 1773, the British government introduced the Tea Act, which made tea expansive for the consumers of another colony of Britain, namely America. This led to discontent amongst the inhabitants of America, when the three ships, namely *Darmouth*, *Elanov* and *Beaver*, loaded with tea from China arrived at Boston. The agitators boarded the ship and dumped the tea. This event is known as the Boston Tea Party in the history of America, which laid the foundation for the independence of America from the British rule (Breen, 2004; Tucker and Handrickson 1982). In 1823, British army officer Robert Bruce discovered tea plants which were growing in the wild in Assam. However, his discovery remained unattended by the officials of the East India Company. There were pressures on the British government to find an alternative location for growing tea to expunge the stigma of illegitimate trading in tea in lieu of opium in China. Governor-General William Bentinck (1774–1839) established a Tea Committee in 1834 to find the possibilities of growing tea in the Indian subcontinent (Ellis, Coultan and Manger, 2015, 211–212). The Tea Committee soon discovered the progress made by Charles Bruce, the younger brother of Robert Bruce, who was also posted in the region by the East India Company. In 1836, Charles Bruce identified a number of locations in Assam where tea plants existed. He also informed that Assam Rajahs did not tax anyone who undertook the effort of cultivating on the hills. In 1830, the government of the Company gave permission to its officials and expatriate British citizens to own land in India. In January 1839, the East India Company auctioned the first consignment of Assam tea in London. This led to the formation of Assam Company. By the 1850s, most of the Assam hills were transformed into tea gardens. Calcutta Port became an important centre of tea exports.

Availability of tea from Assam reduced the dependence of British consumption on China tea. This also made possible the availability of tea at much lower prices to the British consumers. In 1784, Prime Minister William Pitt passed the Commutation Act, which reduced the existing duties on tea. This has been described as 'Democratization of Tea Drinking' in Britain (Ellis et al., 2015, Chapter IX, 179–202). This affected the national life style. As Defoe observed:

> Tea table amongst ladies and coffee house among men seem place of new invention.... What people liked about these new drugs was they offered a very different kind of stimulus from traditional European drug, alcohol. Alcohol is technically a depressant, glucose, caffeine and nicotine by contrast were eighteenth century equivalent of uppers. Taken together, new drugs gave English society an almighty hit. (Furguson, 2004, 115)

The description given above clearly shows that while traditional flexible manufacturing of Dacca was experiencing decline, Calcutta's economy was revived by getting chance to export Assam tea. The phenomenon of de-industrialization has been widely debated in the literature on economic history of the Indian subcontinent.[39] Decline of traditional flexible manufacturing led to decline in the prosperity of Dacca. Decline in traditional flexible manufacturing does not *pari pasu* means decline of handicrafts because traditional flexible manufacturing is just one of the several formats in which handicrafts can be organized. Handicraft format of manufacturing could be embedded in several other forms of organizations. Moreover, some of the products of Dacca had become sociocultural products and their demand persisted. In the section the follows, the debate on de-industrialization has been discussed.

DEBATE ON DE-INDUSTRIALIZATION

As it has been described above, the Indian subcontinent had become an important manufacturer and exporter of manufactured goods during the Mughal Empire. The traditional flexible manufacturing was producing about 25 per cent of the total manufacturing output of the world until the decline of the Mughal Empire began. The percentage share of the manufacturing enterprises of the Indian subcontinent declined significantly.[40] Since the manufacturing sector at that time consisted mainly of handicrafts, decline in the output of manufacturing has been viewed as decline of handicrafts or also as de-industrialization. The phenomenon of de-industrialization was at variance with the experience of British manufacturing, where crafts-based manufacturing was replaced by modern manufacturing during the same historical time. Therefore, the level of output as well as employment in the British manufacturing did not experience any decline. In the case of manufacturing sector of the Indian subcontinent, crafts-based manufacturing registered decline though modern manufacturing did not replace it then. Therefore, in the context of experiences of the manufacturing sector of the Indian subcontinent, decline of handicrafts or de-industrialization represents a movement one stage backward, rather than one stage forward. The process of de-industrialization experienced by Indian manufacturing symbolizes not only the loss in income and employment in the manufacturing sector, but also stands for a process which caused mass deskilling of craftsmen, skills which they had perfected over centuries. Due to all these reasons, the episode of de-industrialization has assumed importance in the writings of economists as well as of historians.

The handicrafts-based mode of production of the India subcontinent had become a globally competitive method of production by evolving the capacity to satisfy the need of mass markets. This had become possible because of its organization of production, which was based on the nexus between merchants and craftsmen, which has been described as traditional flexible manufacturing. Therefore, the process of de-industrialization can be reinterpreted on the premise that so long the nexus between merchants and craftsmen persisted, the traditional flexible manufacturing survived and experienced significant expansion. The decline in traditional flexible manufacturing occurred when historical circumstances were able to break the nexus. Therefore, in this section, the process of de-industrialization has been analysed in terms of the historical conditions which led to the break in nexus between craftsmen and merchants.

The analysis of historical facts clearly reveals that the Mughal Empire provided necessary and sufficient conditions for the expansion of traditional flexible manufacturing. These conditions have been discussed in detail in Chapters 1 and 2 of the present study. It has been debated in this section how after the Battle of Plassey of 1757, when the East India Company began its attempts for territorial expansion and political consolidation in the India subcontinent, the process of de-industrialization set in. This happened because when the East India Company used its political power to achieve monopoly of trade in the manufactured products, it slowly created conditions which isolated Indian merchants from participating in the traditional flexible manufacturing. The isolation of Indian merchants from craftsmen was necessary to (a) make craftsmen dependent on the agents of the company for selling their products and (b) establish the Company's monopoly over the manufactured products. To achieve these objectives, the East India Company had to break the nexus between merchants and craftsmen. The same process has also been explained by some scholars as the decline of Indian merchant capital, because when merchant capital became weaker, it could not maintain the nexus.[41]

The episode of de industrialization had been a recurrent theme in the writings of nationalist scholars. They have used de-industrialization experienced by the economy of the subcontinent as an example of failure of British rule. To explain the failure of the British rule, they have argued that the British government in order to safeguard the interests of British manufacturers exposed the traditional flexible manufacturing of the Indian subcontinent to the products produced by modern manufacturing of Britain. The argument given by the nationalist writers assumes that if there had been present a national government instead of a colonial one, it would have protected the interests of Indian manufacturers from foreign competition. The nationalist interpretation of the episode of de-industrialization began with the writings of Dadabhai Naoroji (Dutt, 1906), R. C. Dutt[42] and Nehru.[43] This is also important to mention that the most important consequence of de-industrialization was the decline in the use of *charkha* (spinning wheel). This became an important symbol of the independence movement led by Gandhi.

It is an important historical fact that the debate on de-industrialization began much earlier than the achievement of independence of India; yet the debate has not been able to resolve the most contentious issue. The most contentious issue of this debate is regarding the timing of the beginning of the process of de-industrialization. The timing of this event is quite relevant, because it will inform us about the main characters who were present at that point in time. The knowledge about the presence of different actors at the time of event will help in identifying the factors that caused de-industrialization. The speculations regarding exact timing of the episode of de-industrialization are spread over the period between 1750 and 1900. Out of this long stretch of time, historians have identified two subperiods. According to one set of scholars, it was the decline of the Mughal Empire which led to the process of de-industrialization. The other group of scholars believe that the process occurred when cheap machine-made products manufactured in Britain began to penetrate the Indian markets.

The scholars who suggest that the process of de-industrialization began after the decline of the Mughal Empire argue that the death of Aurangzeb in 1707 led to fragmentation of the Mughal Empire into several autonomous political entities. Each ruler of the new autonomous political entities became dependent on merchants to protect and expand his territories. The increasing dependence on merchants to finance their wars led to increasing conflicts also between merchants and rulers. In the earlier chapter, several instances have been described when rulers confiscated the properties of merchants. The increasing insecurity regarding their private property, deterioration in the quality of governance, rising instances of banditry put the wealth of merchants into a bottomless pit. In such prevailing conditions, merchants withdrew their financial resources from productive economic activities. Therefore, they also stopped financing networks of craftsmen. This created disconnect between merchants and craftsmen and between craftsmen and mass market. This caused slow decline in the traditional flexible manufacturing. This fact has led some scholars to associate the decline of Mughal power with the decline of traditional flexible manufacturing. However, as it has already been mentioned, the emergence of successor states in Hyderabad, Maharashtra, Punjab, Rajasthan, Mysore and Awadh provided necessary conditions for the continued existence of traditional flexible manufacturing (Marx, 1868, 358).

The relationship between the decline of traditional flexible manufacturing and the penetration of British machine-made goods in the

India subcontinent was highlighted for the first time by William Bentinck, who was the Governor-General of India during 1833–1835. He described, for the first time, consequences of imported mill cloth from Britain on the decline of Indian cotton textile manufacturing. His ideas regarding the role of imports of British mill cloth in the Indian traditional flexible manufacturing of textiles were used as example in the book of Karl Marx, when he stated, 'The bones of cotton weavers are bleaching the plains of India'.[44] He describes again about the event of de-industrialization which was experienced by the manufacturing industry of the subcontinent in his frequently quoted article entitled 'British Rule in India'. In this article, he describes, 'it was the British intruder who broke up Indian handloom and destroyed the spinning wheel. England began with driving the Indian cotton from European markets, it then introduced the very mother country of cotton with cotton'. In the same article, he goes on to add, 'From 1818–1836, the exports of the twist from Great Britain to India rose in proportion to 1:5200'. The outcome of this process was that the 'British steam and Science uprooted over the surface of Hindustan the union between agriculture and manufacturing'.[45] It is interesting to mention that both sets of explanation are ignorant of the fact that during the period (1757–1857), the East India Company was busy in consolidating its political hegemony and had already become an important player in Bengal. It is surprising that historians have not analysed the role of the East India Company in the process of de-industrialization as experienced by the manufacturing industry of the Indian subcontinent.

The debate on de-industrialization resurfaced after the data on census of population, national income and occupation pattern of working population began to appear in the official publications after 1870. Due to this reason, the contemporary debate on the process of de-industrialization could not throw light on the period prior to 1870. The earliest empirical evidence regarding de-industrialization was based on the census reports of 1881 and 1891. This empirical study established that the percentage of population working in the manufacturing, mining and construction sectors registered a decline from 28 per cent to 12 per cent.[46] Another empirical study, which used census date for the period 1881–1931, also recorded decline in the employment in the manufacturing sector from 20 million to somewhere between 13 and 15 million, while number of persons employed in the agricultural sector increased from 62 million to 71 million. The study interpreted the movement of working population from manufacturing to agriculture as de-industrialization (Thorner, 1962).

These estimates were disputed by Daniel Thorner when he obtained results quite contrary to the results reported above. He used revised data of census of population from 1881 to 1931. His estimates established that the extent of working population engaged in the manufacturing sector did not change significantly during the period. Therefore, he did not find any evidence regarding de-industrialization. Hence, he conceded that the event of de-industrialization, if it did occur in the Indian subcontinent, must have happened before 1881.[47] Similar results were also observed by the study of Krishnamurty, when he made an attempt to understand the problem of de-industrialization with the help of its analysis by observing shifts in the occupational pattern of the working population. He found that the occupational pattern was almost stagnant during the period of his study (1881–1951). His study revealed that the percentage of working population engaged in the primary activities remained around 70 per cent, in the manufacturing sector around 10 per cent, and the services occupation accounted for about 20 per cent.[48]

Scholars like Harnetty have used the extent of exports of handloom as a proxy for understanding the process of de-industrialization. He observed that the handloom weaving achieved its peak level in terms of volume in 1802 and in terms of value in 1800. Subsequently, exports of Indian cotton textiles declined due to intensification of competition with British textiles produced by its mills.[49] Simons has used the data gathered by Paul Bairoch regarding global spread of manufacturing enterprises to understand how the birth of modern manufacturing affected the process of de-industrialization in the periphery of the developed economies of Europe. He also observed that 25 per cent of the global output of manufactured goods was produced by the manufacturing sector of the Indian subcontinent in 1750. This proportion declined to 20 per cent in 1800, to 10 per cent in 1860 and became just 3 per cent in 1880.[50] These estimates have not been accepted by

many scholars. The critics argue that percentage share of the manufactured goods produced in the Indian subcontinent in global output
does not appraise accurately the decline of manufacturing in India. It
only shows the percentage share of Indian manufacturing in the global
output. The decline in the contribution of Indian manufacturing to
the global output might have occurred because the rate of growth of
manufacturing in other countries was much faster than its growth in
the Indian manufacturing.

The most elaborate and detailed exercise so far to understand the
process of de-industrialization has been conducted by Clingingsmith
and Williamson. Their empirical exercise covers the period between
1750 and 1913. Their study shows that the manufacturing sector of the
Indian subcontinent experienced the process of de-industrialization
during two subperiods of their entire time series data. The first phase of
de-industrialization occurred during 1750–1810, which he attributes
to the decline in the centralized authority of the Mughal state. The
second sub-period when manufacturing activities experienced decline
is between 1810 and 1860. According to their observation, the second
phase of de-industrialization coincides with increasing competition
faced by the Indian manufacturers from the machine-made goods
produced by British modern manufacturing. The study suggests that
the process of de-industrialization was complete by 1860. Therefore,
it is quite obvious that most of the empirical exercises that have been
described above, which study the Indian experience after 1860, did
not observe the incidence of de-industrialization.[51] These empirical
studies have led a number of scholars to believe that the episode of
de-industrialization might have occurred much earlier.[52]

As it has been mentioned above, most scholars who accept that
de-industrialization in the Indian subcontinent occurred before 1860
explain it by associating it with the decline of the Mughal Empire.[53]
The decline of the Mughal Empire began with the death of Aurangzeb
in 1707. How then could it result in the process of de-industrialization
which started around the 1750s? It is quite obvious that these scholars
are oblivious to the fact that the ascendancy of the East India Company
began from the 1750s onwards. The ignoring of this vital fact by historians has given clean chit to the role of the East India Company in

the process of de-industrialization experienced by the Indian manufacturing. The emergence of the East India Company as a ruler after the Battle of Plassey gave it more capability to exercise monopoly power on the trade of Indian manufactured goods. In order to establish its monopoly over the trade in manufactured goods, it eliminated the role of Indian merchants from the trade of manufactured goods. The marginalization of the role of Indian merchants from the process of production of handicrafts systematically broke a more-than-a-century-old nexus between merchants and craftsmen, which led to the decline of traditional flexible manufacturing.

It is also an important historical fact that just as the hegemony of the East Indian Company began with the occupation of Bengal, the process of de-industrialization also began at Bengal. As it has been described in the earlier section of this chapter, the event of de-industrialization transformed the richest subah of the Mughal Empire into the poorest region of the Indian subcontinent. Manufacturing of Dacca declined significantly and converted this city into an exporter of raw materials. It is not surprising that Bengal experienced famine in 1770. Therefore, it is quite obvious that the decline of traditional flexible manufacturing began with the political ascendancy of the East India Company, and not with the decline of the Mughal Empire. The policies followed by the East India Company, which systematically broke the nexus between merchants and craftsmen, exposed craftsmen to several kinds of risk and uncertainty. The new relationship that emerged between craftsmen and the East India Company, after marginalizing the role of Indian merchants, was similar to the relationship that exists between 'parasite and host' where 'parasite uses the structure of the host for its own sustenance'.[54]

In the new circumstances, while the East India Company reduced the role of merchants in the manufacturing activities, it developed a strong symbiotic relationship with Indian merchants in commodity trading. This is because by this time the Indian subcontinent had been transformed from an exporter of manufactured products into a nation which supplied raw materials for the manufacturers of Britain. India had slowly become an exporter of primary products such as cotton, opium, tea, raw silk and indigo. In order to export these commodities, the East India Company and the agency houses developed strong ties with Indian merchants, who helped them to maintain the supply chain of these commodities from farms to the port. The Indian merchants who became part of this supply chain also accumulated wealth which they subsequently used to promote modern manufacturing enterprises.

Apart from decline in exports of manufactured goods, de-industrialization was also related to certain changes that were occurring inside the economy of the India subcontinent. As it has been mentioned in Chapter 1 of the book, certain segments of traditional flexible manufacturing were engaged in the production of luxury handicrafts for elites and nobles of the Mughal Empire. The emergence of political hegemony of the East India Company eliminated the hierarchy of mansabdars created by the Mughal Empire and replaced it by salaried administrations appointed by the Company. This shift in the composition of elites led to a new consumption pattern. The new elite's consumption pattern brought a significant decline in the demand of luxury handicrafts. It has been estimated by some scholars who expressed that 'perhaps three quarter of the domestic demand of luxury handicrafts, with a magnitude of about five percent of the Mughal national income disappeared'.[55]

This is also an important fact that it is not only the decline in the demand of luxury handicrafts which led to de-industrialization; most of the Indian consumers who could afford cheaper machine-made goods adopted them as part of their consumption. This change in consumption pattern of Indian consumers was also responsible for de-industrialization. Some anthropologists have raised a very relevant issue regarding the adoption of machine-made products in the consumption pattern of an average Indian. The relevant issue is 'How, then do culturally determined consumption pattern changes to accommodate alien, manufacturers in a society in this market itself is not powerful enough to create taste' (Faiz Baksh, 1889, 97, quoted in Appadurai, 1986, 304). It is being explained with the help of an important historical fact that the period after 1750, when British machine-made goods began to enter the market in the Indian subcontinent, coincided with the period of fragmentation of Indian polity. This process created new regional elites. These new regional elites wanted to evolve their own distinct identity, more differentiated and distinct from the Mughal aristocracy. These elites adopted British goods, which provided them an alternative pattern of consumption. This also gave them chance to mix up with the new power elite—the officials of the East India Company.

The changes in the consumption pattern of the new regional elite got manifest when they constructed their new palaces or *havelis*. Their palaces were decorated with several European products. One could see in their residences clocks, curtains, mirrors, paintings, artefacts and other items procured from European sources. The capital of Awadh, Lucknow, emerged as an important market of British glasswares. The Nawab of Lucknow imported in huge quantity sheet glass from Britain. These sheet glasses were used in the construction of Chota Imambara and Bara Imambara. The liberal display of British and European objects by the new elite is also manifest in the artefacts and products which are displayed in the Salarjung Museum of Hyderabad, and other museums and palaces of Rajasthan, Punjab, Awadh and Mysore. The shift in the pattern of consumption of new elites clearly shows a paradigm shift in the nature of consumption, from the consumption of socially embedded *products* to *commodity fetishism*.

During this period, historical circumstances also gave birth to another group of change agents, which also influenced the demand for Indian manufactured goods. These new change agents were several British and French freebooters, who were engaged by the Nizam of Hyderabad, the Marathas and Sikh rulers to provide training to their army for the sake of modernization. These freebooters adopted uniforms for their armies which were made of scarlet English broad cloth. This is how the uniforms of armies of local rulers were made from British textiles. It is how the initial demand for the British machine-made cloth came from the armies of the local rulers. Faiz Baksh, who has recorded several historical facts regarding the Indian subcontinent during the period when the East India Company enjoyed political hegemony over it, describes that 'when eunuch administration of Lucknow, Jawahir Ali Khan's personal soldiers (*sabit-khanis*) were seen in green livery, irregulars in black, and Mewati soldiers in white, it made other rich people envious'.[56]

It must have become clear by now from the discussion above about the process of de-industrialization, which was experienced by the Indian flexible manufacturing, that most of the debate has remained focused on the decline of traditional flexible manufacturing of textiles. This might be because textile manufacturing was the most important part of traditional flexible manufacturing, which provided income as well as employment to large numbers of families at that point in time. Even in textile manufacturing the inter-regional variations are quite evident from the analysis of differences between the experience of Surat and Dacca. In Surat, textile manufacturers succeeded by changing their product mix as well as identifying *niche* markets abroad, where they could sell their products.

Since spinning reduced the cost of yarn significantly with the use of modern machines, it is expected that hand spinning lost competitive advantage in the traditional flexible manufacturing. Spinning was generally a part-time work usually performed by the women of the household. Therefore, the absence of spinning in the household affected the income of the family but did not affect the overall employment. However, availability of cheaper yarn provided opportunity for weavers to substitute machine-made yarn in place of hand-spun yarn. Moreover, some weavers began to weave cloth for products which were not produced by modern mills of Britain. This comprised cloth which was more ethnic in character or was consumed by niche markets, such as *dhotis*, *chaddars*, *dupttas* and the like.

The scholars who have participated in the debate of de-industrialization while focusing on textile manufacturing have ignored varieties of products which were produced by the traditional flexible manufacturing. The Industrial Revolution of Britain had revolutionized the production of a very limited number of products, because modern technology did not affect manufacturing of all the products simultaneously. Therefore, it is expected that the availability of machine-made goods did not affect all industries at the same time and to the same extent. It is quite possible to think that the traditional flexible manufacturing which was engaged in the production of domestic utensils, metalwares, agricultural implements, silver and gold jewellery might have experienced an upward trend because these products were not experiencing any competition from British factory-made products. In the same way, it could be assumed that manufacturing of hide and leather products might have also expanded because of demand for leather products by the expanding army of the East India Company as well as by the armies of the local rulers for saddles, shoes and breaches. One can also speculate that demand for shoes and footwear might have increased due to Westernization of dress code for emerging new professions such as lower and higher bureaucracy, lawyers, teachers and so on.

The analysis presented above shows that the consequences of the rule of the East India Company were different for Surat and Dacca. Since Dacca came under the rule of the Company much earlier than the rest of the Indian subcontinent, and the rule of the East India Company was absolute, its economy was significantly impacted by the rule of the Company. The Company also used different regulations, strategies and practices, which systematically eliminated the role of Indian merchants from participation in the traditional flexible manufacturing, which exposed the craftsmen to several kinds of risks. It at the same time also increased the dependence of craftsmen on the gomastas of the Company. The dependence of craftsmen on the East India Company altered the nature of contract between the craftsmen and the East India Company. The nature of contract increased the power of the Company to impose its monopoly power in terms of pricing of the product. The increasing disadvantages in the nature of relationship might have forced some of the craftsmen to leave their crafts.

In the case of Surat, the powers of the East India Company were not absolute for a considerable period. This happened because of the presence of Marathas in the hinterland of the city. Therefore, the East India Company required the cooperation of Indian merchants to procure important products such as textiles, cotton and opium. This dependence of the East India Company on Indian merchants facilitated the process of accumulation of wealth of Indian merchants. The East India Company encouraged the migration of rich merchants and craftsmen to Bombay because Bombay city could not generate enough resources for its sustenance and growth due to absence of hinterland. Moreover, by the time the East India Company was able to consolidate its political power on the Western coast, after the Third Anglo-Maratha War, it had lost the right of monopoly of trade in the Indian subcontinent. These factors reduced the consequences of the rule of the East India Company on Surat.

It is also worth mentioning that the merchants of Surat migrated to several locations in South and East Africa to develop these places as market of products produced by the traditional flexible manufacturing of Surat. Some of them even migrated to Bombay to exploit new opportunities, which were available there in the form of trade in cotton and opium of Malwa. Craftsmen of Surat also changed the production pattern of their products and customized these according to the consumer preferences of markets in Burma, East Africa and South Africa.

The debate on de-industrialization regarding its appropriate timing suggests that the process occurred during the period between 1750 and 1860. This period coincides with the period when the East India Company established it political hegemony over vast territories of the Indian subcontinent. The longest period of the rule of the Company was experienced by Bengal, where Dacca is located. It was the absolute powers enjoyed by the East India Company which got manifested through several kinds of regulations and practices, which contributed to the decline of traditional flexible manufacturing. Therefore, the scholars who attribute the decline of traditional flexible manufacturing to either decline of the Mughal Empire or the entry of machine-made goods produced by the British mills need certain corrections in their narrative. The role of the East India Company in the process of de-industrialization, especially regarding the manufacturing of Dacca, cannot be ruled out.

The consequences of the rule of the East Indian Company on the economy of the Indian subcontinent have been recorded by two important pieces of art produced during the beginning and near the end of the rule of the Company. They appropriately illustrate that the economy which was full of riches at the time when the East India Company began its territorial occupation was transformed into a dilapidated economy, which has been depicted as a beggar woman. Two decades after the Battle of Plassey (1757), in 1778, a painting was installed on the ceiling of the room in which meetings of the Revenue Committee of the Company were held. This was painted by the artist Spiridione Roma. This painting bears the title *The East Offering Its Riches to Britain*. It depicts three women, who represent three different countries. The most prominent and most beautiful amongst the three represents Britannia, who is confidently looking down upon the other two women. The woman with dark complexion represents India, who is shown offering precious stones and pearls to Britannia. The painting clearly shows how the wealth of the Indian subcontinent was passed on to Britain.[57]

Five years after the end of monopoly over trade bestowed by the royal charter (1813), in 1818, a marble relief was made by a sculptor, Richard Westmacott, in the memory of Alexander Colvin, a British merchant of Calcutta. In this sculpture, India is symbolized by a seated woman who is not wearing any ornaments, and it is shown that her hands are placed on an empty pot (see Note 57). The relief suggests that the process of shifting wealth from India to Britain is complete. After the drain of wealth, the material prosperity of India has already been shifted, and India has been transformed into a woman with begging pot.

NOTES

1. For details regarding annexation of different territories by the East India Company, see Fisher (1993).
2. This conceptualization of the company is given in Travers (2007).
3. This particular term has been used by Stein (2004).
4. The Phrase The Merchant Sovereign has been used by Travers (2007) to describe the rule of the East India Company.
5. Robbins (2006) has used the term corporate state to conceptualize the rule of the East India Company.
6. For this shift with nature of trade, see Dasgupta (1994) and Subramanian (2010, 19).
7. For understanding about these events, see Nightingale (1970) and Bowen et al. (eds) (2012).
8. To know in detail the shifting of Lowji Nessarwanji Wadia to Bombay, see Subramanian (1996).
9. For these facts, see Guha (1984).
10. To understand this process of relocation of cotton textile manufacturing from the Indian subcontinent in general and from Surat in particular, see Reillo and Parthasarthi (eds) (2009), Reillo and Roy (eds) (2009), Parthasarthi (2011, Chapter IV), Beckert (2014) and Seth (2015, 61–63).

11. For the details regarding American cotton cultivation, see Ferguson (2003).

12. For details, see Siddiqi (1982).

13. See earlier chapter and Subramanian (2010, 74–75) and Roy (2013).

14. For these facts, see Subramanian (1996), Nadin (2009), Haynes and Roy (1999) and Haynes (2015).

15. For details, see Heynes (2012).

16. For details, see Dobbin (1972) and Dossal (1991).

17. For these facts, see Farooqi (1995) and (2006).

18. Reference about the family of Readymoney is available in several writings, see Guha (1970, 1984), Kulke (1978) and Tripathi (2004).

19. For the ideas of Smith, see Smith (1776, 2003) and Winch (1978).

20. For this idea, see Robinson (2006), Dirk (2006) and Roy (2012).

21. For details regarding Jamsetji Jeejeebhoy, see Siddiqi (1982) and Subramanian (2014).

22. For details regarding trade in opium and opium wars, see Greenberg (1969), Inglis (1976), Farooqi (2006) and Pichon (2006).

23. For details, see Misra (1991).

24. To know about this term, see Robins (2006, 76).

25. For drain wealth, see Burke (1783, 1981, Vol. V).

26. For the ideas on economic drain of different scholars, see Bolt (1772 [1998]), Dow (1792) and Verelst (1776).

27. For estimates of Habib, see Habib (1965).

28. This term has been used by Om prakash (2007, 151).

29. For details, see Sinha (ed.) (1968).

30. For further information, see Roy (2010).

31. For these facts, see Arasaratnam (1980) and Parthasarthi (2001).

32. For understanding about the conditions of craftsmen in the production centres organized by the East India Company, see Hussain (1958).

33. For details, see Bhatacharya (1982, 273, 288).

34. For these facts, see Dodwell (1922, Vol. I, 2), *Cambridge Economic History of India.*

35. For details, see Dodwell (1922) and Robins (2006, 60).

36. For details, see Bharacharya (1982).

37. For the idea of leading sector, see Rostow (1957).

38. For details, see Hodgson (1938), Singh (1966) and Tripathi (2004).

39. For these facts, see Frank (1998) and Meddison (2003).

40. For understanding the role of merchant capital in the Indian subcontinent, see Perlin (1983).

41. For ideas of Dadabhai Naroji, see Naroji (1901).

42. Ideas of Jawahar Lal Nehru are available in Nehru (1947).

43. For understanding regional experience of Awadh, see Alam (1986) and Murad (2012); for Hyderabad, see Richard (1975) and Leonard (1979); for Bengal, see Omprakhas (1998) and Leonard (1979), and for Punjab see Singh (1991) and Banga and Grewal (1990).

44. For these sentiments of Marx, see Marx (1853), which is included in the collection of writing of Marx on India edited by Husain (ed.) (2006, 16–17).

45. For these estimates, see Clark (1950).

46. For these facts, see Patel (1952).

47. For these estimates, see Krishnamurthy (1982).

48. For this opinion, see Harnetty (1991).

49. For the global data set evolved on this issue, see Bairoch (1982).
50. These estimates have been obtained from Simmons (1985).
51. For these estimates, see Clinging smith and Williamson (2004).
52. The scholars, who believe that event of de-industrialization occurred much earlier are Markovits (2000) and Roy (2006, 2008).
53. For this quotation, see Dewey (1988, 5).
54. These estimates are given in Medison (1973, 34–35), Deavy (1975) and Gadgil (1971).
55. For these ideas, see Appadurai (ed.) (1986, 303).
56. For the painting referred in the text, see Robbins (2006, 2).
57. Details regarding this paintings are available in Groseclose (1990, 50). However, I have obtained its reference from Ramaswamy (2010, 78–79).

Economic Environment During the British Raj

The East India Company was formed through a royal charter in 1600. It began its trading operations in the Indian subcontinent in 1607 from Surat. The Company was experiencing rapid expansion in its business activities at a time when polity, society and economy of Britain were embedded in the ideology of mercantilism. Almost after 150 years of being in the business, it entered in the business of empire building in 1757, after the Battle of Plassey. The East India Company got an opportunity to enter into the business of empire building by occupying political space vacated by the declining Mughal Empire. During this long period of one-and-a-half century, events in Britain were not just frozen in time. As it has been described in Chapter 2 of the book, the British social order was preparing the ground to achieve revolutionary transformation, the kind of transformation never achieved by any other country. The shift had been caused by simultaneous occurrence of several inventions which changed the nature of its manufacturing enterprises. The transformation in the nature of its manufacturing enterprises has been described as the Industrial Revolution.

The birth of Industrial Revolution was accompanied by the emergence of a new social order, where manufacturers or industrialists were viewed as a dominant group in the process of creation of wealth for the economy. It was the increasing importance of manufacturing which was affecting the stance of policymakers in Britain. As it has already been narrated in Chapters 3 and 4, the interest of the East India Company was different from the interests of manufacturers of Britain. As a consequence of these changes in Britain, for the first time, the

East India Company was experiencing a political regime which was not sympathetic to the interests of the Company.

Britain celebrated the global supremacy of its manufacturing sector by organizing the Great Exhibition of its manufactured products in 1851 in Hyde Park in London. The exhibition began on 1 May 1851, and continued till 15 October 1851. The building that was constructed to display the products produced by the British manufacturers was made of 250,000 glass panes and was aptly named Crystal Palace. In this exhibition, 14,000 products were exhibited. All these products were luxury products of yesteryears and were part of consumption pattern of rich and powerful people of Britain. These products were transformed into products of mass consumption by the modern manufacturing enterprises of Britain. This was made possible by the use of machines which helped in the production of large volume of products at cheaper costs.

Just seven years after this historical event, the rule of the East India Company was abolished in the Indian subcontinent, and it came directly under the British Crown and the Parliament through the Better Governance of India Act, 1857. The end of the rule of the East India Company was the beginning of the British Raj. The transfer of power to the British Crown and the Parliament removed the veil from the face of British imperialism, because from then on the Indian subcontinent was ruled directly by the British Crown and the Parliament and was not managed by its proxy, that is, the East India Company.

These two important historical events were consequences of great transformations which the British society, polity and economy were experiencing while the East India Company was playing its historical role of consolidating its territorial occupation of the Indian subcontinent. Transformations were occurring due to shift in the nature of the power elite which was emerging politically and economically more relevant than the elites who were instrumental in the formation of the monopolies like the East India Company. The other potent force which was transforming Britain was created by the revolutionary changes in the methods of production. The revolutionary changes that were occurring in the methods of production were collectively described by historians as the Industrial Revolution. The changes that were occurring in the ideology of new power elites were making the existence of monopolies like the East India Company and other rent-seeking classes irrelevant for the economic prosperity of the British economy. The emerging supremacy of the interest of manufacturers was creating contradiction between the interests of manufacturers and the East India Company. The British manufacturers were viewing the existence of the rule of the Company on the Indian subcontinent as a barrier to get access to the large market of the Indian subcontinent.

The intertwined forces of shift in the ideology of the new elite and the interest of British mill owners provided bases for the emergence of the British Raj. However, the role of catalyst for the event of 1857 was played by the forces which were uniting different interests in the Indian subcontinent against the rule of the East India Company. The rule of The East India Company had emerged by appropriating land and kingdoms of several local political dispensations. The process of de-industrialization has also affected the life of craftsmen. Heavy taxation of landed classes also affected their material life. The collective discontent of these diverse sections of the society got expression in the form of the Sepoy Mutiny (as described by British historians) or the First War of Independence (as described by nationalist historians). The armed revolt against the company began on the night of 10–11 May 1857, when troops of 9th Native Cavalry deserted their army and moved towards Delhi and made the Mughal emperor Bahadur Shah Zafar the leader of the revolt. This historical event has been variously described by different historians depending upon whether their ideas are influenced by the ideology of the imperialist, the nationalist or the rationalist. The interest in this historical event was revived when in 2007 India celebrated 150th anniversary of this event. The new generation of Indians were able to know about the details regarding this episode from the bestselling book *The Last Mughal*, written by William Dalrymple (see Dalrymple, 2006). Since this event has been already analysed in great detail by several historians covering its different dimensions, we do not intend to spend time on its analysis (Bender, 2016; David, 2002; Hibbert, 1978; Joshi (ed.), 2007; Roy, 2008). An important consequence of the event was that it resulted in the end of even the last remnants of the Mughal Empire. In the recently published English translation (by Rana Safvi) of the eye-witness account of the Revolt of 1857, written by Zahir Dehlvi in Persian as *Dastan-e-Ghadar*, it has become quite evident that Mughal emperor Bahadur Shah Zafar had a premonition that the Revolt of 1857 will put the final end to the rule of Mughal dynasty. While describing about the emotions of the emperor when sepoys entered the Red Fort, he writes that emperor said, 'I have realized that the rebellious sky and wicked world (*falak-e-ghadar* or *zamana-e-na-banjar*) want to see my family destroyed' (see Dehlvi, 1914 [2017], 30). The author also mentions that the Mughal emperor often repeated the following phrase (ibid., 297–298):

Meri aulad na-haq aarzu saltanat ki rakhti. Hai yeh karkhana age chalne wala nahin-hai mujh par khatam hai.

—*Az Tiamur, Taha Zafar*

[My children have unjust dreams of kingship. This order can't last for long. It will end with me.]

—*Timur to Zafar* (1914 [2017], 25)

The relevance of this episode for the tale of four cities is that this event became a catalyst in abolishing the rule of the East India Company and establishing the rule of the British Raj.

In the present chapter, we have analysed the forces which helped in the formation of the British Raj. This chapter also analyses how the formation of the British Raj altered the structure of governance in the Indian subcontinent. This is also intended to explain the shifts in the policy regimes during the period of the British Raj (1857–1947). The purpose of this chapter is to make the readers aware about the changes that were occurring during the rule of the British Raj, which affected the tale of the four cities. For the purpose of the analysis, this chapter has been organized into three sections. In the first section, we present different historical forces which led to the shift from the rule of the East India Company to the rule of the British Raj. In the second section, we present the shifts in structure of governance during the British Raj, and finally in the third section, we analyse shifts in the policy regime that occurred during the British Raj.

FORCES WHICH LED TO THE BIRTH
OF THE BRITISH RAJ

Europe in general and Britain in particular was experiencing a shift in the ideological premises to evolve new policies. Physiocracy, an earlier school of thought, denied importance to manufacturing by classifying manufacturing activities as *sterile* economics activities. This school provided an ideology to support and articulate the interests of peasants.[1] Physiocratic tradition emerged in France in the seventeenth and the eighteenth centuries, and soon it spread to different parts of Europe. It originated in the writings of François Quesnay (1694–1774), Mercier de La Rivière (1771–1793) and Pierre Samuel du Pont de Nemours (1739–1817). In order to establish supreme positon of peasants in the economy and society, the physiocrats accepted agriculture as the only productive activity. This was based on the premise that it is only agriculture which had the capacity to produce economic surplus. Therefore, non-agricultural activities were described as sterile economic activities (see Meek, 1962).

It has already been explained in Chapters 3 and 4 that the mercantilist school of thought protected the interest of merchants. According to the famous scholar Heckscher, the term 'mercantilism' was used for the first time by Quesnay Mirabeau (see Mun, 1664 [1928]). The ideas of this school of thought were propagated in Britain by three leading thinkers, namely Thomas Mun, Josiah Child and Jean Bodin. Out of these three, the last two thinkers were associated with the East India Company and occupied the position of directors of the Company. However, the most profound version of mercantilism was articulated in the two important pamphlets written by Thomas Mun. These are *England's Treasure by Foreign Trade* and *Discourse of Trade from England into East India*.[2] Since these pamphlets presented theoretically a better perspective on mercantilism, Adam Smith also evolved his critique of mercantilism based on these two pamphlets. Thomas Mun in these pamphlets established the justification of the policies based on regulated foreign trade by arguing that the strategy of regulated foreign trade is based on the premise 'wherein we must ever observe this rule, to sell more to the strangers yearly than we consume of theirs in value'. He suggested, just as individuals get richer by not spending as much as they earn, the same principle should be used by a country. He also advocated for the development of local resources to reduce dependence on the imports of resources. He was a strong advocator of protection of domestic producers and imposition of tariffs to increase the stock of bullion (Mun, 1664 [1928]).

Adam Smith developed an alternative view about the economic activities. His ideas are contained in his book *The Wealth of Nations*, which appeared in 1776. The ideas presented by Smith in this book became the basic premise on which a new school of thought emerged, known as *Classical Political Economy*. The new school of thought began to challenge the premises on which the ideas of mercantilism were based. Smith found contradiction between the premises laid down by Mun and the activities of the East India Company. He identified this contradiction based on a simple fact that if one follows the principle of wealth creation mentioned by Mun, then it becomes quite difficult to accept the massive export of bullion by the East India Company to India to pay for the merchandize. This act amounts to drain of wealth of the country. However, Mun defended the export of bullion to India on the ground that by re-exporting the merchandize which was purchased by other countries and by paying in bullion at higher prices at higher profits, the stock of bullion in Britain increased. He also explained this process by putting forth that the logic can easily be visualized by any enlightened citizen if he takes into account not only the initial transaction but all other subsequent transactions between the two countries of India and Britain. He further held that if one only focuses on the export of bullion to India in isolation, then it

> misinforms their judgement and leads them to error. For if we only behold the actions of a husbandman in the *seed* time when he casteth away much good corn into ground, we will rather accompt him as a madman rather than a husbandman: but when we consider his labours in the harvest which is the end of his endeavours, we find the worth and plentiful encrease of his actions. (Mun, 1621 [1930], 17, emphasis added)

The ideology of mercantilism guided the policies of the British government for a considerable period to protect the interests of different rent-seeking sections of the society. This is because it was assumed by the British state that by protecting the interests of home producers and home suppliers, they are protecting the national interest. The ideology of mercantilism justified the granting of royal charter to the East India Company in 1600 to give it a monopoly of trade with the East. It also provided logical justification for enacting the English Navigation Act in 1651 to safeguard the interest of British shipping from the formidable competition of the Dutch shipping companies. The same ideology provided support for the imposition of the Corn Laws in 1689 to protect the interests of grain traders and farmers of Britain. For the first time, the premises on which these policies were based were challenged by Adam Smith. His book reflected the new social reality of Britain, whereby policy makers as well as enlightened citizens of Britain began to accept that an economy can become rich not alone by protecting trade; manufacturing is more important because it has capability to increase the wealth of a nation far in excess than can be generated by land and protected trade (Mun, 1664 [1928], 19).

Smith suggested that the ideology which holds that the wealth of a nation is represented by the amount of bullion it possesses is based on the dual role played by gold in any economy. Gold helps in transactions, and it also plays the role of measure of value of all other products. Therefore, if a country possesses more gold, it has capacity to buy more commodities. If we value gold as a store of value, then it only tells us that the country will have more claims on other commodities. However, Adam Smith contended that this argument was intended to draw the attention of the state towards the importance of preserving bullion, but the argument ignores 'how preserving and augmenting the quality of any other commodity, which freedom of trade, without any such attention never fails to supply proper quantity'.[3] He mentioned that such arguments were advanced by the merchants to impress the Crown and the Parliament that restricted trade increases the wealth of a nation. They never provided the bases to explain how free trade increases the wealth of a nation. However, merchants knew that restricted trade increased their personal wealth.

As opposed to the views held by mercantilists, Smith provided an entirely new perspective to the role of foreign trade for an economy. One can understand this perspective from the way it has been narrated by Adam Smith, in his own language, which explains his understanding as well as the extent of conviction in his perspective. He describes:

> Between whatever places foreign trade is carried on, the all of them derive two distinct benefits from it. It carries out that surplus part of the produce of their land for which there is no demand among them and buys back in return for it something else for which there is demand. By means of it the narrowness of the home market does not hinder the division of labour in any particular branch of art or manufactures from being carried to the highest perfection. It encourages them to improve its productive power and augment its annual produce to the utmost and there by *increases real revenue* and *wealth of the society*. (Emphasis added; see Smith 1776 [2003], 539–540)

To illustrate his perspective on the role of foreign trade, he used the example of the nature of trade between Britain and Asia. He narrates:

> The discovery of a passage to the East Indies opened perhaps a still more extensive range of foreign commerce than that of America, notwithstanding the greater distance, the rest were mere savages. But the empires of China, Indostan, Japan, as well as other in the East Indies, without having rich mines of gold and silver, were in every other respect much richer, better cultivated and more advanced in arts and manufactures, rich and civilized nations can always exchange to a much greater value with one another. (Ibid., 546)

In his book, Smith gave emphasis on the notion that it was due to the influence of mercantilism on the policymakers that Britain and several other economies of Europe have not reaped the full potential benefits of foreign trade with the East. This has happened because of creating monopolies of trading companies. He in fact believed that 'no nation in Europe had even yet benefited from free commerce' (ibid., 554). His perspective on foreign trade also challenged the premise that trade was a *zero sum game*, which was founded on the idea that a nation can become rich only by *beggaring thy neighbours*. This thinking has given rise to a belief that gains of trade for other nations amount to their own loss. Therefore, restricted trade is must. The ideas evolved by Smith advocated *free trade*. His perspective was based on the premise of free trade and free market for providing suitable conditions for encouraging the process of creation of wealth in an economy.

For mercantilist thinkers, 'trade was a kind of war' (ibid., 515). Therefore, they justified wars for the sake of procuring, enlarging or securing monopoly right to trade. This notion had established the nexus between the merchant and the Crown. The new perspective on foreign trade believed that 'trade will always follow cheapness not conquest' (see Child, 1668 [1968], 41; Gay, 1969, Vol. II). This is because the new thinking believed in the concept of *doux commerce* (gentle trade). This was based on the proposition that 'peace is the natural effect of trade. Two nations that trade with one another become reciprocally dependent, for if one has an interest in *buying*, the other is interested in *selling*, and thus their union is founded on their mutual necessities' (Tucker, 1763, 53). Adam Smith not only developed an alternative perspective to the worldview about trade based on mercantilist ideas, but he also evaluated the role of merchants in a society. He articulated the critique of the premises on which the old social order, dominated by merchants, was based. He argued that 'the capital of merchants on the contrary, seems to have no fixed or necessary residence anywhere, but may wander about from place to place according as it can either buy cheaper or sell dear'. After stating this, he makes an important comment:

> A merchant, it has been said very properly, is not necessarily a citizen of any particular country. It is in great measure indifferent to him from what place he carries on his trade, a very trifling disgust will make him remove his capital. No part of it can be said to belong to any particular country till it has been spread as it were over the face of that country.

He does not stop here, and goes on to make a strong argument about merchants' capital when he describes 'capital that is acquired by commerce ... is very precarious and uncertain possession until some part of it has been secured and realized in the civilization and improvement out of land'.[4]

The ideas mentioned above provided ideological support to the new thinking and premises which were challenging the idea of mercantilism in general and were arguing against the founding of an empire by the East India Company in the Indian subcontinent. Smith remarked that this kind of empire was a project 'fit for a nation whose government is influenced by shopkeepers'.[5] Famous economic historian Mokyr has described this new thinking as 'Enlightened Political Economy'.[6] It was this enlightened political thinking which wrote the death warrants for all the symbols of mercantilism. The British government systematically abolished all the regulations which gave monopoly power to different rent-seeking classes. For instance, the Navigation Act was abolished in 1822; prohibition on the export of machinery was reduced in 1824 and abolished in 1843; the Corn Laws were repealed in 1846; and the monopoly of the East India Company was abolished in 1813, and it was stripped of all its commercial functions in 1833.

The analysis given above clearly narrates that the intellectuals of the period had slowly begun to think against the whole class of rent seekers, who used political patronage to redistribute wealth in their favour rather than working for increasing the wealth of the nation. The new thinking helped in creating institutional changes which had a long-run impact on the economy. These institutional changes facilitated the process of reorientation of the creative faculties of individuals away from rent seeking and towards creation of wealth. This historical transformation of the social order in Britain establishes that people's beliefs regarding the content of their lives, and principles that they accept as helpful for the creation of life they want to live and being governed, also play a significant role in determining the institutional foundation of the society. This also narrates a new perspective on the basis of institutional change, which believes that institutional changes emerge as a consequence of alliances and contradictions between different interest groups that exist at a point in time in a nation. The new perspective provides us with an alternative understanding, which suggests that sometimes new ideas may also affect changes in the institutions.

It was an irony of history that an institution like the East India Company, which was an important symbol of mercantilism, was slowly losing its significance and relevance in Britain while it was occupying the central stage in the political economy of the Indian subcontinent. Finally, in 1857, public opinion which was fast emerging against the East India Company found an important excuse to do away with the rule of the East India Company and bring all the territories held by the East India Company in the Indian subcontinent under the direct rule of the British Raj.

At that point in time, when Britain was experiencing transition from mercantilism to the supremacy of classical political economy and simultaneously experiencing transition from traditional flexible manufacturing to modern manufacturing, the Indian subcontinent was experiencing decline in its traditional flexible manufacturing. This process has already been described in Chapter 4 of this book. In the case of Britain, traditional flexible industry got transformed into modern manufacturing. This happened because traditional flexible manufacturing came to its logical irrelevance. As it has been mentioned in Chapter 1, the capital employed by merchants was quite large. This capital they gave as advance to household workshops of craftsmen. This form of organization of production did not give them power to supervise each individual unit of manufacturing. The absence of supervision on household workshops also did not provide them control on quality, efficiency and time scheduling of products. Merchants intended to come out of these conditions of helplessness. They were interested to evolve a method of production which would help them in using their managerial skills and provide them control over the organization of production along with ownership of assets.

The evolution of a new method of organization of production required the development of equipment more efficient than the hand tools used by the craftsmen and motivating them to leave their household workshops to work in centralized workshops. Evolving better equipment necessitated the conversion of the circulating capital of merchants into fixed investment. At the same time, to motivate craftsmen to leave their household workshops to work in the factories required payment of higher wages. Therefore, evolution of a method of organization of production which satisfied the needs of merchants had to wait until such equipment was invented which could more than compensate higher costs of the equipment and labour. This transformation was made possible when inanimate sources of power were used to run tools, that is, with the birth of machines. In the birth of factory as a system of production, power-driven machines played an important role. The use of power-driven machines made it possible to under-sell the products produced by the traditional flexible manufacturing.[7] Therefore, to make factories more competitive than household workshops, investment in fixed capital equipment became inevitable As proportions of fixed capital in the process of production increased, it increased the control of owners of capital on the production process. This increased control led to convergence between *ownership* and *control*.

The convergence between ownership and control altered the circumstances in which craftsmen used to work in their household workshops. The introduction of machines removed the craftsman's autonomy in the place of production. This happened because for the first time craftsmen had to leave their houses to work in the factories. In the new situation the *factory* became the place of *production* and *household* became place of *consumption*, because production shifted from household workshops to factories. In these altered circumstances, instead of tools and equipment being owned by the craftsmen, now the tools and equipment provided them employment. When craftsmen began to work in the factories, they lost their freedom regarding work schedules, pace of work and work stoppages. In factories, craftsmen worked in gangs (teams), following similar time schedules, where work began and stopped uniformly for each worker. The pace of work was determined by machines. The most important change that occurred for the craftsmen was that now they had to work under the watchful eyes of the supervisors and the foreman. The circumstances in which craftsmen were now forced to work have been very appropriately described by one of the important economic historians of the Industrial Revolution, David Landes, when he writes about the new situation for workers, 'factory was a new prison, the clock new kind of jailor' (see Landes, 1964, 43–44). However, it should also be mentioned here that the transformation of circulating capital into fixed capital made the capitalist 'prisoner of his investment' (ibid., 43).

The first factories emerged as a consequence of the process of convergence between ownership and control. This process also gave birth to a system of organization of production which was based on the *centrality* of capital and management by the owners of capital. Perhaps due to this centrality of capital and owners of capital in the new system of production, it was subsequently defined as the *capitalist system*.[8] In the beginning, the new methods of production were used in a small geographical area of Britain covering Coalbrookdale in Shropshire, Birmingham, Derby, and Preston in Lancashire.

Cotton textile manufacturing of Britain developed this kind of advantage much earlier than other manufacturing industries. The advantage occurred when there emerged, within a short period of time, several inventions regarding spinning and weaving of textiles along with the invention of steam engine. This invention created advantage of machines over handicraft-based method of production. This advantage materialized when steam power, which was harnessed by Watt's steam engine, was used to run *spinning frame* designed by Richard Arkwright. This was the first experiment to integrate inanimate sources of power and tools. Their integration resulted in the birth of machines. The integration altered the meaning of manufacturing from *made of hand* to *made of machines*. Due to this transformation in the nature of manufacturing, 'shuttle dropped from the fingers of weaver and fell into iron fingers' (see Landes, 1994, 124). The invention of *flying shuttle* by John Kay (1733) had increased the speed of weaving and thereby created a substantial gap between the speed of weaving and speed of spinning. This gap was bridged by the invention of spinning frame of Arkwright (1764). However, after the invention of *spinning jenny* by Hargreaves in 1769, cotton textile manufacturing became more competitive and productive than the traditional flexible manufacturing of textiles. The first modern cotton textile factory was established at Cromford in Derbyshire in 1771.

The adoption of modern manufacturing techniques in the manufacturing of cotton textiles occurred because at that point in time British as well as European consumers were shifting their liking from textiles made of other materials, such as wool, flex and hemp, towards cotton textile. The accessibility of cotton textiles in different qualities, varieties, colours and prices facilitated in the adoption of cotton textiles by all strata of European and British society. The other important characteristics of cotton textiles such as their being light in weight and washable fabric were quite compatible with the idea of cleanliness.[9] The increased demand for cotton textiles created necessary conditions for mechanization of different stages of processing of textiles such as spinning, weaving, finishing and printing.

The process of import substitution of Indian cotton textiles began with production of *fustian*. Fustian was developed as a cotton textile fabric by mixing linen and cotton (see Coleman, 1973; Jenkins, 1994). The production of fustian grew quite rapidly in Britain in areas such as East Anglia and Lancashire. The rapid acceptance of fustian by British customers motivated manufacturers to develop other important substitutes for Indian cotton textiles. The success of cotton textile industry in Britain created possibilities for the growth of other complementary industries, because cotton textile manufacturing became the *leading sector* of British manufacturing.[10] The changes in methods of production of cotton textiles, helped in shifting the global predominance of Indian cotton textile industry to the dominance of British cotton textile manufacturing industry. This shift established the link between the processes of decline of cotton textile in India and the emergence of Industrial Revolution in Britain. The relocation of cotton textile industry from the Indian subcontinent to Britain facilitated the birth of a trajectory of divergence between Indian subcontinent and Britain. It was this divergence which led to enhancement in the prosperity of Britain and underdevelopment of the Indian subcontinent.[11]

The spread of manufacturing in Britain also induced technological changes in other complementary industries such as mining of coal, iron and steel. Coal had emerged as a prime source of inanimate power which was used to run machines, and steel was becoming a metal for developing modern machines and equipment. Later on, expansion of railways also necessitated the production of iron and steel. Abraham Darby developed a process to transform coal into coke, which helped in minimizing the impurities in the making of iron and steel. Coke was also useful in achieving higher levels of temperatures for smelting iron. He experimented with this technique in his workshop at Coalbrookdale. Steam engine was used to pump out groundwaters, which helped in the digging of coal from deeper underground mines. Attempts were also being made by iron masters to reduce the high silicon content from coal pig iron. To reduce this impurity in the making of iron and steel, Charles and John Wood (brothers) invented the stamping and polling technique in 1761. The most important technological change in the manufacturing of iron and steel occurred when Henry Bessemer invented *Bessemer converter* in 1770.[12] The invention of Bessemer converter made the technique of mixing wrought iron with carbon—a process which used more fuel and consumed more time—totally irrelevant. The Bessemer converter instead used pig iron which already had carbon content. The steel produced with the help of Bessemer converter was quite solid and could be used for the purposes of making machines as well as for the construction of bridges and buildings.[13]

The changes in the methods of production caused by a variety of inventions during the Industrial Revolution in Britain transformed the oriental luxuries which were earlier used only by the rich and powerful citizens of Britain into products of mass consumption. These products became part of consumption pattern of different strata of the British society. The transformation of the *luxury products* into *fashionable products* increased the size of market of these products. Expanding markets provided incentive to innovators for inventing new technologies (Berg 2005). Luxury products are *exclusive* by nature, because they emerge when the social order prohibits the consumption of such products by masses. The process of technological change converted these luxury products into more *inclusive* products. Therefore, the products which were source of *pleasure of few* became source of *pleasure for many* (Berg, 2005, 21–46, 85–111). These products which had become objects of mass desire were displayed in the Great Exhibition of 1851.

It is also important to mention here that during the period of Industrial Revolution there emerged specialized manufacturers of machines and equipment. The formulation of the Copyright Act and Patent Law provided motivation to master craftsmen to devote their capabilities to invent and design new sets of machines and equipment which could be used in improving productivity and efficiency in different manufacturing enterprises. The existence of these laws protected the intellectual property of craftsmen and provided them the opportunity of earning returns on their intellectual capital. This trend was a significant departure from the past because earlier craftsmen use to make their own tools. These new manufacturers of capital goods developed machines which were general purpose machines that could be used across several manufacturing industries, as well as specialized machines and equipment which were useful for a specific manufacturing industry. In the new circumstances, even merchants could buy these machines to establish manufacturing enterprises. Historical evidence suggests that the use of modern machines in the British manufacturing enterprises was a long drawn out process rather than a distinct revolutionary event or a sudden break from the past. The process of adoption of modern technology was neither linear nor continuous. In some of the manufacturing units, crafts-based methods of production and use of machines were simultaneously used giving a characteristic of dualism to the British manufacturing enterprises.[14] The widespread adoption and use of modern machines was also hampered for some time by the anti-machinery *Luddite Movement*.[15]

The emergence of ideological changes in the new power elite and birth of modern manufacturing in Britain impacted the tale of the four cities significantly. To understand the significance of these events that occurred in Britain on the tale of the four cities, remembering two important dates is quite relevant. These two dates are 1760 and 1851. It was around the year 1760 when the process of emergence of modern manufacturing began in Britain. The year coincides with the beginning of the geographical expansion of the East India Company in the Indian subcontinent in 1757. This coincidence tells us that while British manufacturers were beginning to influence the British policy-making, at that point in time the Company of merchants of Britain was consolidating its political power in the Indian subcontinent. In fact, the Company was playing an important historical role to convert the Indian subcontinent into a supplier of raw materials and consumer of the products produced by the British manufacturers by means of facilitating the process of de-industrialization.

The second important date which is relevant for the tale of the four cities is 1851. This date is important for British manufacturers because on this date they celebrated the global supremacy of British manufacturing by organizing the Great Exhibition. The significance of this historical event with regard to the four cities is that it almost coincides with the end of rule of the East India Company and the beginning of the British Raj in 1857. It is important to mention here that when the Indian subcontinent encountered the East India Company, the subcontinent was ruled by the Mughal Empire, and was an important place of manufactured goods and also a wealthier place than the British Empire. When the Indian subcontinent came into direct contact with the British Raj, it was gradually converted into an impoverished economy devoid of its manufacturing strength and eventually emerged as a supplier of raw materials. These vital changes had also influenced how an average British citizen perceived the Indian subcontinent.

In the section that follows, we analyse the impact of transfer of power, to govern Indian subcontinent from the East India Company to British Raj, on the economy and polity of the Indian subcontinent. The shift in the political power from the East India Company amounts to analysing the consequences of shift in the dominant interest of merchants to the centrality of the interests of British manufacturers in the policy making in Britain on the Indian subcontinent.

STRUCTURE OF GOVERNANCE
DURING THE BRITISH RAJ

The rule of the East India Company was abolished by the British Crown and the Parliament by the Better Government of India Act, 1858. The transfer of power of administration from the East India Company to the British Crown made the reality quite apparent to Indian masses that now on the Indian subcontinent will be directly governed by the British Raj and not by any of its proxies. The transfer of all the territories ruled by the Company to the British Crown created a unitary political entity called India. This historical change altered the nature of governance in India. Before 1857, the rule of the East India Company was conducted by the Board of Directors, which was elected by the stockholders of the company. The Board of Directors reported to the Board of Control, a body which was set up by the British government in 1784. The Board of Directors run the Company with the help of writers, merchandizers and examiners. The Company's directors also appointed several officials to run the business of the Company in the Indian subcontinent. The highest positon to run the administration of the Company in the India subcontinent was held by the Governor-General, who looked after the operation of the Company from his office at Calcutta. Next in hierarchy were the Governors of the Bombay and the Madras Presidencies. This structure of governance was replaced by a new structure.

In the new structure of governance, the Board of Directors of the Company along with the Board of Control was replaced by the office of Secretary of State and his Advisory Board. The office of Secretary of State was held by a person who enjoyed the confidence of the ruling party in the British Parliament. The office of Governor-General was replaced by the Viceroy. The position of Viceroy was described as 'Incessant grind' because he had to maintain line of information with the British Crown, the Secretary of State, his advisors, governors and residents in different princely sates. Therefore, the person who was appointed as the Viceroy of India expected 'Hard Work and plenty of it was all they could expect'.[16] Similarly, the offices of examiners and writers were replaced by permanent secretaries. Prior to the formation of the new structure of governance, the administration of the Company was quite authoritarian and enjoyed autonomy from any external influence. In the new administrative structure, the ruling political party in the British Parliament assumed importance in policy formulation. The increasing role of the British Parliament in the administration of India provided possibilities for the influence of different pressure groups that existed in the British polity. There existed several pressure groups in the polity of Britain who had interest in the policy formulations regarding the Indian economy. Some of these pressure groups were cotton textile manufacturers of Manchester and Lancashire, jute manufacturers of Dundee, salt manufacturers of Cheshire, and merchants involved in the trading of tea, opium and indigo during the rule of the East India Company. The civil servants who were running the administration of the Company were trained at the East India College, which was located at Haileybury in Hertfordshire. The college was founded in 1805. The civil servants who were trained here used to receive grounding in classical political economy. It is also worth mentioning here that some of the important scholars who made significant contribution to the literature on political economy were holding important positions in the college. In the beginning, between 1805 and 1834, the famous scholar Malthus occupied the chair on political economy. The same chair was occupied by Richard Jones during 1833–1855. The last occupant of this chair was James Stephen who occupied the chair from 1855 to 1858, until the year the college was closed.

The civil servants who ran the governance of the British Raj were selected through a competitive exam. These civil servants were trained to rule not serve, though 'by ruling they served' (see James, 1997, 308). The candidates who were selected for the Indian Civil Service (ICS) were not necessarily great scholars or intellectuals, but were expected to have capability to collect information or data to argue on subjects logically. Collection of data had become their passion, perhaps at that point in time statistics was known as *political arithmetic*. However, some civil servants were at variance with this stereotype. The scholars who have conducted research on the history of the British Raj must be familiar with the writings of Malcom Darling on Punjab, William Todd on Rajasthan and W. W. Hunter's work on Bengal (see Darling, 1926; Hunter, 1868, 1888 [1974]; Todd, 1829). The example of Darling is quite interesting. He joined the ICS in 1905 and found that he and his wife Josie were misfits in the community of civil servants. The posting of Darling in Rajasthan was in fact a punishment posting for his 'refusal to the mores and habits of his colleagues' (see James, 1997, 308).

For students who entered the ICS, the study of the writings of some of the prominent classical political economists was compulsory reading. The most important amongst them were Adam Smith and David Ricardo. The positions in the ICS were generally preferred by the British middle classes, 'bright young sons of provincial professionals' (ibid., 311). This happened because the introduction of open competitive exams replaced nepotism by meritocracy, that is, it provided scope to merit rather than family and kinship connections. Therefore, the principle of *free competition*, which was an important premise on which classical political economy was based, had special appeal for the middle classes. In the British social order of that time, tenants of orthodox Christianity had been replaced by protestant ethic and the existence of all kinds of monopolies was replaced by open access. It is also important to mention here that the principles of political economy became the guiding principles for the formulation of policy in Britain as well as in its colonies. Despite the fact that there existed several strands of thought amongst classical political economists, there also existed certain issues on which there was consensus amongst all political economists. Most of them accepted that policies of the government should not affect the working of free markets; in fact, they advocated that government policies should be used to make markets more efficient. To make markets free and efficient, policymakers of the British Raj advocated for (a) free inter-regional trade, (b) government regulations to be introduced in those areas where market fails and (c) introduction of property rights and regulations to enforce contracts (see Ferguson, 2004, 186).

When the Indian subcontinent came in direct contact with the British Empire, it intended to create its new image through the British Raj. For this, the British Empire wanted to erase the image created by the rule of the East India Company, which acted as an agency of the British Empire to transfer resources from the Indian subcontinent to Britain. The British Raj intended to project itself as an institution which provides impartial justice in a society which was segmented into different religions and was also hierarchical due to the prevalence of caste system. Therefore, unlike the Mughal state which did not legislate by depending on the conventional legal framework that existed in the form of a community-based redressal system,[17] the British Raj believed in legislative state.

In the case of Europe, legislative, judicial and executive powers of the state were enjoyed by the state itself. In Europe, legal experts used their expertise for interpretation and reformulation of laws over time to support the state to enjoy legitimacy, a system which was termed as sovereignty. As a consequence of this process, a high degree of juridification became part of the European political system. Unlike Europe, in India, there was no place for the rulers to act as law givers, because in India law was not within the domain of royal power. In fact, in India, law kept its distance from royal authority.

It obtained legitimacy from an independent source called *Dharma*. 'Dharma is born in a sovereign domain, where king's foot cannot tread'.[18] Therefore, in India, the maxims of the Indian way of life or civil morality remained exclusively under the domain of the *dharma shastras* and thus beyond the purview of powers of the rulers. Due to this reason, despite the fact that traditional written laws are the oldest in India, existence of law has been independent of the state (see Kolff, 2008, 53). Looking at this important characteristic of the Indian state, Hegel described, 'if China may be regarded nothing else but a state, Hindu political existence presents us with a people but not state'.[19] The rulers of Mughal India were also guided by Islamic laws. Therefore, the Mughal state was also not a legislative state. This happened because the Mughal state accepted the supremacy of communities who were guided by their own laws and regulated the conduct of their members. The Mughal state intervened only in instances when there emerged inter-community disputes (Hegel, 1857 [1901], 157).

The British policymakers believed that Indian society needed modern laws, and wanted to project that only the British Raj can provide impartial justice and establish a legal framework, which were necessary for the smooth functioning of the market economy. The British government also intended to establish that British rule was necessary in India, otherwise the fragmented and hierarchical society that exist in the Indian subcontinent would lead to a fragmented polity. The Regulation Act of 1773 laid the foundation for the establishment of the Supreme Court of India. The Court was established to obey the principle of extraterritoriality of all the British citizens in the Indian subcontinent. The attempt was to send the message that British citizens, wherever they lived in the colonies of the British Empire, would be subjected only to British laws. The premise on which this principle was based established that irrespective of the country where British citizens were settled as colonizers, they would be tried by English courts, presided over by British judges, according to British laws, and their cases argued by advocates trained in British laws. The rule of law means equality in justice. This was in reality impossible because British subjects were considered to be above law, and the courts protected their acts of omission and commission.

The first example where the extraterritorial principle was used immediately after the founding of the Supreme Court in India was the case of Nand Kumar. Nand Kumar, who was *diwan* of the Nawab of Bengal, filed a case in the court of Bengal. The case was filed against Warren Hastings, in which he charged him of taking bribe of £35,000 for helping an individual to get appointment in the court of the nawab. The case was filed in the Supreme Court in 1775. In reaction to this case, Warren Hastings sued him for forging the document which Nand Kumar had filed as a proof of the bribe. The first chief justice of India, Elijah Impey, was a close friend of Warren Hastings and gave Nand Kumar death sentence on the charges of forgery. The forging of document was not a serious crime to be punished by death sentence. This was described at that time as a *judicial murder* (see Kolsky, 2010). Similar was the fate of William Orby Hunter, who was an indigo planter when his case was filed in the Supreme Court in 1794. Hunter was charged with the brutal torture of three of his female servants. Even for his brutal act, his punishment was just to pay fine (ibid., 2). To highlight these acts of discrimination by the British court, Bal Gangadhar Tilak aptly described the prevailing reality of the colonial justice system, when he wrote, 'The Goddess of British justice, though blind, is able to distinguish between black and white' (ibid., 4). The British Raj also evolved a legal framework to provide right to property and enforce contracts for the smooth functioning of the market.

The same consequences were experienced when, to regulate the behaviour of indisciplined British citizens and native Indians, British administration began the process of codification of laws in India. For this purpose, the British government promulgated the Indian Penal Code (IPC) in 1860, drafted by Thomas Babington Macaulay. However, Kolsky, one of the scholars who has done detailed analysis of the colonial justice system, tells us that there were 'far more executions of Europeans in India pre-1860 than there were after the promulgation of IPC' (see Kolsky, 2010, 12). Due to the existence of discrimination in the provisioning of justice, the law constructed race in British India' (ibid., 13). The purpose for creating a codified universal logical system of law was to 'protect Indians from a new breed of Brahmins' (see Kolsky, 2010, 69). However, the IPC did not establish uniform laws of jurisdiction; it instead established special privileges for the British, and maintained racial exclusivity of the 'new Brahmins'.

In the perception of the British administration, the Mughal Empire existed in the centrality of the imagination of Indians. Even the East India Company enjoyed diwani right in Bengal granted by the Mughal emperor. Moreover, when several sections of the Indian polity and society organized rebellion against the rule of the Company, they accepted Mughal emperor Bahadur Shah Zafar as their undisputed leader. This fact forced the British government to project the British Raj as a replacement of the Mughal Empire. To project this new idea, the British administration organized the Delhi Darbar in 1876. The Delhi Darbar was organized to revive the Mughal tradition to display the imperial splendour. Around 400 princes were invited to participate in the event. This event was organized to emphasize that the paramountcy of the Mughal Empire had been replaced by the centralized authority of the British Raj. Therefore, all the princes who attended the event henceforth be loyal to the British Raj (see Travers, 2007, 11–19). To this historical event, Sir Dinakar Rao, Chief Minister of Maharaja of Gwalior, commented, 'India has been until now a vast heap of stones some of them small, now from roof to basement, each stone of it is in its right place' (see James, 2003, 316).

In the new circumstances, the direct rule of the British Empire made it obvious that henceforth the interests of British manufacturers will directly influence the British policymaking for the Indian subcontinent. This was apparent because by this time the interests of British manufacturers had assumed importance in the British policymaking. This shift in the priority of the British policymakers had altered the circumstances for the Indian manufacturers. This happened because the buffer that existed between interests of Indian manufacturers and British manufacturers, namely the East India Company, no longer existed. It had gone into oblivion after playing its historical role. In the section that follows, we will see how the shift in the nature of governance during the British Raj affected the policy regime in India.

POLICY REGIME CHANGES
DURING THE BRITISH RAJ

It has already been described in the first section of this chapter that by 1851 British manufacturers had achieved global competitive advantage. They achieved this advantage with the help of several inventions which transformed their traditional flexible manufacturing into modern manufacturing. This gave them competitive advantage over the traditional manufacturing of the Indian subcontinent: As it has been described in Chapter 3 of book, the major portion of the traditional flexible manufacturing industry of India had experienced decline. Therefore, the British policymakers found it most appropriate to follow the policy of free trade, which had ideological support in classical political economy. The East India Company did not exist any longer which had vested interest in challenging free trade. This is because the East India Company used to earn profits from the sale of products made by Indian traditional manufacturers. So long the East India Company existed, it enjoyed monopoly of trade with India, being a company protected by the royal charter. It was this status given to the East India Company which had denied the access of Indian markets to the British manufacturers. After ending the monopoly of trade of the East India Company with India in 1830, the British government granted them open access the Indian markets. Therefore, it was in the interests of British manufacturers that the British government followed the policy of free trade in order to help them get free access to the vast Indian markets.

It is important to mention that the same British manufacturers had achieved competitive advantage by forcing the British government to impose tariffs on import of Indian textiles in particular and other foreign products in general. Not only this, the interests of the infant manufacturing sector of Britain were protected by the British state. It also protected the interests of British manufacturers by waging wars against potential competitive nations. Once British manufacturers had established global competitive advantage, tariffs were not in their interest any longer. Existence of tariff was helping the interest of British landed gentry because it helped them to maintain higher price of food grains and agricultural raw materials. Both the advantages of the landed gentry were working against the manufacturers. The higher prices of food grains increased the level of wages and higher prices of raw materials increased the costs of production. Both the factors increased the prices of manufactured goods. Therefore, by advocating the policy of free trade, they were ensuring and protecting the competitive advantage of British manufacturers. Due to this protected environment, the British manufacturers achieved competitive advantage even during the stage of infancy from regulated trade. Since Industrial Revolution occurred for the first time in Britain, it also became an important example of *infant industry argument* (Dutt 1956, 103). The classical political economists accepted that when manufacturing in any country is at the stage of infancy it needs protection.

The principles of economics provided ideological support to the British manufacturers at both the stages of its evolution. While it was at the stage of infancy, it received support from the mercantilist school which advocated imposing tariffs on imports, and when it reached the stage of maturity, it received support from classical political economy which supported the idea of free trade. Thus, it was ideologically supported by classical political economy. Classical political economy also supported the interests of manufacturers by supporting the formation of institutions and legal framework which would protect private property rights, help in enforcing contracts, provide freedom to enterprise and protect free markets. The classical political economists believed that such institutions were necessary for the smooth functioning of efficient market economies. These economists also advocated that if in any economy such institutions do not exist and existing social framework and belief system act as constraints in the emergence of such institutions, the state should create them through legislations. Their belief was based on the premise that it is the *invisible hand* of the free market which provides freedom of opportunity to create wealth.

Taking support from the principle advocated by classical political economy, the British Raj followed the policy of free trade in India, while all other independent nations of the world were protecting the interests of their home producers by erecting tariff walls on the entry of foreign goods. Tariffs were raised in Germany by Bismarck in 1879, by France in 1881, by Russia in 1882, America in 1890 and Canada in 1897 (see Dutt, 1956). The British government systematically projected that it did not intend to interfere in the working of free market and kept on following the policy of free trade. Because of these reasons 'the role of state was modest one. In no decade between 1872 and 1947 did the state's annual share of GNP average more than 10 percent' (Morris, 1987, cited in Tripathi, 1991, 124). Despite the fact that the role of state during the British Raj was insignificant, its indirect influences on the economy were quite significant. The indirect role of the government emerges as a consequence of sources from where it earns its revenue and where it spends its earning, that is, through the pattern of its earning and expenditure. It is only due to insignificant direct involvement of state in the economy of India it was perceived that in India functioning of the market economy was not impacted by the state. This perception led to misconception that if modern manufacturing did not emerge in India during the British Raj, then its causes should be located in the endogenous factors. The endogenous factors identified by some of the economists were lack of opportunities to invest, segmented markets, absence of capital market, dependence on imported plant and machinery and shortage of managerial talent. These factors were held responsible for the delays in the emergence of modern manufacturing because during the rule of the British Raj 'market was given its head, British India was the great social experiment in letting interest and market forces do virtually everything' (see Morris, 1987). The absence of the role of state during the British Raj has been described as 'night watchman role of state' (ibid., 124; Morris, 1982, 555–675). In fact, the British government played the role of night watchman to provide free market and fee trade in the Indian economy to protect the interests of British manufacturers in disguise.[20] It is also important to inform that while imports from Britain were allowed without tariffs, exports from India to Britain were subjected to tariffs. This was the true face of the colonial government policy of free trade. This discriminating nature of free trade has been described as *one-way free trade* (see Morris, 1987, 154, fn. 4).

This suggests that the view of scholars who advocate that reasons for delay in the emergence of modern industries in India were endogenous to the Indian economy, which restricted the efficient working of market, needs correction. Therefore, the reference to certain supply-side problems such as lack of means of transportation and communication, lack of social and economic infrastructure, and less availability of skilled manpower and managerial talent, and demand-side problems such as existence of mass poverty, income inequalities, and fragmented market as constraints on the growth of manufacturing products of standardized level at large scale needs correction. The absence of several supply factors did not stop the birth of the Industrial Revolution in Britain. It is a hard historical fact that in Britain these preconditions did not exist when modern manufacturing was emerging. The innovations in the means of transportation and communication occurred after the lag of around seven to eight decades. Modern manufacturing evolved around 1760,[21] whereas railways were developed in Britain in the 1830s, telegraph around 1840[22] and global connectivity of telegraph was achieved in 1870.[23] Britain also did not have institutions to impart skills to its manpower. Britain in fact depended on the method of apprenticeship system, where senior craftsmen trained new workers.[24] The most important factor which was missing was the rule of the nation state.

It was the responsibility of the colonial state to develop necessary infrastructure, which was necessary for the development of the economy. The British Raj even safeguarded the interests of the colonial state while developing this infrastructure. This aspect of the colonial state became obvious when the British government took an important decision to develop railways in India. Although it was the East India Company which had initiated the process of developing railways in India in 1845, when the first railway line was constructed between Bombay and Thane. However, development of the railways was strategically used by the British Raj to protect the vested interests of the colonial state. The Sepoy Mutiny or First War of Independence forced the British Raj to develop railways rapidly and at massive scale for the purposes of maintaining administration and defence of the country. This became necessary because railways could help movement of troops, necessary military hardware and officials of the Raj to different locations rapidly and at massive scale. Moreover, by this time the Indian economy had been transformed from a manufacturing economy into a supplier of raw materials for British manufacturing enterprises. Therefore, development of railway connectivity between centres of production of raw materials and port cities for exports was very important for the colonial state. Therefore, initially, the railway connectivity was developed between port cities and important centres of raw material production. To achieve these objectives, three important port cities, which were also Presidency towns of the British Empire, had been already connected with their raw material-producing hinterland during the rule of the East India Company. Bombay was connected with its hinterland in 1853, Calcutta in 1854 and Madras in 1856. In addition, railway expansion became an important means to sell British manufactured goods across different parts of the Indian economy. Hence, railways assumed strategic importance for the British Raj to maximize its political as well as commercial interests.[25]

To reduce the chances of occurrence of another episode like 1857, the British administration wanted to develop and expand network of railways across India in the shortest possible time. Rapid expansion of railways was not possible without having enormous financial resources. To solve the problem of financial constraint, the British government invited private investment in the development of Indian railways. To provide incentive for private investment by British citizens, the British government guaranteed 5 per cent return on their investments. In the event of railway companies not making profits, the British government guaranteed to compensate them. This promise of the government motivated British citizens to invest in the railway companies. The guarantee of return on investment flooded the railway companies with necessary finances. It has to be remembered that such an option was not given to Indians. The guarantee of return on investment given to the private railway companies was based on an understanding that the government had right to buy back the railway lines after the lapse of 25 years. The mode of financing for development of railways in India was perhaps the first historical example of private–public participation (PPP). By following this method of financing development of railways, the government became the owner of 67 per cent of total investment in India by 1921.[26]

The guarantee on the returns on investment by the British government encouraged several private companies to invest in the expansion
of railways. These private companies developed their own network of
railway lines. Each company specialized in developing railways in a
particular region. Some of the important railway companies were East
Indian Railway Company, Great Indian Peninsula Railway Company,
Scinde Punjab and Delhi Railway, and North Western State Railway.
Apart from these major railway companies, some minor railway companies ware also floated which provided railway services to smaller
areas, such as Rajputana–Malwa Railway, East Coast Railway, Bengal
Nagpur Railway and Madras Railway. There also existed a railway
network developed by the British government to earn income for
the government. As a consequence of all these investments, both by
public and private sector companies, by the beginning of the First
World War, the total distance covered by the entire railway network
consisted of 40,000 km.[27]

This is also an important historical fact that while developing the
Indian railways, the government encouraged investments in Britain,
because it purchased most of the machines, equipment, locomotives,
railway wagons, rails, rolling stock and track material, rail signalling
equipment, and the like from British suppliers. Therefore, a very large
part of finances raised in Britain flowed back to Britain. This happened
because all the purchases for developing railways in India were made
by floating tenders only in Britain. This practice also supported the
interests of British manufacturers.[28] By following such discriminatory
policies, the British government denied the Indian economy the economic advantages arising from the development of railways.

Indian railways could have benefited the Indian economy or might
have emerged as a leading sector in the growth process of the Indian
economy as it had emerged in the case of America. This would have
happened provided the British government had initiated a policy for
buying railway equipment from India-based vendors. This policy
would have impacted the growth of Indian manufacturing significantly
by encouraging investment in the manufacturing industries which
have strong technological linkages with the development of railways,
such as iron and steel industry, coal mining, manufacturing of railway

wagons and signalling equipment. If the government of Britain had accepted tenders only from those companies which were based in India, it would have provided incentive to several foreign companies to establish their manufacturing facilities in India, which would have in turn provided learning opportunities to Indian entrepreneurs and development of skills amongst Indians.

The British government not only outsourced all the requirements for developing railways in India, it was also an important feature of the British Raj that it followed the policy of buying stores from Britain. Governments of almost all countries are big buyers of all kinds of indigenously manufactured goods, a policy which provides support to native manufacturers. The policy of buying stores from Britain encouraged the manufacturers of Britain, and it simultaneously reduced the impact of government expenditure on the Indian economy. Government expenditure is an important component of the aggregate demand of the economy, which can be used to take the economy to a higher level of equilibrium. The purchasing of stores from Britain continued from 1858 to 1885. This policy not only affected the process of development of the Indian economy, it also increased the extent of payments made in sterling. This payment in sterling affected the current account balance of the Indian economy. Under these conditions, Lord Salisbury suggested in 1876 that stores should be purchased in India. His suggestions were ignored by the British government. To change the existing policy to buying stores in India rather than from Britain, Lord Ripon introduced an important resolution in 1883 (Sen, 1972, Chapter II; Seth, 1987, 33–34). However, Indian manufacturers had to wait until 1885 to get advantage of government purchases for its requirement.

Apart from discriminating policies which the British government followed, as mentioned above, the government also followed the policy of discriminating freight rates. The freight rates varied for movement of goods from port cities to the inland destinations in comparison to movement of cargo from one city to another. This practice was followed to facilitate the international trade rather than inter-regional trade in the domestic economy. The Indian nationalist leaders provided several examples of this kind of discrimination to British authorities.

One such important anomaly in the freight rates was that the transportation of imported matches from Bombay port to Delhi cost the same tariff as what was charged for transporting them from Ahmedabad to Delhi, despite the fact that the distance between Delhi and Ahmedabad was 483 km less (Rungta, 1970). The facts regarding the development of railways in India amply demonstrate that the main objective of developing railways in India was to facilitate the export of raw materials and control the administration of the Indian subcontinent rather than providing a necessary condition for the growth of the Indian economy. John Keay, a prominent historian, has very appropriately described development of railways in India as 'trains and drains'—to develop trains for drain of resources (see Keay, 2010, 450).

The basic premise on which the policies of the colonial state were based underwent fundamental changes during the First World War. The wartime needs altered global economic forces which compelled the British government to deviate from its basic principle of policy-making. Some policies changed because the British government had to give some concessions to the Indian economy since Indian nationalist leaders helped the British government by supporting the war effort. Therefore, to satisfy some of the demands of the nationalist leaders, the government appointed the Indian Industrial Commission in 1916, followed by forming the Indian Fiscal Commission in 1922, and subsequently their demands were also considered under the Montagu–Chelmsford Reforms in 1921. These committees advocated giving certain amount of autonomy to the policymaking in India rather than it being formulated entirely in Britain. Historians have different views on these events on policymaking. Economic historians such as Amiya Bagchi, Basudev Chatterji, Rajat Kanta Roy and B. R. Tomilson do not believe that these changes in any way altered the policy regime followed by the British Raj.[29] Historians like Dewey argue that these committees and reforms added a certain amount of sovereignty to the policymaking of British administration in India. This partial shift of policymaking in India opened the possibilities for the influence of different pressure groups, which were emerging as a consequence of existence of the Congress party and the associations of different businesses.[30]

For a very short period, the Labour Party formed government in Britain during 1929–1931. The government of Labour Party was a little more sympathetic to the interests of Indian manufacturers and was willing to accommodate their interests. However, global economic environment experienced significant changes during the Great Depression of the 1930s, which affected the economies of Europe as well as Britain. The new circumstances forced the British government to deviate from the policies based on laissez faire and free trade. This happened because each economy wanted to protect its market by imposing tariffs on imports and also necessitated government intervention in running the economies. The Great Depression spread from its centres of the world market to countries which were their peripheries (i.e., colonies) like an epidemic. When the colonies received this virus, the disease became more acute. This is because viruses affect weaker metabolism more seriously and also for a longer duration. By the 1930s, the Indian economy had also internalized modern manufacturing; though it was not very large, nevertheless it required policies to sustain itself. For the first time, the British government imposed tariff on imports, because at the same time the British government had also imposed tariffs to protect its own manufacturers. The imposition of tariffs benefited all these Indian manufacturers who were manufacturing import substitutes. This increased the demand for such products which were produced locally for domestic markets because imported products had become expensive. Therefore, tariff imposed during the Great Depression helped the growth of industries such as cotton textiles, sugar and steel manufacturing.

The Great Depression came to end with the beginning of Second World War in 1939. As a consequence of the War, foreign trade flows experienced cessation due to disruption of sea routes. Moreover, when Japan entered the War, it brought war near the boundaries of India. India under these circumstances became an important military base for defence supplies including arms and ammunition for the operation of allied forces. During this war, ordnance factories started manufacturing several kinds of arms and munition. The emerging situation also necessitated the cooperation of Indian manufacturers to help the British government to fulfil its wartime needs. Therefore, in order to compel Indian manufacturers to work according to wartime needs, the government gave up the policy of laissez faire and imposed several restrictions on the Indian manufacturers by promulgating the Defence of India Act, 1939, and the Rules Made Thereunder. These Rules gave far-reaching powers to the British administration to interfere in the working of Indian manufacturing enterprises. Rule 81 of the Defence of India Rules provided power to the state to regulate or prohibit production of certain products. Similarly, Rule 84 provided authority to prohibit import or export of certain products to control the flow of foreign exchange. The government of the British Raj used provisions laid down in the Defence of India Act to regulate the manufacturing activities in India.[31] It is by using these Rules that the British Raj acquired the plants and machines employed in Jaya Engineering Works and Texmaco for the use of its army during the Second World War (see Piramal, 1998).

The narrative given above clearly establishes that the British Raj followed the policies which are generally followed by a colonial state. It followed the policy of free trade and laissez faire so long it was compatible with the interests of British manufacturers. When it deviated from these policies, the deviation occurred to protect the interests of British manufacturers. The behaviour of the state during the British Raj has been very appropriately been described by Robert Travers, when he writes, 'The British in India were destined to remain a society of temporary exiles rather than settlers, and a class of rulers rigidly separated from those they ruled' (see Travers, 2007, 29).

It is interesting to mention that despite the existence of several types of implicit or explicit discriminations that have been described above, in the policy pursued by the British Raj modern manufacturing enterprises did make their emergence in India. This happened because historical circumstances provided the presence of all important preconditions that are necessary for the emergence of modern manufacturing. There had always existed in India a variety of raw materials and abundant supply of entrepreneur aptitude in the form of several communities of merchants. These merchants had made substantial wealth from long-distance trade in commodities such as cotton, jute and opium, which they could invest in capital needed to float manufacturing enterprises.

Some of the merchants had also earned experience of running businesses by participating in the traditional flexible manufacturing by organizing networks of craftsmen. The communities of merchants who had migrated from Surat to Bombay had accumulated financial resources by trading in cotton and opium. Similarly, there also existed concentration of entrepreneurial talent which was engaged in the running of agency houses in Calcutta. These two groups of merchants located at two different colonial cities promoted two different modern manufacturing industries in India. The Bombay-based merchants established several cotton textile mills, whereas the Calcutta-based agency houses floated several mills to manufacture jute textiles. In the chapter that follows, we look at the experience of the four cities during the British Raj. The purpose is to understand the consequences of changes in the structure of governance and shifts in policy regimes that were affected by the British Raj on the tale of the four cities. This is because in the altered circumstances the destiny of these four cities got embedded in the conditions created by the British Raj.

NOTES

1. For detailed understanding of Physiocratic ideas, see Meek (1962), Robins (1979) and Baumol (2002).
2. For the ideas on mercantilism, see Hecksher (1935).
3. Adam Smith's ideas against mercantilism are available in his book Wealth of Nations, Book IV chapter I, Smith (1776 [2003]).
4. These are the ideas of famous thinker Montesquieu which have been referred in Mokyr (2009, 65).
5. These ideas are given in Smith (1776 [2003], 563) and Winch (1978, 32).
6. The idea of Enlightened Political Economy has been described in Mokyr (2009, Chapter IV, 63–78).
7. To understand how the traditional flexible manufacturing was transformed into modern manufacturing, see Mathias (1959), Redlick (1964) and Seth (2003).
8. For understanding the evolutions of factory system of production, see Seth (2015), Chapter II, 47–57.
9. For detailed understanding of this increasing demand of cotton textile, see Harte (1997) and Lemire (1991, 2004).
10. Rostow has described cotton textile manufacturing industry of Britain as leading sector of the economy, because it provided impetus to several other manufacturing industries, which have strong technological links with it, see Rostow (1957) and Rostow (1963).
11. For the emergence of the process of divergence in detail, which led to growth in Britain and de-industrialization in India, see Riello and Parthsarthi (2009) and Riello and Roy (ed.) (2009).

12. For understanding regarding technological changes that occurred in the manufacturing of steel, see Singer et al. (1950), Vols. I and II.
13. For the knowledge regarding technological changes that occurred during the period of industrial revolution in Britain, see Rider (2007, Vols. I and II), and Horn (2007).
14. For understanding the dualistic nature of British manufacturing enterprises, see Behagg (1998), Triblicock (1969), Berg (1993) and Seth (2015, Chapter II).
15. Anti-machine rhetoric is an on-going theme in the working class movement in Britain. Machine breaking amongst luddites has provided enough material for the historians of British labour movement; for details, see Berg (1980, 15–17).
16. For details regarding the office of Viceroy, see James (2003, 313–315).
17. For these ideas, see Bhattacharya (1965) and Hoznetly (1972).
18. For details, see chapter 1 of the book.
19. For details, see Lingat (1973), Mommsen and Moor (eds.) 1992 and Koff (2008).
20. For this idea, see Ray (1992, 66).
21. According to some of the scholars, industrial revolution began in Britain in 1760; see Neff (1943) and Ashton (1948).
22. American scientist Samuel Morse had developed electric telegraph along with the codes in 1838. It was introduced along the stretch of railway lines out of London in 1839; see Cairncross (2001, 23).
23. In 1857, it took 40 days for news of Indian mutiny to reach London. However after the establishment of several telegraphic lines which connected India with London by 1870, a message from India to London could be conveyed in hours, see Solymar (1999); p.3.
24. For details, see Habakkuk (1962), Smith (1967), Treblicock (1969), Behagg (1998) and Berg (1993).
25. For details, see Macpherson (1955, 180) and Morris and Dudley (1975).
26. For details regarding this practice, see Morris and Dudley (1975), Tomilson (1981, 1993) and Sarkar (1983).
27. For the development of Indian railways, see Thorner (1951), Astha (1976) and Hurd (1982, 758).
28. For details regarding government purchases, see Labman (1965).
29. For the ideas of these economists, see Bagchi (1972), Tomilson (1979) and Chatterjee (1983).
30. For the arguments given by Dewey, see Dewey (1981).
31. For details, see Government of India (1939), Marathe (1986) and Mohan (1992).

Tale of Four Cities and the British Raj

The birth of the British Raj led to a paradigm shift in the nature of governance, and shifts in policy regimes were experienced by the people living in the Indian subcontinent. Since in Britain, predominance of the interests of manufacturers was accepted as a premise for policymaking, it came into direct conflict with the interests of Indian flexible manufacturing. A very large segment of traditional flexible manufacturing of the Indian subcontinent had declined. Britain had developed the capability to supply cheaper and better manufactured products, which had significantly replaced the local crafts-based products produced by its craftsmen. By 1857, the Indian subcontinent had become supplier of raw materials for British manufacturing enterprises. The policies of laissez-faire and free trade provided free access to British manufacturers to the vast continent-sized Indian market. In altered circumstances, Indian merchants had become a part of the supply chain which was established to procure and export Indian raw materials to Britain. The British Raj had created necessary social, legal and economic infrastructure to facilitate this process. In the new political environment, the colonial cities of Bombay and Calcutta assumed greater significance as gateways for the drain of Indian resources. It is thus very appropriate that the British Raj constructed Gateway of India at Bombay. During this period, the cities of Surat and Dacca were still part of the Raj, but had become peripheral to its interests.

We have already described in Chapter 4 of the book that after the end of the monopoly of trade of the East India Company several agency houses were established in India, which were largely located in the Presidency towns of Calcutta and Bombay. These agency houses were either agents of the companies who were selling manufactured items produced by British manufacturers in India, or were agents of British companies to supply them different raw materials. They accumulated large financial resources; some of these big agency houses had Indian partners or promoters. These houses had made profits from the export of opium, indigo and cotton from India. The Indian merchants and British merchants who were participating in these agency houses had accumulated much wealth, which later on provided necessary financial resources for investments in promoting modern manufacturing enterprises.

The Suez Canal, opened in 1869, was designed and constructed by a French engineer Ferdinand de Lesseps and was largely financed by French. When the governments of Egypt and Turkey were under financial crises, in 1874, British Prime Minister Disraeli purchased 44 per cent of the shares of Suez Canal Company from the Khedive of Egypt for £4 million by using the finances of the Rothschilds.[1] The opening of the Suez Canal reduced the distance between Britain and India significantly, which not only reduced the distance but also reduced the travel time significantly. It was at the same time that the inventions of telephone and telegraph were assuming greater importance, because by this time, underwater cable work was complete to link the continents. This suggests that the process of integration of British and Indian markets was almost complete by this time. The development of railways in India had also linked most of the raw material-producing areas with important port cities. The railways had also helped in creating inter-regional connectivity within the Indian subcontinent and had facilitated in the evolution of a national market. Similar was the role of development of telephone and telegraph in India, though the purpose of developing these items of infrastructure was to help the colonial state to appropriate greater volume of resources of the Indian subcontinent and to use them to maintain political hegemony of the British Raj.

All the developments given above were intended to achieve the objectives of the colonial state; however, its unintended consequences were beyond the control of the colonial administration because they were beyond the imagination of colonial administrators. Bombay's significance increased in 1833 after the abolition of monopoly of trade with India given to the East India Company. Its importance further increased when Chinese market was opened by the British army in 1842. These two intertwined changes provided some of the Indian merchants the opportunity to export cotton and opium from Bombay to China. Opium trade became so lucrative that the Bombay merchants became drug barons of the nineteenth century and Bombay became Medellin (Markovits, 2008, 130).

Calcutta being the capital of the British Raj till 1911 had a large number of European settlers and residences of a number of European merchants. The city also had large numbers of agency houses. It also attracted different native business communities, especially merchants from Rajasthan, who were known as *Marwaris*. The communities of native as well as European merchants were engaged in trading of indigo, opium, saltpetre, jute and raw silk. Coalmines, which had become essential for supplying coal, were also located in nearby places. Due to all these reasons, merchants operating from Calcutta had also accumulated financial resources.

In 1848, for the first time, the British government had provided freedom to the exporters of cotton processing machines and equipment used in the cotton textile mills. Until this time, the British government did not permit machine manufacturers to export machines to maintain the monopoly of textile manufacturers of Britain. The liberalization of trade of textile machines occurred because (a) by this time, the manufacturing of cotton textiles had stopped growing in Britain as rapidly as it was growing at the time of beginning of the Industrial Revolution and (b) the textile machinery manufacturers of Germany, Belgium and France had already begun selling cotton processing machines and equipment abroad. Due to these reasons, the British equipment makers forced the British government to permit them to export cotton textile manufacturing machines and equipment.[2] The freedom to export textile manufacturing equipment provided opportunity to some of the equipment producers of Britain to supply them to Indian promoters of textile mills. At that point in time, there existed standard textile machinery and equipment suppliers who also provided turnkey solutions to establish textile mills. These companies also supplied requisite manpower such as skilled workers and managers for the new textile mills. Some of these companies were Platt Brothers, Oldham and John Hetherington & Sons (Gandhi, 1930; Morris, 1965, 12). Similarly, the Dundee mills, engaged in the manufacturing of jute textiles in Ireland, were able to perfect a machine which could spin jute fibre into yarn with the help of a modified power loom. This new machine increased the demand of Indian jute. The agency houses began to supply Indian jute to Dundee mills. These agency houses soon acquired knowledge about jute textile manufacturing (see Hunter, 1886).

Due to the availability of capital and existence of entrepreneurship in the cities of Bombay and Calcutta, there emerged simultaneously two textile mills—cotton textiles and jute textiles—in these two separate colonial cities during the British Raj. These two cities continued to enjoy important place in the manufacturing map of the Indian subcontinent. It is due to the continued dominance of these two cities, in terms of modern manufacturing enterprises for a considerable period during the British Raj, that it has been described as *dual dominance*.[3] The localization of two different manufacturing industries in these two cities was in fact a manifestation of two different patterns of growth of manufacturing and two different kinds of relationship with British manufacturers. In the case of Bombay-based cotton textile manufacturing, entrepreneurship came from Indian merchants who had accumulated financial resources from trading of cotton and opium. In the case of jute textile manufacturing enterprises of Calcutta, promoters of mills were ex-civil servants of the East India Company and agency houses managed by British citizens. It is because of this reason that a part of the investments in jute textile manufacturing was made by British investors. Owing to these reasons, the attitudes of British policymakers and manufacturers were also different. Cotton textile manufacturing enterprises were manufacturing products which were slowly emerging as import substitutes for the textiles manufactured by British textile manufacturers. Therefore, their growth was against the interest of the British manufacturers. On the contrary, jute textile mills of Calcutta were largely promoted by expatriate Britishers, and they were producing products which were becoming a necessary complement to British manufacturing.

It is also important to mention here that to overcome the shortage of capital and managerial talent in the Indian subcontinent, Indian entrepreneurs invented a new form of business organization described as *managing agency system*. This form of organization of business enterprises continued to exist even after independence till the 1960s, when the government finally reformed the laws to discontinue this form of business organization. This system of business organization came into existence in the Indian subcontinent when an agency house initially promoted an enterprise as joint-stock company, and then instead of running this enterprise with the help of elected board members, it acquired the right to manage it as a managing agent on the basis of a commission on total sales of the enterprise. This innovation in the organization of business enterprise occurred for the first time in 1836, when one of the agency houses, Carr Tagore & Company, founded by a partnership between William Carr and Dwarkanath Tagore (grandfather of Rabindranath Tagore), promoted a company called Calcutta Tugg Association, and then assumed its management. Roughly at the same time, another agency house Parry & Company became managing agents of Proto Novo Steel and Iron Company.[4] The managing agency system was a product of circumstances prevailing at that time. The need of large financial resources to establish modern manufacturing enterprises necessitated the pooling of resources of several individuals. Therefore, the joint-stock company format was accepted. The lack of managerial talent necessitated hiring of talent outside the family. Hiring of outsiders created risk associated with agency problem. To overcome the agency problem, promoters were given right to manage the enterprises. This form of organization of business created a unique form of business organization in India, where public funds were managed by private interests. It also gave right to the promoters turned managing agents to earn commission as a fixed percentage of sales of the organization. During the British Raj, several such managing houses became quite important such as Andrew Yule & Company, Bird & Company, Duncan Brothers, Balmer Lawrie & Company, Williamson Magor & Company, C. F. Martin & Company, McLeod & Company, Rolli Brothers, Shaw Wallace & Company, Parry & Company and Williamson Magor & Company.[5] The same pattern of business organization was also used by Indian promoters of modern manufacturing enterprises, such as Nauroji Wadia & Company, Birla Brothers and Tata Sons.

We have described above some of the important changes that occurred in the economic and business environment of the economy of the Indian subcontinent after it came into direct contact with the British Empire. In the rest of the chapter, we will see how these changes impacted the two cities, Bombay and Surat, located on the Western coast of India, and the two other cities, Calcutta and Dacca, located on the Eastern coast. For this purpose, the rest of the chapter has been organized into two sections. The first section describes the tale of the two cities of the Western coast, and in the second section, the experience of Dacca and Calcutta during the British Raj has been narrated.

BOMBAY AND SURAT
DURING THE BRITISH RAJ

Bombay had become an important port city for trade after 1813, when monopoly of trade given to the East India Company by the British government was abolished. This provided space to several Indian as well as British merchants to participate in the activities related to foreign trade. Volume of trade had further increased after the opening of China market by the British army in 1842. The construction of Suez Canal had reduced the distance between London and Bombay ports substantially, which also increased the intensity of trading activities on the Bombay port. Due to this reason, Bombay had assumed the role of a typical colonial city, which was used to export primary products such as cotton and opium. Bombay did not have its own traditional flexible manufacturing; therefore, it emerged as an important city to drain raw materials produced in the hinterland of Bombay. In order to export these commodities, British merchants and agency houses had to depend on Indian merchants to bring these commodities from hinterland to the Bombay port. Some of the Indian merchants withdrew their participation from evolving network of craftsmen to organize traditional flexible manufacturing to participate in the export of commodities. These merchants became important participants and partners with British merchants by helping them to maintain supply chain of these commodities. Through their participation in the commodity trade, merchants of Bombay had accumulated substantial amount of financial resources. They were predominantly engaged in the export of cotton and opium. Accumulation of financial resources by these merchants subsequently helped them in promoting modern manufacturing enterprises in Bombay.

Local administration also helped in establishing financial infrastructure to provide support to the emerging market economy of Bombay. In 1840, Bank of Bombay was established as a Presidency bank (Bagchi, 1987). In 1850, around 20 Indian brokers, who were dealing in exchange of bullion, stocks and shares, formed an institution called Native Shares and Stock Brokers Association. This association was permitted by the Bombay administration to conduct its business under a banyan tree, opposite the Town Hall of the city. This association subsequently was converted into Bombay Stock Exchange in 1875.[6] The city administration had also established the Mayor's Court, which became an important institution for the enforcement of contracts between merchants across communities. With the establishment of institutions which helped in maintaining law and order and enforcement of contracts, and financial institutions such as bank and stock market, Bombay city administration created necessary institutional infrastructure which is necessary for the smooth functioning of a market economy and to promote entrepreneurship.

The liberalization of export of capital goods of British machinery and equipment suppliers by the government facilitated the availability of machinery and equipment to establish modern manufacturing enterprises. Moreover, the existence of firms not only helped in procuring these machines and equipment, but also helped in the construction, installation of machines and equipment. They also provided necessary manpower and facilitated the establishment of modern manufacturing enterprises. Bombay merchants had already accumulated necessary financial resources to invest in modern textile mills. The availability of technology provided them objective conditions to set up modern textile mills in Bombay.

One of the Parsi merchants, Cowasjee Davar, promoted the first successful steam-powered cotton textile mill at Tardeo in Bombay. The mill, established on 7 July 1854, was named Bombay Spinning and Weaving Company. The mill was constructed and operated by experts who were arranged by a British company of Manchester, John Hetherington & Sons. The building of the company was designed by the architect Sir William Fairbairn, and machines and equipment were installed by a team of British technicians consisting of Lambart, Newton and Bear Sell. The mill was operated by Carding Master Green Halms and Spinning Master Knott.[7] This suggests that the entire know-how to establish and run the mill was outsourced from Britain. The construction of another cotton textile mill, Oriental Spinning and Weaving Mill, also began in 1854. This mill was also promoted by a Parsi merchant Maneckji Petit. Subsequently, several other cotton textile mills were established by different Parsi merchants of Bombay in 1860. These mills were Victoria Mill, Bombay United Spinning and Weaving Company by Mangaldas Nathubhai, Maneckji Petit Spinning and Weaving Mills which was promoted by Dinshaw Petit and Bomanji Hormusjee Spinning and Weaving Company established by Bomanji Wadia. Around the same time, Merwanji Bhavnagar and Kapadia promoted Great Eastern Spinning and Weaving Company. During 1861–1862, Maneckji Petit established two other cotton textile mills, namely Royal Mills and Petit Mills (Mehta, 1954).

While Bombay was emerging as an important location of modern cotton textile mills, Surat remained as a centre of production of cotton and silk textiles with the help of its traditional flexible manufacturing. By this time, the British had lost interest in the exports of Indian textiles because these were substituted by textiles produced by British cotton textile mills. This provided opportunity to the merchants of Surat to explore alternative markets for their textiles. In the attempt to discover new market, they explored the markets of East, West and South Africa and Southeast Asia. Some families of Surat merchants migrated to establish trading contact with these countries. In the process, they began to produce textiles which were customized for the customers of these countries. This is how the merchants of textiles of Surat repositioned themselves to survive in the new circumstances.

In Surat and its hinterland, a parallel qualitative change was occurring. James Landen, who had been appointed by the British government in 1840 to help in improving the quality of cotton grown in Gujarat, was involved in experiments to cultivate long-staple American cotton in India. He introduced the American saw gins in Gujarat's cotton-growing areas. The cotton cleaned with the help of saw gins increased the price as well as marketability of cotton grown in Gujarat. Landen also started a cotton textile mill at Broach in Gujarat in 1853. He, along with Captain Fulljames, provided help to a group of Gujarati merchants from Surat who were planning to establish a cotton textile mill called Surat Spinning Association. However, this project was not successfully implemented. Landen was also in touch with another Gujarati entrepreneur, Ranchodlal Chotelal, whom he helped in starting a cotton textile mill at Ahmedabad, but not in Surat. Subsequently, Ahmedabad became an important location of modern cotton textile mills in Gujarat. For a considerable period, Surat had to wait for attracting investment in the modern cotton textile mills.

On 12 April 1861, the American Civil War began which continued till 2 May 1865. During the period of American Civil War, supply of American cotton was suspended to the British cotton textile mills. It has been already described that it was the availability of cheaper cotton from America, grown by cotton planters with the help of African slaves, which provided competitive advantage to British textile mills. Thus the cotton textiles produced by the British mills were much cheaper than those produced in India by its traditional flexible manufacturing. The disruption in the availability of American cotton forced British textile manufacturers to buy Indian cotton. The dependence of British mills on Indian cotton resulted in a substantial increase in the exports of Indian cotton. The exports of cotton increased from £93 lakh in 1861–1862 to £148 lakh in 1862–1863.[8] This new development established a strong linkage between British Manchester and the Indian Manchester (Bombay) because Bombay became an important port to export cotton from India. Due to the possibilities of earning higher profits from the export of cotton, a very large proportion of Indian cotton was directed for export to Britain. Moreover, cotton exports sucked financial resources of some prominent Indian merchants such as Rustamji Jamsetji (who was a son of Jamsetjee Jeejeebhoy, the merchant who had made huge earnings from the export of opium to China), Behramji Hormusji Cama, Khandos Narondos and Karsondas Madhavadas (Dobbin, 1972). Due to these developments, Bombay underwent a metamorphosis during this period due to manifold increase in the wealth of the merchants of the city. A part of the earnings of the Bombay merchants was spent on developing the residencies of rich merchants. Some part of the increased wealth was spent on charities, which helped in the improvement of infrastructure of the city. Bombay also remained brighter in the night due to the introduction of gas lights in 1866 (see Dossal, 1991).

The increasing exports of cotton to Britain also caused certain unintended consequences. Export boom resulted in massive procurement of Indian cotton for exports. This caused shortages in the supply of cotton for domestic consumption. It also increased the domestic price of cotton. Moreover, a very large proportion of financial resources of Indian merchants was diverted to financing export of cotton. These consequences of exports of Indian cotton to Britain slowed down the investment in textiles mills in India. This arrested the expansion of modern textile mills in Bombay. In the absence of investment opportunities, a very large part of the earnings from the exports of cotton by Bombay merchants was directed towards future trading of cotton. At the same time, another important opportunity emerged for speculation. The opportunity arose as a consequence of increased demand for land in order to meet the needs of the expanding city. Due to non-availability of land, the only alternative option was to reclaim land from the sea. Bombay administration found that private initiative for land reclamation will be a better option. For this purpose, Backbay Reclamation Company was formed in 1864 by Premchand Roychand. Roychand was son of a cotton trader of Surat, Deepchand Jain, who had migrated to Bombay like several other merchants to exploit emerging possibilities of business. Over time several such companies were floated to reclaim land from the sea. Realizing that the reclaimed land will be sold at very high prices, many merchants invested in the stocks of these companies. Not only businessmen, even common people began to invest in the stocks of the companies. The Bank of Bombay provided loans to individuals to buy stocks of the companies. The share mania created by these companies provided another source of speculation (see Subramanian, 2012; Tripathi, 2004; Wacha, 1910).

On 2 May 1865, the American Civil War came to an end. This caused a sharp fall in the prices of cotton. This fall in prices led to a serious financial crisis in the Bombay Stock Exchange. The stock market registered free fall in the stock prices. Panic selling of stocks intensified the crisis further. This stock market crash converted several rich merchants of Bombay into paupers. The most affected institutions were Bank of Bombay, Backbay Reclamation Company and the Asiatic Banking Corporation. The 'edifice built on shares and stock and bubble companies collapsed like a house of cards' (Sullivan, 1937, 73). It was due to these reasons that expansion of cotton textile mills in Bombay was almost suspended (a) during the American Civil War when financial resources of the city were used for speculative purpose and (b) after the end of the Civil War investments in industries did not occur as a consequence of loss of financial resources of the merchants based in Bombay after the stock market crash. It took almost a decade for the merchants of Bombay to recover from this financial shock.

Investments in the cotton textile sector resumed only after 1870. Soon 20 new cotton textile mills were added to the existing cotton textile mills. Some of the important cotton textile mills were established during this time. In 1870, Morarji Goculdas, a Kutchi Bhatia merchant, established the Morarji Goculdas Mill. This company ended the monopoly of Parsi merchants in the ownership of cotton textile mills of Bombay. In 1874, another Bhatia merchant, Maneckji Khatau, opened the Khatau Mill. Thereafter Albert Sassoon, a Baghdadi Jew, whose ancestors had migrated to Gujarat, founded the Sassoon Spinning and Weaving Company in Bombay in 1874. The concentration of cotton textile mills in Bombay provided necessary conditions to mill owners, who had common interest and were experiencing common problems, to form Bombay Mill Owners Association in 1875. The new investments in cotton textile manufacturing continued in Bombay for a much longer period. Two British entrepreneurs, George Cotton and James Greaves, established a company, Greaves Cotton & Company, in 1879; similarly, another group of British promoters, Charles Killick and Presto Nixon, launched Kohinoor Mills; Kowasji Naik established Alexandra Mills in 1892. This mill was subsequently taken over by Nusserwanji Tata in 1893. In the 1890s, Nowroj Nusserwanjee Wadia promoted two cotton textile mills—Bombay Dyeing and Century Mills. In the 1890s, the managing agency house of Bradbury and Brady opened several cotton textile manufacturing firms in Bombay (see Gadgil, 1924; Mehta, 1954; Roy, 1993; Tripathi, 2004).

It is important to mention that until the 1890s, Bombay remained the most favoured location for modern cotton textile manufacturing units. At this point in time, cotton textile mills of Bombay were primarily exporting yarn to markets of China and Japan. This suggests that Bombay textile mills were actually only spinning mills. Since most of their output was meant for exports, they found location near Bombay port to be more appropriate. The Indian twist yarn had achieved phenomenal success in Japanese and Chinese markets. The success had become a source of envy for British textile manufacturers, and motivated the Manchester Chamber of Commerce to conduct an enquiry regarding the success of Indian cotton yarn in the markets of Japan and China (see Gadgil, 1924, 76). However, this advantage enjoyed by the Bombay mills was quite temporary. During the 1860s, the spinning of cotton with machines was introduced in Japan. The local production of machine-spun yarn reduced the demand of Indian cotton yarn in Japanese market (see Koh, 1966, 23). In 1894–1895, Japan defeated China in war. The occupation of China by Japan facilitated the dominance of Japanese cotton yarn in the Chinese market. According to available data, until 1893 Indian cotton mills were supplying 96 per cent of the cotton yarn needed by Chinese cotton textile manufacturers; after the occupation of China by Japan, the Indian exports of cotton yarn registered a dramatic decline (ibid., 14).

The loss of the Chinese and Japanese markets for the exports of Indian cotton yarn, manufactured by Bombay mills, created necessary conditions for structural transformation of Bombay-based cotton textile mills. The new circumstances forced reorientation of Bombay mills towards domestic market. Initially they began to target Indian handloom weavers for supplying them machine spun cotton yarn. Handloom weaving still existed at several locations, including Surat and its periphery. The adoption of machine made yarn reduced their costs substantially and gave them new competitive capability against cloth supplied by the British mills.[9] The Bombay mills also adopted the strategy of vertical integration by also weaving cloth to capture the domestic market to supply textiles. This also led to the growth of integrated cotton textile mills. These important structural changes experienced by the Bombay cotton textile mills repositioned the cotton textile production from being an export-oriented industry into an import-substituting industry. The transformation made the Indian cotton textile industry inward looking. This transformation also affected its pattern of location. This happened because cotton textile manufacturers realized that in order to maintain its competitive advantage, it had to spread to different cotton-growing areas of India. This realization led to spatial spread of cotton textile manufacturing from Bombay to other parts of India, such as Nagpur, Ahmedabad, Indore, Gwalior, Kanpur, Delhi, Punjab, Coimbatore and Tripura.[10]

While modern cotton textile manufacturing was spreading to other parts of India, Ahmedabad emerged as an important location of cotton textile mills to take the advantage of cotton grown in Gujarat. Most of the entrepreneurs ignored Surat while promoting modern textile mills in Gujarat. The more obvious reason for preferring Ahmedabad, and not Surat, by Gujarati entrepreneurs is that—unlike Bombay mills which depended on exports of cotton yarn to China and Japan, which might have necessitated location at a port city—Ahmedabad mills had access to several centres of traditional flexible manufacturing of textiles, which provided them a big domestic market since Gujarat mills were linked with the domestic market, the did not require location at the port of Surat. Therefore, the Ahmedabad mills developed a symbiotic relationship with local centres of handloom weaving by supplying them machine-spun yarn. Also, Ahmedabad was well connected by land routes with all the centres of traditional flexible manufacturing of textiles in Gujarat, including Surat.[11] However, as Ahmedabad became congested, cotton textile mills also moved to Surat. The famous cotton textile baron of Gujarat, Gaganbhai Mafatlal, established the first modern cotton textile mill at Surat in 1916. Subsequently, Surat also became an important centre of cotton textile manufacturing.

The emergence of modern cotton textile mills and their rapid expansion in India invited envy of the British cotton textile manufacturers. This happened especially when cloth of Indian produce was slowly replacing cloth produced by British mills in the Indian market. In order to safeguard their interest, they began to influence the policies of the British government. They pressurized the British government to impose discriminatory tariffs on Indian cotton textile manufacturing. The process of discrimination against Indian cotton textile manufacturers began when Lord Lytton in 1878 removed customs duties on British textiles imported in India. British manufacturers were not satisfied with this marginal effort of the British government. They expected much more significant action from the government to diminish the competitive advantage of Indian cotton textiles. In 1890, the mill owners of Manchester secured another important victory when the British government introduced excise duty on the cotton textile mills of India.[12]

British manufacturers of cotton textile began to visualize the cloth produced by Indian cotton textile mills, which were largely concentrated in Bombay, as an import substitute for British textiles. This perception increased the hostility between Indian and British mill owners. The Indian owners of cotton textile mills tried to protect their interest through Bombay Mill Owners Association, which was formed in 1875, and Ahmedabad Mill Owners Association, which was established in 1891. However, their concerns were not addressed by the British administration. Their discontent got transformed into Indian nationalism, because they realized that only the government which will be run by Indians, will protect the interests of Indian manufacturers. These sentiments of nationalism got manifest when the Indian National Congress was formed by a British civil servant, Allan Octavian Hume, in Bombay in 1885. The Indian National Congress was formed to provide a platform for the expression of grievances and concerns of native elites and businessmen to British authorities in order to arrive at possible negotiated benefits for them.

The spread of cotton textile mills across different location in India ebbed the competitive advantage of cotton textile mills located in Bombay. This happened because they had to procure cotton from the same areas in which these mills were located; therefore, they had to incur transportation cost. As cost of living began to rise in Bombay, the cotton textile mills were forced to pay higher wages. Moreover, increasing prices of land also acted as a disincentive to open new cotton textile mills. Due to these reasons, along with increasing discrimination against cotton textile mills by British administration, entrepreneurs of Bombay looked for new avenues for investments, other than cotton textiles. In November 1869, the Suez Canal was opened, which reduced the distance between London and Bombay and other port cities of Europe substantially. Within a year, in 1870, 436,000 tons of merchandize passed through this canal (Williams, 1965, 276).

The increased connectivity of Bombay with other European port cities can be visualized with the fact that Louis Lumière, who invented cinematography and exhibited his two films *Arrival of Train* and *Leaving Lumière Factors* in France in 1895, exhibited the same films at Hotel Watson in Bombay in July 1896. These shows fired the imagination of several entrepreneurs and creative artists associated with theatre to evolve their own film industry. The film industry of Bombay evolved out of folk theatre and Parsi theatre of Bombay. Jamsetjee Jeejeebhoy had purchased an English theatre in auction in 1835 and renamed it as Grand Road Parsi Theatre Company in 1853. To make the theatre production commercially successful in a vastly cosmopolitan city, Parsi theatre evolved its own language which was a mixture of Persian, Urdu and Hindi. Dadasaheb Phalke adopted the popular story of Raja Harish Chand from folk theatre and used the language evolved by Parsi theatre to give birth to a pan Indian cinema industry with the release of the film *Raja Harish Chand* in 1913.[13] This film paved the way for the emergence of the popular pan Indian film industry. Presently, Indian cinema is largely associated with Bombay and is popularly known as Bollywood, rhyming pretty well with Hollywood, which is the Mecca of the global film industry. Investments were made to establish several film studios, which attracted writers, song writers, directors, musicians, actors and artists from different parts of India. Investments were also made to construct new cinema halls to exhibit films not only in Bombay but also in different parts of India. Around the same time, in 1897, Ardeshir Burjorji Godrej founded a company in collaboration with Boyce & Company called Godrej Boyce & Company to manufacture a new product—namely safety locks. He also introduced another manufacturing industry in Bombay when he started Godrej Soaps Limited in 1919 to manufacture soaps.[14]

The process of diversification of investment continued. The Tatas, who had most of their investments in cotton textiles, made huge investment in opening the Taj Mahal Palace Hotel in Bombay in 1903. The idea to construct a hotel came to the mind of Jamsetji Tata when, one day, he along with one of his foreign friends went for dinner at Pyrk's Apollo Hotel. The guard at the entrance of the hotel did not allow Tata to enter the hotel, because this hotel was open exclusively for Europeans only. This incident motivated Tata to construct the best hotel in the city of Bombay. For this purpose, Jamsetji purchased land at Apollo Bunder and started the Indian Hotels Company Ltd in 1902. At that point in time, the Gateway of India was not yet built. During his foreign travels, he collected finest equipment for the hotel, best even according to the European standards. The Taj Hotel was the first building in Bombay which was lit by electricity. It is still an important landmark of the city of Bombay. It is because of its long heritage and being an expression of Indian nationalism that it became an object of envy for the terrorists, who attacked the hotel on 29/11.

The Tatas also entered the business of electricity generation and distribution. Here the purpose was to supply cheaper electricity to Bombay city and to several textile mills which were still using coal as a source of power. Jamsetji established The Tata Hydro-Electric Power Supply Company in 1910. For generating electricity, the Tatas build an artificial reservoir in the Western Ghats at Wal Wahen near Lonavala. Later on, the Tata Power Hydro-Electric Power Supply Company was renamed as Tata Power Company in 1911. This company was quite ahead of its time because textile mills of Bombay took several years to shift from using steam power to electricity.[15] The economy of Bombay was significantly impacted by the circumstances that emerged during the First World War (1914–1918). This happened because wartime compulsions forced British policymakers to deviate from the professed ideological commitment for free trade and laissez-faire. The departure in the policy began with the appointment of the Industrial Commission in 1916 and the Indian Fiscal Commission in 1922. Despite the disruption that foreign trade flows experienced during the War, it did not significantly affect the economy of Bombay.

In the 1930s, the British economy, along with other European economies, experienced the worst economic crisis ever, known as the Great Depression. This crisis resulted in very high levels of underutilization of industrial capacity, resulting in very high levels of unemployment. This crisis forced the British government to give up the policy of free trade and to introduce tariffs for the first time. These tariffs to protect Indian manufacturing enterprises promoted the process of import substitution and provided opportunities to Indian manufacturers to diversify and promote Indian manufacturing enterprises, which can replace imports. These circumstances encouraged Indian entrepreneurs to enter into the manufacturing of new products. Simultaneously, these circumstances also motivated several European and American enterprises to establish their businesses in India to overcome barriers created by tariff walls. Both the possibilities significantly influenced the growth of Bombay city.

The process of foreign direct investment began when the company Swedish Match, which was the largest supplier of safety matches in India, opened its subsidiary, Western India Match Company (WIMCO), in 1923 at Bombay. In 1928, General Motor Company of the USA established its assembly plant in Bombay to assemble trucks and cars from CKD (completely knocked down) Kits. Ford Motor Car Company also opened its assembly unit at Bombay in 1931. International General Electric of the USA established its Indian subsidiary International General Electric Corporation (India) Ltd in 1930 at Bombay. Unilever, an Anglo-Dutch company, promoted its subsidiary Lever Brothers India Ltd in 1931 to produce the Lifebuoy and Lux brands of soap at Bombay. It also promoted another company, Hindustan Vanaspati Manufacturing Company, at Bombay to produce the Dalda brand of vegetable oil in 1931. Goodlass Wall & Co. Ltd was promoted in Bombay in 1933 to produce paints. Turner & Newall Ltd floated its subsidiary unit at Bombay called Asbestos Cement Company Ltd. in 1934. Crompton Parkinson Ltd promoted Crompton Parkinson Works Ltd in 1937 to manufacture electrical equipment in Bombay.

Firestone Tyre and Rubber Company also established its subsidiary company in Bombay called Firestone India Ltd in 1939. Around the same time in 1938, two Danish engineers, namely Henning Holck-Larsen and Søren Kristian Toubro, founded Larsen & Toubro at Bombay. These Danish engineers had come to India as representatives of a Danish company, FLSmidth & Co., which supplied equipment for erecting cement plants.[16] The details given above regarding foreign direct investments in Bombay during the period of Great Depression of the 1930s (1930–1939) clearly establishes that the imposition of tariffs encouraged foreign companies to set up their enterprises in India. This was facilitated by the prevailing depressed conditions in Europe and America, which forced the companies of these countries to explore new markets like India.

The end of depression coincided with the outbreak of the Second World War (1939–1945). This time cessation of foreign trade was almost complete due to disruption of sea routes. The disruption of trade provided natural protection to the Indian manufacturing enterprises. This situation created circumstances for promoting import-substitution kind of manufacturing. In fact, the circumstances created by the Second World War not only promoted the process of industrialization in India, but it also facilitated the emergence of the process of industrialization in several colonies of European countries. This phenomenon later led to a belief amongst policymakers in the developing countries, after their independence, to encourage development of their manufacturing sector by raising very high tariff walls. This environment also encouraged several Indian entrepreneurs to establish manufacturing enterprises to replace imports. At this point in time, the Birlas opened Hind Cycle Company to manufacture bicycles at Bombay, because bicycles had become an essential means of transportation of the Indian middle classes, and India was importing large numbers of bicycles from Britain. This was more beneficial for the British manufacturers. Walchand Hirachand, an important entrepreneur of Bombay, who had already promoted Hindustan Aircraft Limited at Bangalore, also used the same managing agency company Walchand–Khatau–Kilachand to promote Premier Automobiles Ltd at Kurla near Bombay in 1944. He entered into contract with Chrysler

Corporation to assemble Plymouth cars and with Dodge Brothers Company to assemble their trucks.[17]

These developments created a highly diversified economic base for the city, increased its population and transformed Bombay into the financial capital of India and one of the leading places of manufacturing activities. The increasing size of the city in terms of geography and population resulted in growth of several services, which are necessary for the smooth functioning of a commercial city, such as administration, police, court, municipality, education, health, hospitality, retailing, transportation and so on. These services also provided source of livelihood to a substantial number of families. These employment opportunities attracted people living in different parts of India to migrate in the city. These migrants also led to cultural diversity of the city and evolved it into one of the most important cosmopolitan cities of India. Bombay thus emerged as a land of opportunities.

However, factors such as the existence of mass poverty, extreme income inequalities and fragmented markets due to varieties of regional taste and preferences divided along caste lines and religions reduced the demand for standardized products produced by modern manufacturing industries. Moreover, the factor prices (prices of factor of production like land, labour and capital) also worked against rapid expansion of modern manufacturing. These factors have provided scope for the coexistence of modern large, medium and small enterprises along with traditional flexible manufacturing and crafts-based traditional manufacturing. The existence of the railway network facilitated the mobility of labour along with migrations of craftsmen from different parts of India. The migration was quite significant in the case of weavers who migrated from different centres of traditional flexible manufacturing, which had experienced decline, to new centres of production of textiles. These weavers migrated in large numbers to several towns of Western India such as Sholapur, Malegaon, Bhiwandi, Burhanpur and Surat (Haynes and Roy, 1999; Markovits 2000; Roy, 1999). Some of these weavers purchased power looms which were being discarded by modern textile mills. These weavers not only used their own labour but also employed available cheap labour to establish small textile manufacturing units. This sector is now popularly known as 'power loom sector'.

In new circumstances, the city of Surat was left way behind in wealth and prosperity by Bombay. Surat was also facing imminent decline as a port city because it could not provide scope for anchoring big ships. The sizes of ships had increased substantially after the introduction of steam ships. Moreover, the level of silt had increased in the Tapi river. Despite these disadvantages, the enterprising spirit of the merchants of Surat helped them in maintaining certain level of economic prosperity by producing products for niche markets abroad and innovating new formats of conducting businesses by migrating to cities in South, East and Western Africa, Hong Kong and Burma.

DACCA AND CALCUTTA AND THE BRITISH RAJ

In 1757 when the process of territorial occupation of Bengal by the East India Company began, Britain was beginning its journey towards of industrialization. By the time the rule of the East India Company came to an end and the British Raj began, Bengal had experienced de-industrialization, and from the city of Dacca the production of Dacca muslin had totally disappeared. The industrial Britain did not need its textiles because it had already become largest exporter of cotton textiles and had also begun to produce silk textile. In these circumstances Dacca and its peripheral areas had become sources of procurement of raw silk for British silk mills. To improve the quality of raw silk Britain had introduced filature silk. Introduction of filature silk had replaced the work of traditional silk reelers (nacauds) (see Bhattacharya, 1966, 1982; Roy 1999 and Seth 2015, Chapter III). However, Dacca weavers also adopted filature silk for weaving silk textiles. Despite the fact Dacca's traditional flexible manufacturing industry had lost export market, it did survive by catering to domestic demand by producing ethnic textiles, which were not supplied by the British mills. For a considerable period, population of Bengal in particular and that of the rest of India in general did not en masse adopt Western dress code, especially in the eastern part of India.

When Dacca and Calcutta came under the direct rule of the British Raj, the East India Company had already transformed the economy of Bengal into a supplier of raw materials and other primary commodities which were being demanded in Britain. Dacca and the rest of Bengal had become exporters of jute, indigo, raw silk, tea, saltpetre and opium, and importer of British textiles and other manufactured products. Bengal, which was one of the richest provinces during the Mughal Empire, had been converted into one of the poorest regions of the Indian subcontinent. The city of Dacca which had lost in the race of prosperity was able to maintain its survival only at the margins of the Indian economy.

The British Raj enhanced the economic and political importance of Calcutta by making it the capital city of the Raj. It is quite ironical that the city of Calcutta grew on three villages—namely Sutanuti, Gobindapur and Kolikata—which Job Charnock had acquired through a Zamindari right from a family of the Mujumdars, a Bengali Zamindar family, in 1690, for ₹1,300 (see Hasan, 1992). These villages did not stand in comparison to the prosperity of Dacca during this period. However, 100 years of rule of the East India Company had transformed Calcutta into a big city, which enriched itself by redirecting all the exports of the region through Calcutta Port—initially by exporting products produced by the traditional flexible manufacturing of Dacca, and later by exporting raw materials and primary commodities such as opium, jute, indigo, tea and saltpetre to Britain. Therefore, at this point in time, when the region came under the rule of the British Raj, historical forces had already reversed the process of development. Calcutta had become the centre of prosperity and Dacca had become its satellite or periphery. The merchants of Calcutta had acquired substantial amount of wealth by trading in commodities which were being exported through the port of Calcutta. The British administration had established Presidency Bank of Calcutta in 1806, which was subsequently known as Bank of Bengal since 1809. Bank of Bengal was opened with a significant amount of deposits of native merchants; however, a large proportion of loans were advanced to British merchants (MacPherson, 1955; Morris and Dudley, 1975).

Importance of Calcutta also increased when the city was connected with other parts of the Indian subcontinent by the railways. Railway connectivity was partly increased for the purposes of defence administration and also to transport large volumes of primary products from different peripheral areas of Calcutta for exports. Although the process of construction of railways began during the rule of the East India Company, when Calcutta was connected by railways, it received momentum only during the British Raj (see Bagchi 1987). During the British Raj, the connectivity of Calcutta with the rest of the Indian subcontinent increased because Calcutta had become the capital of the British Raj. As it has been already described in an earlier section of this chapter, to increase inter-regional connectivity through the railway network in the shortest possible time, the British Raj encouraged private investment in railways. Therefore, some of the private companies such as Bengal–Nagpur Railway Company and East Indian Railway Company played an important role in connecting Calcutta with different locations in India.[18] The British administration also increased the city's connectivity with its hinterland by developing a pontoon Bridge over the Hugli river in 1874. The city's infrastructure improved significantly when it was lit with electricity in 1891.

Another significant development that occurred in Calcutta was the emergence of the managing agency system, which in fact originated in Calcutta, when an agency house first promoted a joint-stock company and afterwards it acquired the right to manage that company on the basis of commission as a percentage of total sales. This happened in 1836, when the agency house of Carr Tagore & Company founded by William Carr and Dwarkanath Tagore (grandfather of Rabindranath Tagore) promoted Calcutta Tugg Association and became its managing agents (Blair, 1969). These agency houses were established by forming partnership between Bengali and British merchants. These agency houses traded in raw silk, indigo, opium, British textiles and saltpetre. These partnership companies formed by Bengali entrepreneurs and British merchants were not based on complete trust. This mistrust existed because British partners used to run away to Britain as and when an agency house experienced financial crises. In such a situation, all liabilities of the company were passed on to the Indian partners. Palmer & Company experienced such a crisis in 1830 and Union Bank in 1847. The crises experienced by these companies affected the alliance between Bengali and British merchants (Sinha, 1992, cited in Ray, 1992). Thereafter, most of the agency houses were formed solely by British merchants to overcome this problem. The British administration passed the Companies Act in 1850, but it became more important during the British Raj. This Act gave birth to limited liability companies.

During this period, a large number of Marwari merchants also migrated to Calcutta. These merchants had very strong community networks to conduct their businesses. This important characteristic of communities of merchants has been described in greater detail in Chapter 1 of the book. These Marwari merchants had earned substantial amount of wealth by participating in the supply chains of different commodities which were exported from Calcutta. Hence, when the British Raj began in Calcutta, two sets of people were wealthy—the British agency houses, which had monopolized trade, and the Marwari merchants. Initially, British agency houses used managing agency form of organization of business to promote modern manufacturing enterprises in Calcutta.

Trading in jute was important both as a raw material and in the form of products such as ropes and cordage. Until 1830, Dacca and its peripheral areas had monopoly of traditional flexible manufacturing of jute products. The Dundee mills of Ireland were able to successfully convert the jute fibre into yarn with the help of a modified loom. This led to increase in the demand for raw material for jute textile industry. This necessitated the import of jute from India. However, the Dundee mills depended to a very large extent on Russian hemp. The Crimean War, which began in 1854 and continued till 1856, affected the regular supply of Russian hemp for the Dundee mills.[19] The disruption in supply of Russian hemp gave to Bengali jute a near monopoly position. This boom in the demand of jute gave opportunity to the agency houses of Calcutta to make huge profits. Since the Marwari merchants were important participants in the entire supply chain of procurement, baling and bringing jute to Calcutta for exports, they also earned large incomes. These agency houses had contact with the

Dundee mills; therefore, they were able to acquire necessary technical knowledge to start jute textile mills in Calcutta.[20] The opportunity to make profits by opening jute textile mills at a place which had abundant supply of jute motivated George Auckland, a Scot, to start a jute textile mill called Auckland & Company at Rishra near Srirampur in 1854. This company laid the foundation of establishing modern jute textile manufacturing units. It was the birth of modern jute textile mills which transformed Calcutta from being merely a trading city into a manufacturing city. This small beginning gave advantage to Calcutta to grow faster in terms of wealth and prosperity.

After a gap of several years, Thomas Duff, a British entrepreneur, who promoted jute textile mill, which was registered in the London Stock Exchange as Champdany Jute Mill in 1872. The companies which were registered in London were called sterling companies. He promoted another sterling company called Sanmuggar Jute Company at Hugli in 1873. In the same year, Calcutta-based agency house Kettle Buller & Company established Gloster Jute Mill. British entrepreneur MacAlister started Oriental Jute Company in 1875. Thereafter several agency houses of Calcutta opened jute textile companies. Jardine Skinner & Company started a jute textile mill in 1876, and Gillanders Arbuthnot & Company opened their jute textile mill in 1883. The opening of so many jute textile mills in Calcutta resulted in excess capacity in the manufacturing of jute textile. This happened because demand of jute textiles was not rising with the same speed. This situation continued during 1884–1895. As the demand situation became favourable, the jute-growing areas of Bengal experienced famine from 1895 to 1900, which also arrested the expansion of capacity in the jute textile manufacturing.[21]

It is only after 1900, when the situation became better, that several agency houses of Calcutta such as Andrew Yule & Company, Shaw Wallace & Company, James Finlay & Company, Bird & Company, Rolli Brothers, McLeod & Company and Graham & Company promoted various jute textile manufacturing mills. As a consequence of this rapid expansion in the production capacities in jute textile manufacturing mills, by the time of the beginning of the First World War (1914), there existed dominance of British managing agency houses in the manufacturing of jute textiles in Calcutta. This particular monopoly position of the British agency houses was highly dependent on a parallel monopoly position enjoyed by the Marwari merchants of Calcutta. The entire supply chain through which jute textile mills were getting supply of raw jute was monopolized by the Marwari merchants. Apart from supplying jute, these merchants owned most of the baling houses. They also enjoyed an important position in the overall jute economy of Bengal as brokers, agents and subagents.

However, the dominance of British agency houses in the jute textile manufacturing did not last long. This happened because Marwari merchants were slowly getting foothold in the industry. Their importance in jute textile manufacturing increased substantially. To enter into the manufacturing of jute textiles, Marwari merchants used two different strategies. One of the strategies was to acquire large proportion of shares of the jute mills owned by British promoters. The prevailing method used by the British agency houses to buy jute helped them to acquire large volumes of stocks of jute mills. These houses used to allot blocks of shares of their companies to jute suppliers to meet the requirement of working capital. The practice of getting supply of jute by allotting blocks of shares was popularly described as *fatka* system. Since the Marwari merchants were supplying jute to the houses for processing in the mills, they slowly became the owners of large numbers of stocks. The ownership of such large numbers of shares gave them opportunity to become members of the board of directors and sometimes even the director of the company. Using this fatka system, the Bangurs took over the Kettlewell Bullen & Company, the Kedias took over a jute mill owned by Anderson Wright & Company, the Bajorias took over Begg, Dunlop & Company, Keshav Prasad Goenka took over Duncan, and Radhakissan Kanoria took over the management of McLeod & Company. The other strategy which the Marwari merchants adopted was to float Indian-owned and managed companies. Some of the Marwari merchants who promoted such jute mills were G. D. Birla, Swaroopchand Hukumchand and Badridas Goenka.[22]

We have already explained about the birth of tea plantation in Assam with the help of the Botanical Survey of India. The entire output of tea was also supplied to Britain from the Calcutta Port.

However, when Bengal came under the rule of the Raj by the 1860s, exports of cotton from Bombay and tea from Calcutta assumed greater importance.[23] The British administration increased the connectivity of Calcutta with the tea-growing districts by developing railways or by introducing steamer services. As a consequence of these facilities, the area under tea plantation increased manifold. Tea occupied an important position in the transportation network between Assam and Calcutta. It is important to mention here that the share of tea exported from Calcutta to Britain increased from 7 per cent in 1868 to 54 per cent in 1896 (see Roy, 2006, 266–268). Tea which was associated with China in the consciousness of British consumers, slowly got replaced because now tea was being produced within the geographical boundaries of the British Empire. The emerging importance of Indian tea led to debate in Britain on the issue—which one of them, India or China, produces better tea. One of the important participants in the debate was Edward Money, who wrote a book in 1884 titled *Tea Controversy (A Momentous Indian Question)*, where he described that 'The Indian (tea) is grown and manufactured on large estates under superintendence of educated Englishmen and skill and capital are combined to produce best possible article'. In comparison to the Indian tea, 'China tea by contrast is produced by poor artisans in the rudest way'. This is how the Indian tea produced by intelligent Englishmen in mechanized factories, and grown in bigger tea estates, was getting ideological support from the Empire.[24]

As Calcutta began its journey towards being an industrialized city of the Indian subcontinent the administrative needs of city necessitated the spread of modern education. The use of English language by native as well as British intellectuals was establishing dialogue between them to evolve new ideas. Bengal renaissance got boost with the founding of the Asiatic Society of Bengal on 15 January 1784. The society was formed by civil servants of the East India Company. Some of the prominent members of the society were William Jones, Henry Colebrooke and Charles Wilkins. The society played an important role in the rediscovery of India, for instance, William Jones, the founder of the society, discovered the linkage between Sanskrit, Greek and Latin, which are known as the Indo-European group of languages.

The explorations by the members of the society established the importance of Indian civilization in terms of its prevalence even before the birth of Christ and its rich literary achievements. These findings increased the self-esteem of the people of Bengal and made them take pride in their nation. Emergence of national pride is a precondition for the emergence of nationalism. While paying tribute to various British scholars who enriched the understanding about India amongst Western scholars, John Keay in his book *India Discovered: A Recovery of a Lost Civilization* writes that for a considerable period, India was perceived by Western scholars as the *exotic East*, which was known for the wealth of its rulers and for animals such as elephants, tigers and snakes 'like some glorious and glittering *circus*'. After the efforts of the Asiatic Society of Bengal, the image of India underwent metamorphism and 'now in place of circus, we have a museum' (Keay, 1981 [2013], 13; Schwab, 1984). In 1818, Raja Ram Mohan Roy founded the Brahmo Samaj movement in Calcutta, which tried to combine the Hindu way of life with Western liberal ideas. This movement laid the foundation of *Bengal Renaissance*, much ahead than any other part of the Indian subcontinent. The Bengal Renaissance created cultural awakening amongst the Bengali middle classes, which gave birth to the spirit of nationalism. The new social and cultural ecosystem got its manifestation in a literary movement which got expression in the form of poetry, short stories, novels and plays. It was the evolution of this new social and cultural ecosystem that subsequently facilitated the birth of cinema in Calcutta. Films historians believe that Hiralal Sen was in fact the first film-maker. Hiralal Sen (1866–1917), along with his brother Motilal Sen, established the first film-making company, the Royal Bioscope Company, in 1898 in Calcutta. In 1903, the company produced the movie *Alibaba and Forty Thieves*. It was around the mid-phase of this movement that the famous novel *Anandamath* (The Abbey of Bliss), written by Bankim Chandra Chattopadhyay, appeared in 1882, which provided to the Indian nationalist movement their first battle cry *Vande Mataram*—a long poem which occurred as a part of the novel. The novel is about revolt by ascetic warriors against an abstract nation. Three years after the publication of this novel, in 1885, the foundation of the Indian National Congress (INC) was laid in Bombay. Rabindranath Tagore transformed this poem into a song, and this song was sung for the first time in the Calcutta session of the Indian National Congress held in 1896 (see Eck, 2012; Lipner, 2005). This song inspired the imagination of eminent Bengali painter Abanindranath Tagore to conceptualize Bharat Mata in the form of a painting in 1906.[25]

It is important to mention here that the Bengali nationalism was inspired by *Anandmath*, which advocated for achieving independence even by using means of violence. This might have happened because Bengal was ruled by the East India Company for the longest duration, and therefore had experienced the worst form of colonial administration. The kind of nationalism that was initiated by the formation of the INC in Bombay initially was more like the idea of nationalism associated with *mercantilism*. Therefore, it concentrated on getting negotiated concessions for Indian businesses, such as concessions on tariffs and taxation, and ease for conducting businesses for Indian entrepreneurs. Due to the mercantilist bias of its strand of nationalism, it attracted participation by several business houses of Bombay. These business houses also provided it necessary financial resources to continue its struggle. It is due to this distinct character of the INC, it believed in gradual movement towards achieving independence by negotiation and coercion by peaceful struggle and moral pressure. On the contrary, the idea of nationalism that emerged in the city of Calcutta got manifested in the formation of several revolutionary groups which were involved in the struggle for independence. The climax of this difference came when Subhas Chandra Bose severed his association with the INC and formed the Indian National Army.

These small beginnings were giving rise to the idea of India as a Nation. This idea was beyond the expectations of nineteenth-century British and European scholars. These scholars believed that India was a geographical area, but not a nation. Because the Indian subcontinent was devoid of a common language, cultural and ethnic commonality, and a common religion. Despite all these notions amongst these scholars, nationalist feeling did emerge amongst the Bengal middle classes and educated Bengalis. These feeling, which were incipient, came on the surface when Bengal was partitioned by Viceroy Lord Curzon into 1905 in two parts. One part consisted of Chittagong,

Dacca and Rajshahi divisions, and districts of Hill Tippera and Malda, and was called East Bengal. These were predominantly Muslim majority areas. The rest of Bengal, including Bihar and Orissa, which were Hindu majority areas, was called West Bengal. The division of Bengal led to a sustained struggle, part peaceful, part militant and assumed the proportion of the independence movement. The movement forced the British government to abandon the idea of partition of Bengal. As a consequence of all the political events which occurred due to the emergence of nationalistic feelings in Calcutta, the British Raj shifted its capital from Calcutta to Delhi in 1911, taking away from the city its political significance, which it had enjoyed being the capital city of the Raj. However, it did not affect its economic significance, because the preconditions that are necessary and sufficient for achieving growth and development were already sown in the soil of Calcutta city.

One of the important forms of struggle adopted by the people of Bengal was to boycott the consumption of British-made goods, which is described as the *Swadeshi* movement. This social preference for Indian goods encouraged several entrepreneurs to open new manufacturing enterprises which could replace foreign goods. This was a form of *social protection* rather than *protection through tariffs* for made in India products. It is quite interesting that up to this time the role of Bengali entrepreneurship was almost negligible in the process of industrialization of Bengal. Bengalis were busy in accumulating human capital. The accumulation of human capital provided a distinct advantage to the people of Bengal over the people of other regions, when modern education began to spread in other parts of the Indian subcontinent with the opening of several universities such as universities of Dacca, Banaras, Allahabad and Lahore. Bengali academics occupied most of the faculty positions in these universities and in their affiliated colleges. It is in this unique way that Bengalis participated in the process of economic development of the Indian economy by participating in colleges, universities and scientific institutions. By this time, Calcutta had schools which were spreading knowledge about mathematics and basic science. The city already had Hindu College and Presidency College, which were giving quality education to the students. Subsequently, Calcutta Medical College was set up in 1857.

The Indian Association for the Cultivation of Science was also opened in Calcutta in 1876. Moreover, quite a large number of students who graduated from the educational institutions of Calcutta went abroad for higher studies. Earlier, the educated Bengali elite class was seeking jobs in colleges, universities, government departments, railways and companies promoted by Indian and British entrepreneurs. Law had also become an important profession in Calcutta.

The Swadeshi movement encouraged some of these educated Bengalis to promote companies which required understanding of science and technology to produce high-technology products which had become part of consumption of the middle classes. Two Bengali entrepreneurs established Bande Match Factory and Oriental Match Factory in 1906. It is also important to mention that two persons, P. Ayya Naidu and his cousin A. Shanmuga, developed skills for making safety matches while working in Bande Match Factory at Calcutta. On their return, they established a match factory in Sivakasi. They were manufacturing handmade safety matches using the brand name Bengal Light. Later on, these two brothers opened factories to produce fireworks with the brand name Peacock and Cock. Eventually, Sivakasi became the capital of fireworks production in India (Damodaran, 2008, 138–142).

Around the same time, Prafulla Chandra Roy, trained as an experimental chemist, with a PhD degree in chemistry from the University of Edinburgh, along with another well-known scientist of Bengal, Jagadish Chandra Bose, established Bengal Chemicals & Pharmaceutical Works Ltd. Later on, Prafulla Chandra Roy also established Bengal Immunity to manufacture vaccines. Kiran Shankar Roy, who had studied at Oxford University, established Bengal Lamps Ltd to produce electric bulbs. However, he could not sustain this enterprise for a long time due to financial problems. This enterprise was later purchased by Lala Shri Ram. Manindra Chandra Nandy, the Maharaja of Kasimbazar, started Bengal Pottery. The Mitra family set up Calcutta Chemical Company to manufacture soap, toothpaste and herbal cosmetics, and the family of the Dasguptas established Bengal Waterproof Ltd, which manufactured the Duckback brand of raincoats and gumshoes.[26] The Bengali entrepreneurs who promoted these enterprises were professionals, scientists and middle-class educated individuals who did not have financial resources to expand the scale of operations. This limitation became an important disadvantage when they experienced stiff competition from several multinational corporations who had established their units in Calcutta after the First World War. These multinationals were producing the same products with better technology and huge financial resources. As a consequence of this limitation, most of the enterprises which were floated by the Bengali entrepreneurs in Calcutta did not survive for long. However, some of the enterprises that emerged in response to the Swadeshi movement have survived till now. These enterprises are those which are producing products such as Jabakusum (C.K. Sen and Co. Pvt. Ltd) and Keo Karpin brands of hair oil (Dey's Medical) and Boroline (GD Pharmaceuticals) (see Majumdar, 2012, 122; Seth, 2015, Chapter 5).

The multinational corporations began their operations in Calcutta after the 1920s, when the government of the British Raj imposed tariffs on the imports of manufactured goods during the First World War. These tariffs were not imposed to protect the Indian manufacturers but to protect Indian market from the manufactures produced by several European countries and America, which had by this time achieved industrialization.[27] Most of the multinational companies which opened their enterprises in India were interested to jump tariff walls erected by the British Raj to enter into a large continental-size market. Calcutta became an important location of these firms. The importance of Calcutta remained because it was quite a large metropolitan city with large numbers of consumers, both native and British. Moreover, it was a port city well connected with its hinterland.

The multinational enterprises which opened their businesses in Calcutta were Jenson and Nicholson, which was established in 1922; Imperial Chemical Industries (ICI) in 1923; Siemens, a German multinational, opened its subsidiary unit also in 1923. Britannia Biscuit Co. Ltd in 1924; Dunlop Rubber Company (India) Ltd in 1926; and Imperial Tobacco Company which began its operation in Calcutta in 1928. Colgate–Palmolive Company opened its Indian operations in Calcutta in 1930. In 1931, three multinational companies opened their enterprises in India. These were International General Electric

Corporation (India) Ltd, Bata India Ltd, Philips India Ltd and Lever Brothers.[28] Philips India cannibalized the market of Bengal Lamps. Multinational enterprises such as Colgate–Palmolive and Lever Brothers changed the consumption preference of the Indian middle classes significantly. It is due to the quality of their products, scale of their operations and advertisement capabilities that not only Indian middle classes, but also natives of different countries had begun to believe that their products are an essential part of maintaining cleanliness. They gave up the use of their native products which they used earlier for cleanliness. There emerged a myth 'Lifebuoy Men and Lux Women'.[29] Under these circumstances, the Bengali entrepreneurs could not sustain their enterprises; only recently, Patanjali brand floated by Baba Ram Dev has challenged the myth created by Lever regarding Life Buoy and Lux.

Calcutta remained as an important location for several multinational enterprises. For instance, Metal Box Ltd established its subsidiary Metal Box Company of India in Calcutta in 1933. Eveready Company Ltd opened its operation by forming National Carbon Company to manufacture the Eveready brand of electric batteries in Calcutta. In 1934, Goodlass Wall & Co Ltd opened its first enterprise called D. Waldie & Co. in 1934 in Calcutta. Thereafter, it started two other subsidiaries in 1939 at Calcutta for manufacturing different chemicals. Godfrey Philips Ltd established its subsidiary Godfrey Philips India Ltd to manufacture cigarettes in Calcutta. British Canadian multinational Aluminium Company of Canada started its subsidiary, Aluminium Production Company of India Ltd, at Calcutta in 1938 to manufacture aluminium sheets.[30]

It is important to mention that the attraction of Calcutta for foreign multinationals lasted only during the inter-war period (1920–1939). Suddenly the inflow of foreign investment declined with the beginning of the Second World War. This phenomenon needs explanation. One set of scholars believe that with the emergence of several modern manufacturing enterprises floated by Indian entrepreneurs, subsequently developing their specific needs prompted them to come closer to the nationalist movement. Slowly they developed their own associations.

The nationalist leaders had accepted the participation of India in the First World War on the promise that they would get certain amount of autonomy in the governance of India. To this effect, the British administration had introduced the Montague–Chelmsford Reforms in 1917. Therefore, foreign multinational enterprises were uncertain about their future in India (Kidron, 1965). Another strand of thought existing on this issue explains the decline of foreign firms by tracing problems such as shortage of capital (Tomilson, 1981, 1993), which were endogenous to the operation of firms. Some scholars believe that the proportion of foreign holding of stocks in these companies declined as the number of shareholders increased substantially. They were aware that due to wider spread of their holding there was no threat to take over. These foreign enterprises consciously diluted their holding and invested their resources at other more competitive locations.[31]

The spread of modern manufacturing in Calcutta and its hinterland increased the demand for equipment and machines, that is, capital goods. This provided motivation to established enterprises to produce capital equipment which were in demand amongst the manufacturers of Calcutta. As a consequence of this increase in demand for capital goods, P. N. Datta & Company of Calcutta started production of machine tools in 1930. The Birlas opened Textile Machinery Corporation (Texmaco) at Calcutta. However, this unit was taken over by the British administration immediately after its formation under the Defence of India Rules for using its machinery and equipment to produce goods required during the Second World War. Due to this reason, this enterprise could begin to produce ring frame looms only after 1945, when the British administration gave back the possession of the plant (Kenny and Florida, 1993).

The end of the Second World War was the beginning of American supremacy in the manufacturing field. The competitive advantage of the US manufacturing over British and European manufacturing emerged when one of its manufacturing enterprises, Eli Whitney, in its gun manufacturing factory located at New Haven, Connecticut, introduced the assembly line method of production. This method helped in the *mass production* of standardized goods using interchangeable parts.[32] This method facilitated the emergence of large-scale enterprises, financed by pooling resources of thousands of investors in the joint-stock format of organization of business enterprise. The existence of large-scale enterprises created necessary conditions for use of methods evolved by Frederick Winslow Taylor, which are now being described as *Taylorism*.[33] The joint-stock companies needed pools of managers to run the businesses, which led to *managerial revolution*.[34] These distinct characteristics of the American manufacturing enterprises established the global competitive advantage of American enterprises. These techniques were employed by Henry Ford in Ford Motor Company in 1911, which helped him to produce the cheapest car in the world. Since then, this approach is also known as *Fordism* (Collins and Lapierre, 1975, 13).

The period immediately after the Second World War, had significantly impacted the economies of Europe in general and economies of Britain in particular due to wartime destruction. The city of London has been described by some noted authors of modern history in the following words: 'It was the smell of charred ruins up like an autumn mist from thousands of bombed out buildings' (Bagchi, 1972; Tomilson, 1978, 1993). These economies were busy in the process of post-War reconstruction. This period provided opportunities to entrepreneurs in Calcutta to establish enterprises to produce some of the consumer durables. Demand for such products had increased in India, which was met by importing these products from abroad. Looking at the huge demand–supply gap, entrepreneurs of Calcutta began to enter into the production of consumer durables. Ford Motor Company established it assembly unit in Calcutta. In 1942, the Birlas promoted Hindustan Motors in Calcutta to assemble Morris Cars and Studebaker Trucks from CKD kits. Around the same time, Ramprasad Basil, an engineer working in the department of telegraph, designed the first sewing machine and established Jaya Engineering Company to manufacture sewing machines. Earlier, sewing machines of the Singer brand were imported from America (Travers, 2007, 29). The developments discussed above demonstrate how Calcutta emerged as a rich prosperous city, with a diversified industrial base, urban infrastructure and educational institutions. These developments increased the economic gap between Dacca and Calcutta. Dacca, which was once economically a much better city during the Mughal Empire and was the capital of Bengal, lost its economic prosperity to a city established by the colonial power. Prosperity of Calcutta also had spillover effects on the economy of Dacca. Dacca and its hinterland started producing raw materials which were required in the manufacturing sector of Calcutta and other parts of Bengal. Dacca also continued to manufacture textiles, not for export but needed by the population of Bengal which remained wedded to ethnic choices. Despite the impact of Westernization on Bengal, a very large part of the population remained attached to the traditional consumption pattern, especially in terms of choices regarding textiles. Partly, it was a product of the increased sense of nationalism promoted by the Swadeshi movement. These sentiments of the population helped in the continuous production of certain items in the handicraft mode. As education spread in Bengal, it also affected Dacca. Dacca had its own university. However, concentration of several modern manufacturing units in Calcutta gave birth to a trajectory of divergence in prosperity between Dacca and Calcutta. The tales of the two cities of the Eastern coast of India amply demonstrates how the shift in the policy regimes affected the fortunes of the cities of Dacca and Calcutta. The policy regimes destroyed the traditional flexible manufacturing of Dacca and facilitated the emergence of modern manufacturing in Calcutta. This can be seen as a process of *creative destruction*, which substantially affected the fortunes of these two cities.

On 15 August 1947, the Indian subcontinent came out of the shadow of the British Raj, when it achieved independence. However, it was partitioned into two independent nations, India and Pakistan, on religious grounds. It is quite saddening to note that while this led to extreme form of communal violence, all the British expatriates left the Indian subcontinent en masse. This was quite a peculiar behaviour on the part of the Britishers, because they never left their other colonies, till today, like the USA, Canada, Australia, New Zealand and South Africa. The question is why they abandoned the Indian subcontinent. One of the historians of the British Empire has very appropriately described that 'The British in India were destined to remain a society of temporary exiles rather than of settlers' (Acemoglu and Robinson 2001). One tentative explanation for this peculiar behaviour on the part of the British expatriates has been advanced by some historians, based on some historical facts. On the basis of these facts, they have identified two different forms of interaction between the colonialized and the colonizers.

In one of the forms, colonizers set up *extractive states*, where the main objective of the colonial state was to transfer economic surplus and materials of the colony to the imperial state. These were the colonies which were not hospitable for the settlement of citizens of the colonial state. Therefore, in the absence of desire to settle permanently, the colonial state intended to transfer riches from the colonies to the imperial state. In another form of colonization, the imperial powers found suitable environment for large settlement of their citizens. Anticipating long-term stay in such colonies, these expatriates created similar institutions that were existing in the states of colonizers. It is here that they developed the economy and stayed back). This simplistic explanation does not explain the experience of the Indian subcontinent. This needs elaborate research. Since this is not precisely the place to explore the answer to this pertinent question, we are leaving it for readers to imagine different possible scenarios.

The partition of the Indian subcontinent in 1947 separated these two cities and allocated them to two different nations. Bengali nationalism was able to prevent the partitioning of these two cities of the Indian subcontinent in 1905. But Independence of India in 1947 could not stop this separation. As a consequence of the Partition, Dacca became the capital of East Pakistan and Calcutta became the capital of West Bengal, one of the several states which formed the Indian Union. Contemporaneously, Dacca is known as Dhaka and is the capital city of the youngest nation of the Indian subcontinent, Bangladesh. Due to unlimited supply of cheap labour, it has emerged as an important centre of production of apparels. The city is producing apparels for almost all the important brands of the West. This is how the industry which was transplanted in Manchester and Lancashire has travelled back to its original location, again in search of cost advantage. Jeremy Seabrook has very passionately described this phenomenon in his book

The Song of the Shirt: 'Bangladesh today does not clothe the nakedness of the world, but provides it with limitless cheap garments through Primark, Walmart, Benetton, Gap' (Seabrook, 2014, Jacket of the book).

Calcutta, now known as Kolkata, is stagnating because its most important manufacturing industry, namely jute textiles, is slowly going into oblivion. Scientific and technological advances have made available several cheaper substitutes for jute textiles. Most of the jute textile mills have been closed down. One of the oldest and main slums of Calcutta, Anand Nagar, has grown at a site where two jute textile companies lodged their workers. The slum Anand Nagar (City of Joy) has been immortalized by Dominique Lapierre's novel *City of Joy*, which appeared in 1985. Continuous rule of the Left parties since the 1960s pampered workers to the extent that the workers forgot their work ethic, which facilitated flight of capital, decline of old factories and arrested the growth of new enterprises. At the turn of the century, people of Calcutta elected a new party, Trinamool Congress, to make the city more open to investments. The new party also has a Left-like attitude, which has not provided conditions for the growth of new industries. These circumstances have made Kolkata a place of tired, greying population, as percentage share of people above the age of 60 is very high, where young people are waiting for a prophet who will reinvent the city and take it to a new path. The city has no shortage of human capital, but *das capital* is missing. Once there emerges complementarity between the two, the city will again come to life.

After independence, Surat automatically became part of Gujarat, one of the states of the Indian Union, but Bombay's future hung in the air till 1956. The problem occurred because Bombay since 1500 until 1947 was under foreign occupation, that is, during the entire period of my tale of the four cities. It was earlier occupied by the Portuguese and then by the British. Moreover, it was a cosmopolitan city, where persons belonging to different faiths, religions and speaking different languages lived together. Due to this reason, there emerged two different opinions regarding its allocation to different political units created by State Reorganizing Committee. One of these two opinions were represented by Bombay Citizens' Committee, consisting of residents of Bombay city, whose families had contributed significantly to the development of the city. This group was represented by Shri Purushottamdas Thakurdas and the Tatas. They submitted their memorandum to the State Reorganizing Committee in 1954. The other point of view was articulated by Samyukta Maharashtra Samiti. Please and its memorandum was prepared by Shankarrao Deo and a noted economist of Pune, Dr D. R. Gadgil.

The Bombay Citizens' Committee was interested to make Bombay as an autonomous city state because it was not dominantly a Marathi-speaking region, it was cosmopolitan in character and was the commercial capital of India. Geographically also, it was a separate and distinct region from Marathi-speaking areas, almost like an island city separated by the sea and mountains. The exclusivity of Bombay from Marathi-speaking regions and its unique character was very aptly articulated by S. K. Patil in the Parliament. He described that Bombay was 'a melting pot which will evolve a glorious new civilization ... will set the pace for other states in the practice of secularism and mutual understanding'.[35] On the contrary, the Samyukta Maharashtra Samiti. Please argued that Bombay should become part of the Marathi-speaking state called Maharashtra, and the city should be made its capital. The formation of this state will strengthen the federal character of the Indian Constitution by bringing together all the Marathi-speaking people within a single political unit.

After deliberating on different strands of thought on the issue, the State Reorganizing Committee proposed that a separate state with the name Vidarbha be created consisting of Marathi-speaking areas. The Bombay state will remain as it is. But recommendations of the Committee were ignored under the pressure of agitation organized by Samyukta Maharashtra Samiti. Please during the annual session of the Congress party, which was held in Bombay in 1956. Under this mounting pressure, Bombay was joined with Maharashtra. History has proved how erroneous this decision was, taken under pressure. This is because quite often the peace and tranquillity of this cosmopolitan city is disturbed by the violent agitations organized by the regional parties of Maharashtra, which want to impose Marathi language on the people living in Bombay. These parties also harass the migrants to the city who have come in pursuit of their dreams. They perceive these migrants as persons who are taking away their economic opportunities.

NOTES

1. For details regarding Suez Canal, see Ferguson (2004, 130–132).
2. For these facts, see Tripathi (2004).
3. It was observed in early 1880s that Calcutta and Bombay had emerged on two nodal centres of trade, without parallel in any other country. How these two cities enjoyed double dominance, see Hunter (1888) and Markovits (2000, 2008).
4. For the evolution of managing agency system, see Blair (1969).
5. For details regarding the functioning of the managing agency system, see Nigam (1957), Basu (1958), Singh (1966) and Sethia (1969).
6. For details, see Wacha (1910).
7. These facts have been taken from Gandhi (1930, 52).
8. For this data, see Mehta (1954, 27–29).
9. For details, see Parathasarthi (2001), Riello and Roy (2009), Riello and Parathasarthi (2009), Roy (1993) and (1999).
10. For the spatial spread of Indian after textile manufacturing in India, see Bagchi (1972), Seth (1987, 2015), Chandavarkar (1994), Mahadevan (1999), Chari (2004) and Damodaran (2008).
11. The symbiotic relationship that existed between modern textile manufacturing mills of Ahmedabad and traditional flexible manufacturing textile mill of Gujarat, see Roy (1982).
12. For these discriminating policies of the British government on Indian cotton textile mill, see Mehta (1954) and Morris (1965).
13. For details knowledge about Bombay film industry, see Hanson (2011) and Mazumdar (2007).
14. To know in detail the contribution of Godrez in the economic and social life Bombay, see Karanjia (1997).
15. For understanding in detail about the House of Tata's, see Johnson (1966) and Lala (1981).
16. For details regarding foreign investments, see Kidron (1965), Bagchi (1972) and Tomilson (1978).
17. To know in detail about these enterprises, see Piramal and Herdeck (1986), Tripathi and Mehta (1990), Piramal (1998) and Tripathi (2004).
18. For details, see Tomilson (1981, 1993) and Hurd (1982, 758).
19. For the consequences of Crimean War on the demand for Dacca jute, see Williams (1965, 254).
20. To know in detail regarding the beginning of jute textile mills in Calcutta, see Hunter (1888, 1974).
21. For details regarding jute-textile manufacturing industries, see Wallace (1928) and Buchanan (1966).
22. See for details regarding these facts, see Goswami (1982, 1985, 2011).
23. For the detailed history of tea plantation on in India, see Eliss et al. (2016) and Griffiths (1967).

24. See Money (1841), statements are quoted in Ellis et al. (2015, 239–240).
25. For this painting, see Ramaswamy (2011).
26. For details regarding their companies, see Roy (1999).
27. For details, see Rosen (1958, 20–30) and Roy (2006).
28. How multinational companies like Lever Brother created this myth around the world amongst all the third world countries, see Burke (1996).
29. For details regarding foreign investments in India, see Kidron (1965), Tomilson (1978, 1993) and Tripathi (2004).
30. For this strand of thought, see Roy (1979) and Kidron (1965).
31. For details, see Khanolkar (1969) and Piramal (1998).
32. For understanding Taylorism, see Taylor (1885 [1919], 1947).
33. For understanding about managerial revolution, see Morris (1979) and Chandler (1977).
34. To know about Fordism, see Amin (1995).
35. See Guha (2007, 195) for the statement of S.K. Patil.

EPILOGUE

Cities of a region are embedded in social and economic forces that are evolved by the political regime that governs its manifestation of peaks of civilizing factor of a polity. As political regimes alter, these socio-economic forces also undergo change. Therefore, cities are significantly impacted by changes in the political regimes. In the present book, my attempt was to understand how colonial power altered the nature of the economy of the Indian subcontinent and reorganized it to meet the needs of imperial economy. While reorganizing the economy, colonial power also affected the spatial distribution of economic activities. It was the spatial redistribution of economic activities that shifted the location of wealth and prosperity. The shifts in location of wealth and prosperity that occurred as a consequence of policies pursued by the colonial power resulted in the decline of native cities and prosperity in the colonial cities. However, while researching for the book, I observed that reality may not necessarily conform to historical stereotypes.

Historians have developed certain stylized facts regarding conse-quences of colonialism on the native economy. These stylized facts establish uniformity regarding these consequences. This perspective gives a false confidence that past is known, while future is uncertain. However, my exploration provided contrary evidence and forced me to believe that even past is uncertain because past can also be variously described. The objective analysis of past may also provide several out-comes, where each one of them appears valid description of the past. Therefore, the main objective of writing this book was to illustrate the variety in regional experiences of colonialism. These variations have been explained with the help of narrating the tale of four cities.

Dear readers, I am really grateful to all of you who have read the book so far and have arrived at this section. You have read the tale that I have been able to write from my exploration of existing sources. While telling the tale, I have tried my best to let the facts speak for themselves. To avoid my personal biases and prejudices, I have used material drawn from the works of several scholars, irrespective of their ideological premises. We are human beings and have capacity to understand things according to our own capabilities, experiences and exposure. Therefore, I do not rule out certain amount of subjectivity in narrating the tale.

In order to minimize subjectivity, I have not included in the book a final chapter titled 'Lessons Learnt from the Tale of Four Cities' that I had initially planned. This is because, after writing this chapter, I realized that it contains those lessons that I have learnt from the tale. This chapter contained purely my own subjective assessment of the experience of four cities. My assessment may be one of the several evaluations which can be arrived at by different individuals. Therefore, instead of that chapter I have written this epilogue. I have done this strictly following the tradition of storytelling, as it evolved in India and in some other oriental countries. This tradition is manifest in the stories told in *Panchatantra, Jataka Kathas, Arabian Nights, Maznun and Laila, Heer Ranjha* and several such stories. This tradition is based on the premise that the role of storyteller or writer is just to narrate the story, thereby giving total freedom to the listener or reader of the story to interpret and learn lessons from the story according to his own cir-cumstances, understanding and purpose. Therefore, I am also giving complete freedom to your imagination to draw your own conclusions and learn your own lessons from this tale of four cities.

Wish you all the best for learning your own lessons.

BIBLIOGRAPHY

Acemoglu, Daron, and James A. Robinson, 2012, *Why Nations Fail: The Origins of Power, Prosperity and Poverty*. New York, NY: Crown Business.
———, 2008, 'Political Loosers as Barriers to Economic Development.' *The American Economic Review* 90, no. 1: 126–130.
Acemoglu, Daron, Simon Johnson, and James A. Robinson, 2001, 'The Colonial Origins of Comparative Development: An Empirical Invitation'. *The American Economic Review*, 91, no. 5: 1369–1401.
———, 2002, 'Colonial Origins of Comparative Development: An Empirical Investigation.' *The American Economic Review* 91, no. 5: 1369–1401.
Acemoglu, Daron, and James A. Robinson, 2008, 'Political Loosers as Barriers to Economic Development', *American Economic Review*, 90, no. i: 126–130.
Alam, Ishrat, 2012a, 'Iron and Steel Fabrication Technology in Medieval India.' In *History of Technology in India*, Vol. 1, edited by Harbans Mukhia, 467–482. New Delhi: Indian National Science Academy.
———, 2012b, 'Textile Technology in Medieval North India.' In *The History Technology in India*, Vol. 2, edited by Harbans Mukhia, 341–354. New Delhi: Indian National Science Academy.
Alam, Muzaffar, 1986, *The Crisis of Empire in Mughal North India: Awadh and Punjab 1707–1748*. New Delhi: Oxford University Press.
Alam, Muzafar, and Sanjay Subrahmanyam, eds., 1998, *The Mughal State 1526–1770*. New Delhi: Oxford University Press.
Alchian, Armen, and Harold Demsetz, 1972, 'Production Information Costs and Economics Organization.' *The American Economic Review* 62, no. 5: 777–795.
Alesina, Alberto, and Paola Giuliano, 2015, 'Cultures and Institutions.' *Journal of Economic Literature* 53, no. 4: 898–944.
Ali, Daud, 2004, *Courtly Culture and Political Life in the Early Medieval India*. Cambridge, UK: Cambridge University Press.
Allami, Abul Fazal, 1927, *The Ain-i-Akbari*, Vols. I–II. Edited by Colonel D. H. Phillot and translated from Persian by H. B. Blichmann. New Delhi: Oriental Books Reprint Cooperation.

Allami, Abul Fazal, 1956, *Akbarnama*, Vols. I–III. Translated from Persian by H. B. Blichmann. New Delhi: Bibliotheque.

Alvi, Seema, ed., 2002, *The Eighteenth Century India*. New Delhi: Oxford University Press.

Al-Sharif, Idrish, 1960, *Kitab Nuzahat-ul-mushtaq*. English translation with commentary by S. Maqbul Ahmad. Leiden: Palgrave Macmillan.

Ambirajan, S., 1987, *Classical Political Economy and British Policy in India*. Cambridge, UK: Cambridge University Press.

Amin, Ash, ed., 1995, *Post Fordism: A Reader*. Oxford, UK: Blackwell Publishing.

———, 1989, 'Flexible Specialization and Small Firms in Italy: Myth and Reality.' *Antipode* 21, no. 1: 13–24.

Amin, Ash, and Joanne Roberts, eds., 2008, *Community, Economic Creativity, and Organization*. New York, NY: Oxford University Press.

Anderson, Gary M., and Robert D. Tollison, 1982, 'Adam Smith's Analysis of Joint Stock Companies.' *Journal of Political Economy* 90, no. 6: 1237–1256.

Anderson, Gary M., Robert E. McCormick, and Robert D. Tollison, 1983, 'The Economic Organization of the English East India Company.' *Journal of Economic Behavior and Organization* 4, no. 2–3: 221–238.

Aneja, Atul, 2016, '"Silk Road" Train to Reach Afghanistan on Sept. 9.' *The Hindu*, 28 August.

Anthony, Pagden, 2001, *People and Empire: A Short History of European Migration, Exploration and Conquest: From Greece to Present*. New York, NY: Modern Library.

Appadurai, Arjun, ed., 1986, *The Social Life of Things: Commodities in Cultural Perspective*. Cambridge, UK: Cambridge University Press.

Aquil, Raziuddin, 2008, 'On Islam and Kufr in Delhi Sultanate: Towards a Re-interpretation of Ziya Al-Din Barmi's *Fatwa-i-Jahandari*.' In *Rethinking a Millennium: Perspectives on Indian History from the Eighth to the Eighteenth Century: Essays for Harbans Mukhia*, edited by Rajat Datta. New Delhi: Aakar Books.

Arasaratnam, S., 1979, 'Trade and Political Dominion in South India 1750–1790: Changing British–India Relationship.' *Modern Asian Studies* 13, no. 1: 19–40.

———, 1980, 'Weavers, Merchants and Company: The Handloom Industry in South India 1750–1790.' *The Indian Economic and Social History Review* 17, no. 3: 257–281.

Aristotle, 340 BC (2001), *Basic Works of Aristotle*. New York, NY: Modern Library.

Arrow, Kenneth J., 1985, 'The Economics of Agency.' In *Principals and Agents: The Structure of Business*, edited by J. Pratt and R. Zeckhauser, 37–51. Boston, MA: Harvard Business School Press.

Ashton, T. S., 1948, *Industrial Revolution 1760–1800*. Oxford, UK: Oxford University Press.

———, 1960, *Industrial Revolution 1760–1800*. Oxford, UK: Oxford University Press.

Astha, Mahesh Chandra, 1976, 'Railway Rates and Fares in India 1849–1922: A Historical cum Analytical Study.' PhD thesis, Department of Economics, Delhi School of Economics New Delhi.

Athar Ali, M., 1978, 'Eighteenth Century: An Interpretation.' *The Indian Economic and Social History Review* 5, no. 1–2: 175–186.

———, 1975, 'The Passing of Empire: The Mughal Case.' *Modern Asian Studies* 9, no. 3: 385–396.

———, 1986–1987, 'Recent Theories of Eighteenth Century India.' *Indian Historical Review* 13, no. 1–2: 102–110.

Babur, Zahiruddin Mohammad, 1996, *The Baburnama: Memoirs of Babur, Prince and Emperor*. Translated by Wheeler M. Thackston. New York, NY: Modern Library.

———, 2002, *The Baburnama: Memoirs of Babur, Prince and Emperor*. Translated by Wheeler M. Thackston. New York, NY: Modern Library.

Bagchi, Amiya Kumar, 1972, *Private Investment in India 1900–1939*. Cambridge, UK: Cambridge University Press.

———, 1978, 'De-industrialization in India in the Nineteenth Century: Some Theoretical Implications.' *The Journal of Development Studies* 12, no. 2: 135–164.

———, 1987, *The Evolution of State Bank of India*, Part 1: *The Roots 1806–1879*. Bombay: Oxford University Press.

Bairoch, P., 1982, 'International Industrialization Levels from 1750–1980'. *Journal of European Economic History*, II: 10269–10333.

Baker, S. G., 1935, *Report on Scientific and Technical Development of the Jute Manufacturing Industry in Bengal*. Calcutta: Indian Jute Mills Association.

Balfour, Edward, 1885, *The Cyclopædia of India and of Eastern and Southern Asia, Commercial, Industrial, and Scientific*. London: B. Quaritch.

Balhatchet, K., and J. Harrison, eds., 1980, *The City in South Asia: Premodern and Modern*. London: Curzon Press.

Banarsidas, 2009, *Ardhakathanak: A Half Story*. Translated from Braj Bhasa by Rohini Chawdhury. New Delhi: Penguin India.

Banga, Indu, 1978, *Agrarian System of Sikhs*. New Delhi: Oxford University Press.

Barani, Zia-ud-din, 1357 (2015), *Tarikh-in Firoz Shahi*. Translated by Istiyaq Ahmad Zilli. New Delhi: Primus Books.

Barnes, Ruth, 1997, *Indian Block Printed Textiles in Egypt: The Newbery Collection in the Ashmolean Museum*. London: Oxford University Press.

Barnett, Richard B., 1980, *North India Between Empires: Awadh, the Mughals and the British, 1720–1801*. Berkeley, CA: University of California Press.

Basu, S. K., 1958, *The Managing Agency System*. Calcutta: World Press.

Bauman, Christopher, 2000, *Southern Silk Road*. Bangkok: Orchid Press.

Baumol, William J., Robert Litan, and Carl J. Schramm, 2007, *Good Capitalist, Bad Capitalist and Economic Growth*. New Haven, CT: Yale University Press.

Baumol, William J., Robert Litan, and Carl J. Schramm, 2012, 'Four Types of Capitalism, Innovations and Economic Growth. In *The Oxford Handbook of Capitalism*, edited by Dennis C. Mueller, 115–228. New York, NY: Oxford University Press.

, C. A., 1983, *Townsman and Bazars: North Indian Society in the Age of British Expansion*, Cambridge, UK: Cambridge University Press.

———, 1986, 'The Origin of Swadeshi (Home Industry): Cloth and Indian Society 1700–1930.' In *The Social Life of Things: Commodities in Cultural Perspective*, edited by Arjun Appadurai, 285. Cambridge, UK: Cambridge University Press.

———, 1987, *Indian Society and Making of the British Empire*. Vol. I: *The New Cambridge History of India*, Part 2, 127–155. Cambridge, UK: Cambridge University Press.

———, 1988a, *The British Empire and the World 1780–1830*. Oxford, UK: Oxford University Press.

———, 1988b, *The Indian Society and the Making of British Empire*, Vol. II: *The New Cambridge History of India*, Part 1. Cambridge, UK: Cambridge University Press.

Bayly, C. A., and Sanjay Subrahmanyam, 1988, 'Portfolio Capitalists and the Political Economy of Early Modern India.' *The Indian Economic and Social History Review* 25, no. 4: 401–424.

Beckert, Sven, 2014, *Empire of Cotton: A New History of Global Capitalism*. London: Penguin Books.

Behagg, Clive, 1998, 'Mass Production Without the Factory: Craft Producers, Guns and Small Firm Innovation, 1790–1815.' *Business History* 40, no. 3: 1–15.

Behera, Subhakanta, 2002, 'India's Encounter with the Silk Road.' *Economic & Political Weekly* 37, no. 51(21 December): 4485–4987.

Bender, Jill C., 2016, *The 1857 Indian Uprising and the British Empire*. Cambridge, UK: Cambridge University Press.

Benjamin, N., 1976, 'Arab Merchants of Bombay and Surat (1800–40).' *The Indian Economic and Social History Review* 13, no. 1: 85–95.

Benning, J., 1982, 'Silver in Seventeenth Century Surat: Monetary Circulation and Price Revolution in Mughal India.' In *Precious Metals in the Later Medieval and Early: Modern Worlds*, edited by J. F. Richards. Durham, NC: Carolina Academic Press.

Berg, Maxine, 1980, *Machinery Question and Making of Political Economy*. Cambridge, UK: Cambridge University Press.

———, 1993, 'Small Producers Capitalism in Eighteenth Century England.' *Business History* 35, no. 1: 17–39.

———, 2005, *Luxury & Pleasure in Eighteenth-century Britain*. Oxford, UK: Oxford University Press.

———, 2012, 'Luxury, the Luxury Trade, and the Roots of Industrial Growth: A Global Perspective.' In *The Oxford Handbook of History of Consumption*, edited by Frank Trentmann, 173–191. Oxford, UK: Oxford University Press.

Berle, A., and G. C. Means, 1932, *Modern Corporation and Private Property*. New York: Macmillan.

Berman, Harold J., 1983, *Law and Revolution: The Formation of the Western Legal Tradition*. Cambridge, MA: Harvard University Press.

Bernier, François, 1670 (2011), *Travels in the Mughal Empire*. Translated by Irvin Brock. Cambridge, UK: Cambridge University Press.

Boyer, R., 1988, *The Search for Labour Market Flexibility: The European Economies in Transition*. Oxford: Clarendon Press.

Bhardwaj, Atul, 2016, 'Belt and Road Initiative: Potential to Tame American Imperialism.' *Economic & Political Weekly* 51, no. 43: 12–13.

Bhardwaj, H. C., 1982, 'Development of Iron and Steel Technology in India During 18th and 19th Century.' *Indian Journal of History of Science* 17, no. 2: 222–237.

Bhattacharya, S., 1965, 'Laissez Faire in India.' *The Indian Economic and Social History Review* 2, no. 1: 1–22.

———, 1966, 'Cultural and Social Constraints on Technological Innovation and Economic Development.' *The Indian Economic and Social History Review* 3, no. 3: 242–256.

———, 1982, 'Regional Economy 1757–1857: The Eastern India.' In *The Cambridge Economic History of India*, Vol. II, c. 1757–c. 1970, edited by Dharma Kumar, 270–331. Cambridge, UK: Cambridge University Press.

Bhatia, B. M., 1974, *History and Social Development*, Vol. 1. New Delhi: Vikas Publishing House.

Bird, Anthony, and Ian Hallows, 1984, *The Rolls-Royce Motor Car*. London: B.T. Batsford.

Biswas, Arun Kumar, 2001, *Minerals and Metals in Pre-modern India*. New Delhi: Oxford University Press.

Blair, Kling B., 1969, *Partner in Empire: Dwarkanath Tagore and the Age of Enterprise in Eastern India*. Berkeley, CA: University of California Press.

Blake, Stephen, 2008, 'Nav Ruz in Mughal India.' In *Rethinking a Millennium: Perspectives on Indian History from the Eighth to the Eighteenth Century*, edited by Rajat Datta, 121–138. New Delhi: Aakar Books.

———, 1960, *British India Centenary 1856–1956*. London: Orient Longman.

Bolts, William, 1772 (1998), 'Considerations on Indian Affairs.' In *The East India Company 1600–1858*, edited by Patrick Tuck. London: Routledge.

Bordien, Pierre, 2005, 'Principles of an Economic Anthropology.' In *The Handbook of Economic Sociology*, edited by Neil J. Smelser and Richard Swedberg, 75–89. Princeton, NJ: Princeton University Press.

Boserup, F., 1965, *The Conditions of Agricultural Growth: The Economics of Agrarian Change Under Population Pressure*. London: Allen & Unwin.

Baumol, W. J., 2002, 'Services as Leaders and Leaders of Services.' In *Productivity, Innovation and Knowledge in Services*, edited by Jean Gadrey and Faiz Gallouj, 147–163. Cheltenham, UK and Northampton, MA: Edward Elgar Publishing.

Bowen, H. V., 1987, 'Lord Clive and Speculation in the East India Company Stocks 1766.' *The Historical Journal* 30, no. 4: 890–927.

———, 1989, 'Investment and Empire in the Later Eighteenth Century: East India Stock Holding, 1756–1791.' *The Economic History Review* 42, no. 2: 186–206.

Bowen, H. V., 2006, *The Business of Empire: The East India Company and Imperial Britain, 1756–1833*. Cambridge, UK: Cambridge University Press.

Bowrey, T., 1905, *A Geographical Account of Countries Round the Bay of Bengal 1669–1679*. Cambridge, UK: Hakluyt Society.

Braudel, Fernand, 1982, *Civilization & Capitalism 15th–18th Century*, Vol. II: *Wheels of Commerce*. London: William Collins Sons & Co.

Breen, T. H., 2004, *The Market Place of Revolution: How Consumer Politics shaped American Independence*. New York: Oxford University Press.

Brenning, Joseph A., 1990, 'Textile Producers and Production in Late Seventeenth Century Coromandel.' In *Merchants, Markets and the State in Early Modern India*, edited by Sanjay Subrahmanyam, 66–89. New Delhi: Oxford University Press.

Brent, Peter, 1976, *The Mongol Empire: Genghis Khan, His Triumphs and His Legacy*. London: Weidenfeld and Nicolson.

Broeze, Frank, ed., 1989, *Brides of the Sea: Port Cities of Asia from the 16th to 20th Centuries*. Kensington, NSW: University of New South Wales Press.

Buchanan, Daniel Huston, 1966, *The Development of Capitalist Enterprises in India*. London: Frank Cass & Co.

Burke, Edmund, 1783 (1981), 'Ninth Report of Select Committee, June, 1783.' In *The Writings and Speeches of Edmund Burke*, Vol. V, edited by P. J. Marshall. Oxford, UK: Clarendon Press.

Burke, Peter, 1979, *The New Cambridge Modern History*, Vol. XIII (companion volume). Cambridge, UK: Cambridge University Press.

Burke, Timothy, 1996, *Lifebuoy Men and Lux Women: Commodification of Consumption and Cleanliness in Modern Zimbabwe*. Durham and London: Duke University Press.

Burt, Roger, 1998, 'Proto-industrialization and Stages of Growth in the Metal Mining Industries.' *The Journal of European Economic History* 27, no. 1: 85–104.

Burton, Andrey, 1993, 'Bukhara Trade 1558–1718.' Paper on Inner Asia No. 23. Bloomington, IN: Indian University Institute for Inner Asian Studies.

Cairncross, Frances, 2001, *The Death of Distance: How the Communications Revolution Is Changing Our Lives*. London: Texere Publishing.

Calkins, Phillips, 1970, 'The Formation of a Regionally Created Ruling Group in Bengal, 1700–1740.' *The Journal of Asian Studies* 29, no. 4: 799–806.

Carlos, Ann M., 1991, 'Agent Opportunism and the Role of Royal African Companies Compared.' *Business and Economic History* 20, 142–151.

———, 1992, 'Bonding Versus Internal Promotion and Trust: Evidence from the Royal African Company 1672–1691.' Department of Economics, University of Colorado. Mimeo.

———, 1992, 'Principal–Agent Problem in Early Trading Companies: A Tale of Two Firms.' *The American Economic Review* (Papers and Proceedings) 82, no. 2: 140–145.

Carlos, Ann M., and Stephen Nicholas, 1988, 'Giants of Early Capitalism: The Chartered Trading Companies or Modern Multinational Corporation.' *Business History Review* 62, no. 3: 398–419.

Carlos, Ann M., and Stephen Nicholas, 1990, 'Agency Problems in Early Chartered Companies: The Case of the Hudson's Bay Company.' *The Journal of Economic History* 50, no. 4: 853–875.

———, 1993, 'Managing the Manger: An Application of Principal–Agent Model to the Hudson Bay Company.' *Oxford Economic Papers* 45, no. 2: 243–256.

Cartledge, Paul, Edward E. Cohen, and Lin Foxhall, eds., 2002, *Money, Labor and Land: Approaches to the Economies of Ancient Greece*. Oxford, UK: Oxford University Press.

Casas-Arce, Pablo, and Hajeebu Santhi, 2004, 'Job Design and Benefits of Private Trade.' Working Paper, Oxford Economics Working Paper Series Peg. 204, Oxford, UK.

Cassels, Nancy Gardner, 2010, *Social Legislation of the East India Company: Public Justice Versus Public Instruction*. New Delhi: SAGE.

Caton, H., 1985, 'Pre-industrial Economics of Adam Smith.' *The Journal of Economic History* 45, no. 4: 833–853.

Chakravarti, Ranabir, 2009, 'Visiting Faraway Ports: India's Trade in the Western Indian Ocean, ca. 800–1500 CE.' In *Rethinking a Millennium: Perspectives on Indian History from the Eighth to the Eighteenth Century: Essays for Harbans Mukhia*, edited by Rajat Datta, 249–274. New Delhi: Aakar Books.

Chandavarkar, Rajnarayan, 1994, *The Origins of Industrial Capitalism in India: Business Strategies and the Working Class in Bombay, 1900–1940*. Cambridge, UK: Cambridge University Press.

Chandler, Alfred, 1962, *Strategy and Structure: Chapters in the History of the American Industrial Enterprise*. Cambridge, MA: MIT Press.

———, 1977, *The Visible Hand: The Managerial Revolution in American Business*. Cambridge, MA: Harvard University Press.

Chandra, Satish, 1973, 'Social Background to the Rise of the Maratha Movement During the 17th Century in India.' *The Indian Economic and Social History Review* 10, no. 3: 209–217.

———, 1998, 'Review of the Crisis of the Jagirdari System.' In *The Mughal State, 1526–1750*, edited by Muzaffar Alam and Sanjay Subrahmanyam, 347–360. New Delhi: Oxford University Press.

Chari, Sharad, 2004, *Fraternal Capital: Peasant-workers, Self-made Men, and Globalization in Provincial India*. Ranikhet: Permanent Black.

Chatterji, Bankimcandra, 1882 (2005). *Anandmath, or the Sacred Brotherhood*. Translated by Julius J. Lipner. New York, NY: Oxford University Press.

Chatterji, Basudev, 1983, 'The Political Economy of "Discriminating Protection": The Case of Textiles in the 1920s.' *The Indian Economic and Social History Review* 20, no. 3: 239–276.

Chaudhuri, B. B., ed., 1997, *Economic History of India from Eighteenth to Twentieth Century*. New Delhi: Manohar Publishers.

Chaudhuri, K. N., 1966, *The English East India Company: The Study of an Early Joint-Stock Company 1600–1640*. London: Frank Cass & Co.

———, ed., 1971, *The Economic Development of India Under the East India Company 1814–1858*. Cambridge, UK: Cambridge University Press.

Chaudhuri, K. N., 1978, *The Trading World of Asia and the East India Company 1660–1760*. Cambridge, UK, and New York, NY: Cambridge University Press.

———, 1979, 'Markets and Traders in India During the Seventeenth and Eighteenth Centuries.' In *Economy and Society: Essays in Indian Economic and Social History*, edited by K. N. Chaudhuri and C. J. Dewey. New Delhi: Oxford University Press.

———, 1985, *Trade and Civilisation in the Indian Ocean: An Economic History from the Rise of Islam to 1750*. Cambridge, UK: Cambridge University Press.

———, 1990, *Asia Before Europe: Economy and Civilisation of the Indian Ocean from the Rise of Islam to 1750*. Cambridge, UK: Cambridge University Press.

Chaudhuri, K. N., 1974, 'The Structure of Indian Textile Industry in the Seventeenth and Eighteenth Centuries.' *The Indian Economic and Social History Review* 11(June–September): 23–35.

Chaudhury, Sushil, 1972, 'Merchants, Companies and Rulers: Bengal in the Eighteenth Century.' *The Journal of Economic and Social History of the Orient* 31, no. 1: 71–85.

———, 1995, *From Prosperity to Decline: Eighteenth Century Bengal*. New Delhi: Manohar Publishers.

Child, Sir Joshia, 1668 (1968), 'A New Discourse on Trade.' In *Joshia Child Selected Works 1668–1697*. Farnborough: Gregg Press/University of London.

Chopra, Preeti, 2011, *A Joint Enterprise: The Creation of New Landscape in British Bombay, 1839–1918*. Minneapolis, MN: University of Minnesota Press.

Christian, David, 2004, *Maps of Time: An Introduction to Big History*. Berkeley, CA: University of California Press.

Clark, C., 1950, *The Conditions of Economic Progress*. London: Mac Millan.

Clingingsmith, David, and Jeffery G. Williamson, 2004, 'India's De-industrialization Under British Rule: New Ideas, New Evidence.' Working Paper No. 10586. Cambridge, MA: National Bureau of Economic Research.

———, 1983, 'Proto-industrialization: A Concept Too Many.' *The Economy History Review* 36, no. 3: 435–448.

Coleman, D. C., 1973, 'Textile Growth.' In *Textile History and Economic History*, edited by N. B. Harte and K. G. Ponting. Manchester: Manchester University Press.

Collins, Larry, and Dominique Lapierre, 1975, *Freedom at Midnight*. New York: Simon and Schuster.

Clutton-Brock, Juliet, 1992, *Horse Power*. Cambridge, MA: Harvard University Press.

Commander, Simon, 1983, 'Jajimani System in North India.' *Modern Asian Studies* 17, no. 2: 283–311.

Cooper, Randolf G. S., 2003, *The Anglo-Maratha Campaigns and the Contest for India: The Struggle for Control of the South Asian Military Economy*. New York, NY: Cambridge University Press.

Clunas, Craig, 2007, *Empire of Great Brightness: Visual and Material Cultures of Ming China, 1368–1644*. London: Reaktion Books.

Dale, Stephen F., 1994, *Indian Merchants and Eurasian Trade, 1600–1750.* Cambridge, UK: Cambridge University Press.

Dale, Stephen F., 2008, 'Empires and Emporia: Palace, Masque Market and Tomb in Istanbul, Isfahan Agra and Delhi.' *The Journal of Economic History of the Orient* 53, no. 1–2: 15–38.

Dalrymple, William, 2006, *The Last Mughal: The Fall of a Dynasty, Delhi 1857.* New Delhi: Penguin Viking.

Dalrymple, William, and Anita Anand, 2016, *Kohinoor: A Story of the World's Most Infamous Diamond.* New Delhi: Juggernaut Books.

Damodaran, Harish, 2008, *India's New Capitalists: Cast, Business and Industry in a Modern Nation.* Ranikhet: Permanent Black.

Darling, Malcolm, 1926, *Punjab Peasantry in Prosperity and Debt.* London: Oxford University Press.

Das Gupta, Ashin, 1967, The Crisis at Surat 1730–173. *Bengal Past and Present* 86, Part II: 158–175.

———, 1970, 'The Merchants of Surat, c. 1700–1750.' In *Elites in South Asia,* edited by E. Leach and S. N. Mukherjee. Cambridge, UK: Cambridge University Press.

———, 1994, *Indian Merchants and the Decline of Surat: c. 1700–1750.* New Delhi: Manohar Publishers.

———, 2001, *The World of Indian Ocean Merchants 1500–1800.* New Delhi: Oxford University Press.

Dasgupta, Subrata, 2007, *The Bengal Renaissance: Identity and Creativity from Ram Mohan Roy to Rabindranath Tagore.* New Delhi: Permanent Black.

David, M. D., 1973, *History of Bombay 1661–1708.* Bombay: University of Bombay.

David, Saul, 2002, *The Indian Mutiny.* New Delhi: Penguin India.

Davis, Gerald F., 2003, 'Firms and Environment.' In *The Handbook of Economic Sociology,* edited by Neil J. Smelser and Richard Swedberg, 478–502. Princeton, NJ: Princeton University Press.

Davis, J. H., F. D. Schoorman, and L. Donaldson, 1997, 'Towards Stewardship Theory of Management.' *Academy of Management Review* 15, no. 3: 369–381.

Daw, Alexander, 1792, *The History of Hindostan, from the Death of Akbar, to the Complete Settlement of the Empire Under Aurangzeb.* Dublin: Luke White.

Deavy B., 1975, *The Economic Development of India: A Marxist Analysis.* Nottingham: Spokesman Books.

Dehlvi, Zahir, 1914 (2017), *Dastan-e-Ghadar.* Translated from Persian into English by Rana Safvi. New Delhi: Penguin India.

Derrett, J. D. M., 1976, 'Rajdharma.' *The Journal of Asian Studies* 35, no. 4: 597–609.

Desai, Ashok V., 2011, 'The Parsis: Entrepreneurial Success.' In *The Oxford India Anthology of Business History,* edited by Medha M. Kudaisya, 122–137. New Delhi: Oxford University Press.

Desai, Meghnad, 2009, *The Rediscovery of India.* New Delhi: Allen Lane/Penguin India.

de Sousa, J. P., 1961, *History of the Chemical Industry in India*. Bombay: Technical Press Publications.

Dietmar, Rothermund, 1988, 'Problem of India's Arrested Development Under British Rule.' In *Arrested Development in India: The Historical Dimension*, edited by Clive Dewey, 3–11. New Delhi: Manohar Publishers.

Devare, Hema, 2016, *Ganga to Mekong: A Cultural Voyage Through Textiles*. New Delhi: Manohar Publishers.

Devra, G. S. L., 1987, 'The Mughal State and Indian Business.' In *State and Business in India: A Historical Perspective*, edited by Dwijendra Tripathi, 1–24. New Delhi: Manohar Publishers.

Dewey, Clive, ed., 1988, *Arrested Development in India: The Historical Dimension*. New Delhi: Manohar Publishers.

Dey, Hirendra Lal, 1933, *The Indian Tariff Problem in Relation to Industry and Taxation*. London: Allen & Unwin.

Diamond, Jared, 2005, *Guns, Germs and Steel: A Short History of Everybody for the Last 13,000 Years*. London: Vintage.

Dirk, Nicholas B., 2006, *The Scandal of Empire: India and the Creation of Imperial Britain*. Ranikhet: Permanent Black.

Dittle, J. H., 1920, 'The House of Jagat Seth.' *Bengal Past and Present* 20: 111–120.

Divekar, V. D., 1982, 'The Emergence of an Indigenous Business Class in Maharashtra in the Eighteenth Century.' *Modern Asian Studies* 16, no. 3: 302–330.

Dobb, M. H., 1963, *Studies in the Development of Capitalism*. London: Routledge & Kegan Paul.

Dobbin, Christine, 1972, *Urban Leadership in Western India: Politics and Communities in Bombay City*. London: Oxford University Press.

Dodwell, H., 1922, *Madras Weavers Under the Company*. Proceedings of the Indian Historical Research Commission. Calcutta: Government Press.

Dore, Ronald, 1986, *Flexible Rigidities*. Stanford, CA: Stanford University Press.

Dossal, Mariam, 1991, *Imperial Designs and Indian Realities: The Planning of the Bombay City 1845–1875*. Bombay: Oxford University Press.

Dossal, Meriam, and Alice Thorner, eds., 1996, *Bombay: Metaphor for Modern India*. Bombay: Oxford University Press.

Dugrid, Paul, 2008, 'Community of Practice Then and Now.' In *Community, Economic Creativity, and Organization*, edited by Ash Amin and Joanne Roberts, 1–10. New York, NY: Oxford University Press.

Dutt, R. C., 1906, *The Economic History of India in the Victorian Age*. London: Kegan Pal.

———, 1916, *The Economic History of India Under Early British Rule: From the Rise of the British Power in 1757 to the Accession of Queen Victoria in 1837*, 103. London: Kegan Paul.

Eck, Diana L., 2012, *India: A Sacred Geography*. New York, NY: Harmony Books.

Ekelund, Robert B., and Robert D. Tollison, 1981, *Mercantilism as a Rent-seeking Society*. College Station, TX: Texas A&M University Press.

Ekelund, Robert B., and Robert D. Tollison, 1997, *Politicized Economics: Monarchy, Monopoly, and Mercantilism.* College Station, TX: Texas A&M University Press.

Ellis, Markman, Richard Coulton, and Matthew Mauger, 2015, *Empire of Tea: The Asian Leaf That Conquered the World.* New Delhi: Speaking Tiger.

Eraly, Abraham, 2003, *The Mughal Throne: The Saga of India's Great Emperors.* London: Phoenix.

Estall, R. G., and Oglive R. Buchanan, 1946, *Industrial Activity and Economic Geography.* London: Hutchinson University Library.

Fama, E., 1980, 'Agency Problem and the Theory of Firm.' *The Journal of Political Economy* 88, no. 2: 288–307.

Farooqui, Amar, 1995 'Opium Enterprise and Colonial Intervention in Malwa and Western India, 1800–1824.' *The Indian Economic and Social History Review* 32, no. 4: 450–572.

———, 2006, *Opium City: The Making of Early Victorian Bombay.* Gurgaon: Three Essays Collective.

Fateh, Sonya, 2012, 'Tracing the Origins of Pak's Doom and Gloom.' *The Times of India,* 14 June.

Fei, John C. H., and Gustav Ranis, 1969, 'Economic Development in Historical Perspective.' *The American Economic Review* (Papers and Proceedings) 59, no. 2: 286–400.

Ferguson, Niall, 2002, *Empire: The Rise and Demise of the British World Order and Lessons for Global Power.* New York, NY: Basic Books.

———, 2004, *Empire: How Britain Made the Modern World.* London: Penguin.

———, 2011, *Civilization: The West and the Rest.* London: Allan Lane/Penguin Books.

Findlay, Ronald, and Kevin H. O'Rourke, 2008, *Power Plenty: Trade, War, and the World Economy in the Second Millennium.* Princeton, NJ: Princeton University Press.

Findlay, Ronald, and Mats Lundahl, 2006, 'The First Globalization Episode: The Creation of Mongol Empire, or the Economics of Chinggis Khan.' In *Asia and Europe in Globalization: Continents, Regions and Nations,* edited by Göran Therborn and Habibul Haque Khondker, 13–54. Leiden: Brill.

Fisher, Michael H., 1987, *The Clash of Cultures: Awadh, the British and the Mughals.* New Delhi: Oxford University Press.

———, 1993, *The Politics of the British Annexation of India, 1757–1837.* Oxford, UK: Oxford University Press.

Florida, Richard, Charlotta Mellander, and Patrick Adler, 2015, 'Creativity in the City.' In *The Oxford Handbook of Creative Industries,* edited by Candace Jones, Mark Lorenzen, and Jonathan Sapsed, 96–118. Oxford, UK: Oxford University Press.

Fogel, R. W., 1964, *Railroads and American Economic Growth: Essays in Econometric History.* Baltimore, MD: Johns Hopkins University Press.

Folz, Richard C., 1999, *Religions of the Silk Road: Overland Trade and Cultural Exchange from Antiquity to the Fifteenth Century.* New York, NY: St. Martin's Griffin.

Foster, W., ed., 1906–1972, *The English Factories in India: A Calendar of Documents in the India Office*, Vols. 1–13. Oxford, UK: British Museum and Public Records Office.

Frank, Andre Gunder, 1990, 'On the Silk Road: An Academic Travelogue.' *Economic & Political Weekly* 25, no. 46 (17 November): 2536–2539.

———, 1998, *Reorient: Global Economy in the Asian Age*. New Delhi: Vistar Publications.

Franck, Irene M., and David M. Brownstone, 1986, *The Silk Road: A History*. Oxford and New York, NY: Facts On File.

Freeman, C., and F. Louca, 2001, *As Time Goes By: From Industrial Revolution to the Information Revolution*. Oxford, UK: Oxford University Press.

Freudenberger, Hermann, and Fritz Redlich, 1964, 'The Industrial Development of Europe: Reality, Symbols, Images.' *Kyklos* 17: 372–402.

Fruin, W. Mark, 1983, *Kikkoman: Company, Clan, and Community*. Cambridge, MA: Harvard University Press.

———, 2008, 'Business Groups and Inter-firm Networks.' In *The Oxford Handbook of Business History*, edited by Geoffery G. Jones and Jonathan Zeitlin, 244–268. New York, NY: Oxford University Press.

Fukazawa, H. K., 1972, 'Rural Servants in Maharashtrian Village, Demiurgic or Jajmani System.' *Hitotshubashi Journal of Economics* 13: 108–124.

Fuller, C. J., 1989, 'Misconceiving the Grain Heap: A Critique of the Concept of the Indian Jajmani System.' In *Money and Morality of Exchange*, edited by J. Parry and M. Bloch, 50–62. Cambridge, UK: Cambridge University Press.

Furber, Holden, 1970, *John Company at Work: A Study of European Expansion in the Late Eighteenth Century*. New York, NY: Octagon Books.

———, 2004, *Maritime India*. Reprint of *Rival Empires of Trade in the Orient, 1600–1800*. New Delhi: Oxford University Press.

Gadgil, D. R., 1924, *The Industrial Evolution of India in Recent Times, 1860–1939*. Milford: Oxford University Press.

Galenson, David W., 1986, *Traders, Planters and Slaves: Market Behavior in Early English America*. Cambridge UK: Cambridge University Press.

Gandhi, M. P., 1930, *The Indian Cotton Textile Industry: Its Past, Present and Future*. Calcutta: The Book Company.

———, 1934, *Indian Sugar: Its Past, Present and Future*. Calcutta: Government of India Press.

Gardner, Brian, 1971, *The East India Company: A History*. London: Hart-Davies.

Gay, Peter, 1969, *The Enlightenment: An Interpretation*, Vol. II: *Science and Freedom*. New York, NY: W. W. Norton.

Gilbert, Erik T., 2004, *Africa in World History*. Upper Saddle River, NJ: Pearson Prentice Hall.

Gokhale, Balkrishna Govind, 1979, *Surat in the Seventeenth Century: A Study in Urban History of Pre-modern India*. Scandinavian Institute of Asian Studies, Monography Series No. 28. London: Curzon Press.

Gopal, Surendra, 1984, 'Jain Merchants in Eastern India Under the Great Mughals.' In *Business Communities of India: A Historical Perspective*, edited by Dwijendra Tripathi, 69–82. New Delhi: Manohar Publishers.

Gordon, Stewart, 1977, 'The Slow Conquest: Administrative Integration of Malwa into the Maratha Empire, 1720–1760.' *Modern Asian Studies* 11, no. 1: 1–40.

———, 1993, *The Marathas, 1600–1818*. Vol. II, Part 4, *The New Cambridge History of India*. Cambridge: Cambridge University Press.

Goswami, Chhaya, 2011, 'Khojas: A Historical Overview of Their Settlements Overseas.' In *Gujarat and the Sea*, edited by Lotika Varadarajan, 627–650. Vadodara: Darshak Itihas Nidhi Publishers.

Goswami, Omkar, 1982, 'Collaboration and Conflict: European and Indian Capitalists and the Jute Economy of Bengal, 1919–1939.' *The Indian Economic and Social History Review* 19, no. 2: 141–179.

———, 1985, 'Then Came the Marwaris: Some Aspects of the Changes in the Pattern of Industrial Control in Eastern India.' *The Indian Economic and Social History Review* 22, no. 3: 225–249.

———, 1989, 'Sahib, Babus, and Banias: Changes in Industrial Control in Eastern India, 1918–1950.' *The Journal of Asian Studies* 48, no. 2: 289–309.

———, 2011, 'From Bazar to Industry.' In *The Oxford India Anthology of Business History*, edited by Medha M. Kudaisya, 235–257. New Delhi: Oxford University Press.

Gotthold, Julia J., 1987, *Indian Ocean: Bibliography*. Oxford: Clio Press.

Government of India, 1878, 'Custom Notification on N043 March 18, 1978.' Calcutta: Government of India Press.

———, 1939, *Defence of India Act*. Shimla: Government of India Press.

———, 1952, *Large Industrial Establishments in India in 1947*. New Delhi: Government of India Press.

Gower, L. C. B., 1969, *The Principles of Modern Company Law*. London: Stevens & Sons.

Greenberg, Michael, 1969, *British Trade and the Opening of China 1800–42*. Cambridge, UK: Cambridge University Press.

Grewa, J. S., and Indu Banga, 1990, *The New Cambridge History of India*, Vol. II, The Sikhs of the Punjab. Cambridge: Cambridge University Press.

Grewal, J. S., 1995, *The Sikhs of Punjab*. New Delhi: Manohar Publishers.

Greif, Avner, 1993, 'Contract Enforceability and Economic Institutions in Early Trade: The Maghribi Traders' Coalition.' *The American Economic Review* 83, no. 3: 525–548.

Griffiths, Sir Percival Joseph, 1967, *The History of the Indian Tea Industry*. London: Weidenfeld & Nicolson.

Groseclose, Barbara, 1990, *British Sculpture and the Company Raj: Church Monuments and Public Statuary in Madras, Calcutta and Bombay*. Newark, NJ: University of Delaware Press.

Grossman, S., and O. Hart, 1983, 'An Analysis of the Principal–Agent Problem.' *Econometrica* 51, no. 1: 7–45.

Grove, B.R., 1963, 'The Nature of LAND Rights in Mughal India'. *Indian Economic and Social History Review*, I, no. 1: 1–20.

Guha, Amalendu, 1970, 'Parsi Seths as Entrepreneurs 1750–1850'. *Economic and Political Weekly*, 5, no. 48: 32–46.

———, 1984, 'More About the Parsi Sheths: Their Roots, Entrepreneurship and Comprador Role, 1650–1918.' In *Business Communities of India: A Historical Perspective*, edited by Dwijendra Tripathi, 109–150. New Delhi: Manohar Publishers.

Guha, Ramchandra, 2007, *India After Gandhi: The History of the World's Largest Democracy*. New Delhi: Picador India.

Guha, Sumit, 1989, 'The Handloom Industry of Central India 1825–1950.' *The Indian Economic and Social History Review* 26, no. 3: 355–425.

———, 2004, 'Civilization Markets and Services: Village Servants in India from the Seventeenth to the Twentieth Centuries.' *The Indian Economic and Social History Review* 41, no. 1: 79–101.

Gupta, Brijen, 1966, *Sirajuddaulah and the East India Company 1756–1757: Background to the Foundation of British Power in India*. Leiden: Brill.

Gupta, Ranjan Kumar, 1980, 'Iron Manufacturing Industry in Birbhum: A Study of Growth and Evolution.' *Journal of Indian History* 38: 94–106.

Guy, John, 1989, 'Sarasa and Patola: Indian Textile in Indonesia.' *Orientations* 20, no. 1: 38–56.

Habakkuk, H. J., 1962, *American and British Technology in the Nineteenth Century*. Cambridge, MA: Cambridge University Press.

Habib, Irfan, 1964, 'Banking in Mughal India.' In *Contribution to Indian Economic History*, Vol. 1, edited by Tapan Raychaudhuri. Calcutta: Firma K.L. Mukhopadhyay.

———, 1965, *The Agrarian System of Mughal India 1556–1707*. London: Asia Publishing House.

———, 1982, *An Atlas of the Mughal Empire*. New Delhi: Oxford University Press.

———, 1987, 'A System of Trimetalism in the Age of "Price Revolution": Effects of the Silver Influx on the Mughal Monetary System.' In *The Imperial Monetary System in Mughal India*, edited by John F. Richards, 137–170. New Delhi: Oxford University Press.

———, 1987, 'Agrarian Economy Under the Sultanate.' In *The Cambridge Economic History of India*, Vol. I, edited by Tapan Raychaudhuri and Irfan Habib. Cambridge, UK: Cambridge University Press.

———, 1990, 'The Merchant Communities in Pre-colonial India.' In *The Rise of the Merchant Empire: Long-distance Trade in the Early Modern World 1350–1750*, edited by James D. Tracy. Cambridge, New York, NY: Cambridge University Press.

Haider, Najaf, 2012, 'Minting Technology in Mughal India.' In *History of Technology in India*, edited by Harbans Mukhia, 222–247. New Delhi: Indian National Science Academy.

Hajeebu, S., 2005, 'Contract Enforcement in English East India Company'. *Journal of Economic History*, 65, no. 2: 496–523.

Halil, Inalcik, 1971, *The Ottoman Empire: The Classical Age 1300–1660*. Oxford, UK: Oxford University Press.

Hall, Peter A., and David Soskice, 2001, *Varieties of Capitalism: The Institutional Foundations of Comparative Advantage*. New York, NY: Oxford University Press.

Hall, H. D., 1955, *North American Supply*. London: Her Majesty's Stationery Office.

Hall, Peter, 1978, *Cities in Civilization*. New York, NY: Pantheon.

Hall, Richard, 1996, *Empire of the Monsoon*. New York, NY: HarperCollins.

Haellquist, Karl Reinhold, ed., 1991 *Asian Trade Routes: Continental and Maritime*. London: Routledge, Scandinavian Institute of Asian Studies.

Hambly, Gavin R. G., 1982, 'Towns and Cities: Mughal India.' In *The Cambridge Economic History of India*, Vol. I, edited by Tapan Raychaudhuri and Irfan Habib, 434–457. Cambridge, UK: Cambridge University Press.

Hammond, Mason, 1972, *The City of the Ancient World*. Cambridge, MA: Cambridge University Press.

Hanes, W. Travis, and Frank Sanello, 2003, *The Opium Wars*. London: Robson Books.

Hansen, Kathryn, 2011, *Stages of Life: Indian Theatre Autobiographies*. Ranikhet: Permanent Black.

Hannah, Williard, 1978, *Indonesian Banda: Colonialism and Its Aftermath in the Nutmeg Islands*. Philadelphia, PA: Philadelphia Institute for the Study of Human Issues.

Harte, Negley B., ed., 1997, *The New Draperies in the Low Countries and England 1300–1800*. New York, NY: Oxford University Press.

Hardgrove, Anne, 2004, *Community and Public Culture: The Marwaris in Calcutta c.1897–1997*. New York, NY: Columbia University Press.

Harnetty, P., 1991, 'De-industrialization Revised: The Handloom Weavers of the Central Provinces of India.' *Modern Asian Studies* 25, no. 3: 455–510.

Hasan, Aziz, 1967, 'Mints of Mughal Empire.' In *Partials Proceedings of Indian History Compress*, 29 Secession, 329–349.

Hasan, Farhat, 1992, 'Indigenous Cooperation and Birth of a Colonial City: Calcutta.' *Modern Asian Studies* 26, no. 2: 360–392.

Hasan, Nurul, 1964, 'The Position of Zamidars in Mughal Empire', *Indian economic and Social History Review*, II, no. 1, 30–49.

Haynes, Douglas, and Tirthankar Roy, 1999, 'Conceiving Mobility: Migration of Handloom Weavers in Precolonial and Colonial India.' *The Indian Economic and Social History Review* 36, no. 3: 35–67.

Haynes, Douglas E., 1991, *Rhetoric and Ritual in Colonial India: Shaping of Public Culture in Surat City 1852–1928*. Berkeley, CA: University of California Press.

Haynes, Douglas E., 1996, 'The Logic of Artisan Firms in Capitalist Economy: Handloom Weavers in Western India c. 1880–1947.' In *Institution and Economic Change in South Asia*, edited by Burton Stein and Sanjay Subrahmanyam. New Delhi: Oxford University Press.

Haynes, Douglas E., 2012, *Small Town Capitalism in Western India: Artisans, Merchants and Making of the Informal Economy, 1870–1960.* New York, NY: Cambridge University Press.

————, 2015, 'Surat City: Its Decline and the Indian Ocean.' In *Port Towns of Gujarat*, edited by Sara Keller and Michael Pearson, 43–56. New Delhi: Primus Books.

Heath, J. M., 1839, 'Indian Iron and Steel Industry.' *Journal of the Royal Asiatic Society* 5, no. 3: 390–399.

Heckscher, E. F., 1931, *Mercantilism.* Translated by Mendel Shapiro. London: Allen & Unwin.

Hegel, G. W. Friedrich, 1857 (1900), *The Philosophy of History.* Translated by J. Sibree. New York, NY: Colonial Press.

————, 1956, *The Philosophy of History.* Reprint of the translation by J. Sibree. New York, NY: Dover Publications.

Heiser, Charles B., Jr, 1990, *Seed to Civilization: The Story of Food.* Cambridge, MA: Harvard University Press.

Henderson, William O., 1975, *The Rise of German Industrial Power, 1834–1914.* Berkeley, CA: University of California Press.

Hibbert, Christopher, 1978, *The Great Mutiny: India 1857.* London: Allen Lane.

Hicks, John, 1969, *A Theory of Economic History.* Oxford, UK: Clarendon Press.

Hill, C. W., and T. M. Jones, 1992, 'Stakeholders Agency Theory.' *Journal of Management Studies* 29, no. 1: 131–154.

Hill, Christopher, ed., 1967, *Reformation to Industrial Revolution*, Vol. II. Harmondsworth: Penguin Books.

Hill, S. C., 1905, *Bengal, 1756–57*, Vol. III. London: John Murray.

Hinnells, John, and Allan Williams, eds., 2008, *Parsis in India and the Diaspora.* London: Routledge.

Hobbes, Thomas, 1651 (1974), *Leviathan.* Edited and abridged with an introduction by John Plamenatz. Glasgow, UK: Collins/Fontana.

Hobhouse, Henry, 1999, *Seeds of Change: Six Plants that Transformed Mankind.* London: Papermac.

Hobsbawm, E. J., 1954, 'The General Crisis of European Economy in the Seventeenth Century.' *Past and Present* 5, no. 1: 33–53.

————, 1968, *Labouring Men.* London: Weidenfeld & Nicolson.

————, 1968, *Industry and Empire: An Economic History of Britain Since 1750.* London: Weidenfeld & Nicolson.

————, 1975, *The Age of Capitalism: 1848–1875.* London: Abacus Books.

Hodgson, G. H., 1938, *Thomas Parry: Free Merchant.* Madras: Higginbotham's.

Holmstrom, B., 1979, 'Moral Hazard and Observability.' *The Bell Journal of Economics* 10, no. 1: 74–91.

————, 1982, 'Moral Hazard in Teams.' *The Bell Journal of Economics* 13, no. 2: 324–340.

Holzman, James M., 1926, *The Nabobs in England.* New York: Oxford University Press.

Hopkins, Peter, 1980, *Foreign Devils on the Silk Road*. Oxford, UK: Oxford University Press.

Horn, Jeff, 2007, *The Industrial Revolution: Milestones in Business History*. London: Greenwood Press.

Horvath, Ronald J., 1969, 'In Search of a Theory of Urbanization: Notes on the Colonial City.' *East Lakes Geographer* 5, no. 1: 70–92.

Horton, M. C., and J. Middleton, 2000, *The Swahili: The Social Landscape of a Mercantile Society*. Oxford, UK: Blackwell Publishing.

Hansmann, Henry, 1996, *The Ownership of Enterprise*. Cambridge, MA: Harvard University Press.

Howe, Anthony, 2002, 'Restoring Free Trade: The British Experience, 1776–1873.' In *The Political Economy of British Historical Experience, 1688–1914*, edited by Donald Winch and Patrick O'Brien, 193–213. Oxford, UK: Oxford University Press.

Howkins, J., 2003, *The Creative Economy: How People Make Money From Ideas*. London: Penguin Books.

Hozenetty, Peter, 1972, *Imperialism and Free Trade: Lancashire and India in the Mid-nineteenth Century*. Manchester: University of Manchester Press.

Hudson, Pat, 1996, 'Proto-industrialization in England.' In *European Proto Industrialization*, edited by Sheilagh C. Ogilvie and Marcus Cerman, 49–66. Cambridge, UK: Cambridge University Press.

Hunter, W. W., 1868, *The Annals of Rural Bengal*. New York, NY: Leypoldt and Holt.

———, 1874, *Famine Aspects of Bengal Districts*. London: Turner & Co.

———, 1888 (1974), *Statistical Accounts of Bengal*, Vol. IX. New Delhi: Concept Publishing Company.

Hurd, John M., 1982, 'Railways.' In *The Cambridge Economic History of India*, Vol. II, c. 1757–c. 1970, edited by Dharma Kumar, 737–761. Cambridge, UK: Cambridge University Press.

Husain, Iqbal, ed., 2006, *Karl Marx on India*. New Delhi: Tulika Books.

Hussain, Hameeda, 1958, *The Company Weavers of Bengal: The East India Company and the Organization of Textile Production in Bengal 1750–1813*. New Delhi: Oxford University Press.

Jacob, J., 1961, *The Death and Life of Great American Cities*. New York, NY: Random House.

———, 1969, *The Economy of Cities*. New York, NY: Random House.

Jaffrelot, Christophe, 2017, 'Corridor of Economic Uncertainty.' *The Indian Express*, Tuesday, 13 June.

Jahangir (1603–1627), 2006, *The Tuzuk-i-Jahangiri* (or *Memoirs of Jahangir*). Translated by Alexander Rogers. New Delhi: Low Priced Publication.

Jain, L. C., 1929, *Indigenous Banking in India*. London: Macmillan.

James, Lawrence, 2003, *Raj: The Making and Unmaking of British India*. London: Abacus.

Janaki, V. A., 1974, *Some Aspects of the Historical Geography of Surat*. Baroda: The M. S. University of Baroda Press.

Jenkins, D. T., ed., 1994, *The Textile Industries*. Oxford, UK: Blackwell Publishing.

Jenkins, David, ed., 2003, *The Cambridge History of Western Textiles*, Vol. I. Cambridge, UK: Cambridge University Press.

Johnson, William A., 1966, *The Steel Industry of India*. Cambridge, MA: Cambridge University Press.

Jones, S. R. H., and Simon P. Ville, 1996, 'Efficient Transactors or Rent-seeking Monopolists? The Rationale for Early Chartered Trading Companies.' *The Journal of Economic History* 56, no. 4: 898–915.

Jones, T. M., and A. C. Wicks, 1999, 'Convergent Stakeholder Theory.' *Academy of Management Review* 24, no. 1: 200–221.

Jorgenson, D. W., 1961, 'The Development of a Dual Economy.' *Economic Journal* 71, no. 282: 309–334.

Joshi, Arun, 1955, *Lala Shri Ram: A Study in Entrepreneurship and Industrial Management*. London and New Delhi: Orient Longman.

Joshi, P. C., ed., 2007, *Rebellion 1857*. New Delhi: National Book Trust.

Hoppit, Julian, and E. A. Wrigley, 1994, 'Introduction.' In *The Industrial Revolution in Britain*, edited by Julian Hoppit and E. A. Wrigley, X–XXXI. Oxford, UK: The Economic History Society, in association with Blackwell Publishers.

Juvani, Ata-Malik, 1997, *Genghis Khan: The History of the World-conqueror*. Translated by J. A. Boyle. Manchester, UK: Manchester University Press.

Kahn, Paul, 1984, *The Secret History of Mongols: The Origin of Genghis Khan*. San Francisco, CA: North Point Press.

Karanjia, B. K., 1997, *Godrej: A Hundred Years*, Vols. I–II. New Delhi: Viking.

Katz, L. F., 1986, 'Efficiency Wage Theories: A Partial Evaluation.' In *NBER Macroeconomics Annual*, edited by S. Fisher, 235–289. National Bureau of Economic Research. Cambridge, MA: MIT Press.

Kayoko, Fujita, 2009, 'Japan Indianzed: The Material Culture of Imported Textiles in Japan.' In *The Spinning World: A Global History of Cotton Textiles 1200–1850*, edited by Giorgio Riello and Prasannan Parthasarathi, 205–226. New York, NY: Oxford University Press.

Keay, John, 1981 (2013), *India Discovered: The Recovery of a Lost Civilization*. London: HarperCollins.

———, 1993, *The Honorable Company*. London: HarperCollins.

———, 2010, *India: A History from the Early Civilization to the Boom of Twenty-first Century*. London: Harper Press.

Kenny, M., and R. Florida, 1993, *Beyond Mass Production*. Oxford, UK: Oxford University Press.

Khan, Safat Ahmed, 1927, *The East India Trade in 17th Century*. Oxford, UK: Oxford University Press.

Khanolkar, G. D., 1969, *Walchand Hirachand: The Man, His Times and Achievements*. Bombay: Walchand & Company.

Kidron, Michael, 1965, *Foreign Investments in India*. London: Oxford University Press.

Kindleberger, Charles P., 1976, 'The Historical Background: Adam Smith and the Industrial Revolution.' In *Market and State: Essays in Honour of Adam Smith*, edited by Thomas Wilson and Andrew Skinner. Oxford, UK: Oxford University Press.

King, Blair, 1966, 'The Origin of the Managing Agency System in India.' *The Journal of Asian Studies* 26, no. 1: 120–130.

Knudsen, Daniel C., 1996, *The Transition to Flexibility*. Norwell, MA: Kluwer Academic Publishers.

Koh, S. J., 1966, *Stages of Industrial Development is Asia: A Comparative History of Cotton Textiles in Japan, India, China and Korea*. Philadelphia, PA: University of Pennsylvania Press.

Kolff, Dirk H. A., 2008, 'A Millennium of Stateless Indian History?' In *Rethinking a Millennium: Perspectives on Indian History from the Eighth to the Eighteenth Century: Essays for Harbans Mukhia*, edited by Rajat Datta. New Delhi: Aakar Books.

Kolsky Elizabeth, 2010, *Colonial Justice in British India: White Violence and the Rule of the Law*. New Delhi: Cambridge University Press.

Kosambi, Meera, 1980, *Bombay and Poona: A Socio-ecological Study of Two Indian Cities, 1650–1900*. Stockholm: Stockholm University Press.

Kosambi, Meera, and John E. Brush, 1988, 'Three Colonial Port Cities in India.' *Geographical Review* 78, no. 1: 32–47.

Kriedte, P., H. Medick, and J. Schlumberger, 1981, *Industrialization Before Industrial Revolution*. Translated from German by Beate Schen. Cambridge, UK: Cambridge University Press.

Krishnamurty, J., 1982, 'Occupational Structure.' In *The Cambridge Economic History of India*, Vol. II, c. 1757–c. 1970, edited by Dharma Kumar. Cambridge, UK: Cambridge University Press.

Kudaisya, Medha M., 2011, *The Oxford India Anthology of Business History*. New Delhi: Oxford University Press.

Kulkarni, A. R., 1996, *The Marathas*. New Delhi: Book & Books.

Kulke, Eckehard, 1978, *The Parsees in India: A Minority as Agent of Social Change*. New Delhi: Vikas Publishing House.

Kust, Matthew J., 1983, *Man and Horse in History*. Alexandria: Plutarch Press.

Lach, Donald F., 1965, *Asia in the Making of Europe*, Vol. I. Chicago, IL: University of Chicago Press.

Lahiri Choudhury, Deep Kanta, 2010, *Telegraphic Imperialism: Crisis and Panic in the Indian Empire, c. 1830–1920*. London: Palgrave Macmillan.

Lal, Deepak, 2004, *In Praise of Empires: Globalization and Order*. New York, NY: Palgrave and Macmillan.

———, 2007, *The Hindu Equilibrium*. Oxford, UK: Oxford University Press.

Lala, R. M., 1981, *The Generation of Wealth: The Tata Story*. Bombay: IBH Publishing.

Lala, R. M., 2007, *The Romance of Tata Steel*. New Delhi: Penguin Viking.

Lamb, Helen B., 1955, 'The Rise of Indian Business Communities.' *Pacific Affairs* 23, no. 2: 93–126.

Landes, David S., 1969, *The Unbound Prometheus*. Cambridge, UK: Cambridge University Press.

———, 1994, *The Wealth and Poverty of Nations*. New York, NY: Abacus.

Landy, C., 2008, *The Creative City: A Toolkit for Urban Innovations*. London: Earthscan.

Latham, A. J. H., 1981, *The Depression and the Developing World, 1914–1939*. London: Croom Helm.

Lawson, Philips, 1993, *The East India Company: A History*. London: Longman.

Lazonick, William, 1990, *Competitive Advantage of the Shop Floor*. Cambridge, MA: Harvard University Press.

———, 1991, 'Institutional Foundations of Industrial Dominance and Decline.' In *Business Organization and Myth of the Market Economy*, edited by William Lazonick, 23–58. Cambridge, MA: Cambridge University Press.

Lebman, Friedrich, 1965, 'Great Britain and the Supply of Railway Locomotives to India: A Case Study of Economic Imperialism.' *The Indian Economic and Social History Review* 2, no. 4: 297–306.

Leick, Gwendolyn, 2002, *Mesopotamia: The Invention of the City*. London: Penguin Books.

Lemire, Beverly, 1991, *Fashion's Favorite: The Cotton Trade and the Consumer in Britain, 1650–1800*. Oxford, UK: Oxford University Press.

———, 2004, 'Fashion and Tradition: Wearing of Wool in England During Consumer Revolution.' In *Wool: Products and Markets (13th–20th Century)*, edited by Giovanni Luigi Fontana and Gerard Gayot, 577–594. Padua: CLEUP.

———, 2009, 'Revising Historical Narrative: Indian, Europe and Cotton Trade c. 1300–1800.' In *The Spinning World: A Global History of Cotton Textiles, 1200–1850*, edited by Giorgio Riello and Prasannan Parthasarathi, 205–226. New York, NY: Oxford University Press.

Leonard, Karen, 1979, 'The Great Theory of the Decline of the Mughal Empire.' *Comparative Studies in Society and History* 21, no. 2: 161–167.

———, 1990, 'The Great Firm Theory of the Decline of Mughal Empire.' In *The Mughal State 1526–1750*, edited by Muzaffar Alam and Sanjay Subrahmanyam, 398–148. New Delhi: Oxford University Press.

Levine, David, 1977, *Family Formation in the Age of Nascent Capitalism*. New York, NY: Monthly Review Press.

Levis, Scott, 1999, 'India, Russia and the Eighteenth Century Transformation of Central Asian Carvan Trade.' *Journal of Economic and Social History of the Orient* 42, no. 4: 519–548.

Levis, Scott, C., 2002, *The Indian Diaspora in Central Asia and its Trade, 1550–1900*. Leiden: Brill.

Levis, Scott, C., ed., 2007, *Indian and Central Asia—Commerce and Culture, 1500–1800—Debates in Indian History and Society*. New Delhi: Oxford University Press.

Levkovsky, A. I., 1965, *Capitalism in India*. Bombay: Popular Prakashan.

Lewis, W. A., 1954, 'Economic Development with Unlimited Supply of Labor.' *The Manchester School of Economic and Social Studies*, 22, no. 2: 139–192.

Licht, Walter, 1995, *Industrialization of America: The Nineteenth Century*. Baltimore, MD: John Hopkins University Press.

Liedholm, Carl E., 1972, *The Indian Iron and Steel Industry: An Analysis of Comparative Advantage*. East Lansing, MI: Michigan State University.

Lingat, Robert, 1973, *The Classical Laws of India*. Berkeley, CA: University of Berkeley Press.

List, F., 1841, *Das Nationale System der Politischen Oekonomie*. Translated as *National System of Political Economy*. London: Longman.

Liu, Xinru, 1996, *Silk and Religion*. New Delhi: Oxford University Press.

Lokanathan, P. S., 1935 (1965), *Industrial Organization of India*. London: Orient Longman.

Louca, F., 2007, 'Long Waves: The Pulsation of Modern Capitalism.' In *The Elgar Companion to Neo-Schumpeterian Economics*, edited by Horst Hanusch and Andreas Pyka, 766–774. Cheltenham, UK and Northampton, MA: Edward Elgar.

Ludden, David, 1996, 'Caste Society and Units of Production in Early Modern South India.' In *Institutions and Economic Change in South Asia*, edited by Burton Stein and Sanjay Subrahmanyam, 105–133. New Delhi: Oxford University Press.

Lundvall, Bengt-Aka, 2007, 'National Innovation Systems: From List to Freeman.' In *The Elgar Companion to Neo-Schumpeterian Economics*, edited by Horst Hanusch and Andreas Pyka. Cheltenham, UK and Northampton, MA: Edward Elgar.

Machado, Pedro, 2004, 'A Forgotten Corner of the Indian Ocean: Gujarati Merchants, Portuguese India and the Mozambique Slave-Trade, c. 1730–1830.' In *The Structure of Slavery in Indian Africa and Asia*, edited by Gwyn Campbell, 17–32. London: Frank Cass & Co.

———, 2009a, 'A Regional Market in a Globalized Economy: East, Central and South Eastern Africa and the Textile Industry in Eighteenth and Nineteenth Centuries.' In *How India Clothed the World: The World of South Asian Textiles, 1500–1850*, edited by Giorgio Riello and Tirthankar Roy, 53–84. Leiden and Boston: Brill.

———, 2009b, 'Awash in Sea of Cloth Gujarat, Africa and Western Indian Ocean.' In *The Spinning World: A Global History of Cotton Textiles, 1200–1850*, edited by Giorgio Riello and Prasannan Parthasarathi, 161–180. New York, NY: Oxford University Press.

———, 2009c, 'Cloths of a New Fashion: Indian Ocean Networks of Exchange and Cloth Zones of Contract in Africa and India in the Eighteenth and

Nineteenth Centuries.' In *How India Clothed the World: The World of South Asian Textiles, 1500–1850*, edited by Giorgio Riello and Tirthankar Roy. Leiden and Boston: Brill.

Macpherson, W. J., 1955, 'Investment in Indian Railways 1845–1875.' *Economic History Review*, 2nd Series, 8, no. 2: 177–187.

MacGregor, Neil, 2010, *A History of the World in 100 Objects*. London: Penguin Books.

MacNeish, Richard S., 1992, *The Origins of Agriculture and Settled Life*. London: University of Oklahoma Press.

Maddison, Angus, 1971, *Class Structure and Economic Growth: India and Pakistan*. London: Allen & Unwin.

———, 2003, *The World Economy: A New Millennial Perspective*. New Delhi: Overseas Press.

Mahadevan Raman, 1992, 'Pattern of Industrial Control in Colonial Madras: Some Critical Observations on the Relative Position of Indian and Foreign Capital, 1930–1950.' In *Indian Industrialization: Structure and Policy Issues*, edited by Arun Ghosh, 336–364. New Delhi: Oxford University Press.

———, 1984, 'Entrepreneurship and Business Communities in Colonial Madras c. 1902–1929: Some Preliminary Observations.' In *Business Communities of India: A Historical Perspective*, edited by Dwijendra Tripathi, 225–239. New Delhi: Manohar Publishers.

———, 1999, 'Southern Region.' In *Footprints of Enterprise: Indian Business Through the Ages*, edited by FICCI. New Delhi: Oxford University Press.

Majumdar, Sumit, 2012, *India's Late, Late Industrial Revolution: Democratizing Entrepreneurship*. New Delhi: Cambridge University Press.

Malabari, Phiroz D. M., 1910, *Bombay in Making*. London: T. Fisher Unwin.

Malekandathil, Pius, 2000, *The Portuguese Casados and the Intra-Asia Trade: 1500–1663*. Proceedings of Indian History Congress 61st Session, Kolkata.

Malleson, G. B., 1901, *History of the French in India c. 1674 to c. 1961*. Edinburg: John Grant.

Maloni, Ruby, 2003, *Surat: Port of the Mughal Empire*. Bombay: Himalaya Publishing House.

———, 2015, 'Surat in the Seventeenth Century: A Pre-modern Urban Phenomenon.' In *Port Towns of Gujarat*, edited by Sara Keller and Michael Pearson, 273–284. New Delhi: Primus Books.

Manchester, William, 1992, *A World Lit Only by Fire*. New York, NY: Little Brown & Co.

Mandeville, Bernard, c. 1714 (1989), *The Fable of the Bees*. London: Penguin Classics.

Marathe, Sharad S., 1986, *Regulation and Development: India's Policy Experience of Controls over Industry*. New Delhi: SAGE.

Marco Polo, 1998, *The Book of Ser Marco Polo*, Vols. I–II. Translated and edited by Henry Yule. New Delhi: Oriental Reprints.

Markovits Claude, 2000a, 'Colonialism and Traditional Crafts.' *Economic & Political Weekly* 35, no. 45: 3939–3940.

———, 2000b, *The Global World of Indian Merchants, 1750–1947: Traders of Sind from Bukhara to Panama.* Cambridge, UK: Cambridge University Press.

———, 2008, *Merchants Traders and Entrepreneurs: Indian Business in Colonial Era.* New Delhi: Permanent Black.

———, 2011, 'Premier Industrial Centres: Bombay and Calcutta.' In *The Oxford India Anthology of Business History*, edited by Medha M. Kudaisya, 281–292. New Delhi: Oxford University Press.

Marris, Robin, 1964, *The Economic Theory of 'Managerial' Capitalism.* London: Macmillan.

Marshall, Peter J., 1975, 'Economic Expansion: The Case of Awadh.' *Modern Asian Studies* 9, no. 4: 465–482.

———, 1976, *East Indian Fortunes: The British in Bengal in the Eighteenth Century.* Oxford, UK: Clarendon Press.

———, 1987, *Bengal: The British Bridgehead: Eastern India 1740–1828.* Cambridge, UK: Cambridge University Press.

———, ed., 2003, *The Eighteenth Century in Indian History: Evolution Revolution.* New Delhi: Oxford University Press.

Martin, Mariana, 2004, 'Hundi/Hawala: The Problem of Definition.' *Modern Asian Studies* 43, no. 4: 909–937.

Marx, Karl, 1853, 'The British Rule in India.' *New York Daily Tribune*, 25 June. In *Karl Marx on India* (2006), edited by Iqbal Husain, 11–17. New Delhi: Tulika Books.

———, 1853, 'The East India Company: Its History and Results.' *New York Daily Tribune*, 24 June.

———, 1853, 'The Future Results of British Rule in India.' *New York Daily Tribune*, 8 August. Reprinted in *Karl Marx on India* (2006), edited by Iqbal Husain, 46–51. New Delhi: Tulika Books.

———, 1868 (1978), *Capital*, Vol. 1. Moscow: Progress Publishers.

Mathew, K. S., 1986, *Portuguese and the Sultanate of Gujarat, 1500–1573.* New Delhi: Manohar Publishers.

———, 1987, 'Business in Portuguese India: The Sixteenth and Seventeenth Centuries.' In *State and Business in India: A Historical Perspective*, edited by Dwijendra Tripathi, 22–58. New Delhi: Manohar Publishers.

Mathias, Peter, 1959, *The Brewing Industry in England 1700–1830.* Cambridge, UK: Cambridge University Press.

Mazumdar, Ranjani, 2007, *Bombay Cinema: An Archive of the City.* Ranikhet: Permanent Black.

McCloskey, Deirdre, N. 2010, *Bourgeois Dignity: Why Economics Can't Explain the Modern World.* Chicago, IL: Chicago University Press.

McFetridge, D., 1995, 'Knowledge, Market Failure and Multinational Enterprise: A Comment.' *Journal of International Business Studies* 26, no. 2: 409–406.

McGraw, Thomas K., ed., 1988, *The Essential Alfred Chandler: Essays Toward a Historical Theory of Big Business*. Boston, MA: Harvard Business School Press.

McNiell, William H., 1989, *The Age of Gunpowder Empires, 1450–1800*. Washington, DC: American Historical Association.

Meek, Ronald, 1962, *The Economics of Physiocracy: Essays and Translations*. New York, NY: Allen & Unwin.

Mehta, S. D., 1954, *Cotton Mills of India 1854–1954*. Bombay: Textile Association.

Mehta, M., 1991, *Indian Merchants and Entrepreneurship in Historical Perspective*. New Delhi: Academic Foundation.

Mehta, Shirin, 2011, 'Socio-economic Origins of a Business Community: The Bhatias of Kutch as Overseas Merchants.' In *Gujarat and the Sea*, edited by Lotika Varadarajan, 613–626. Vadodara: Darshak Itihas Nidhi Publishers.

Mendels, Franklin F., 1972, 'Proto-industrialization: The First Phase of the Industrialization Process.' *The Journal of Economic History* 32, no. 1: 241–261.

———, 1982, *Proto-industrialization: Theory and Reality*. General Report, Eighth International Economic History Congress, Budapest.

Metcalf, Barbara, 1993, 'Norms of Comportment Among Imperial Mughal Officers.' In *Power, Administration and Finance in Mughal India*, edited by John. F. Richards, 255–289. Aldershot: Variorum Collected Studies Series.

———, ed., 1984, *Moral Conduct and Authority: The Place of Adab in South Asian Islam*. Berkeley, CA: Berkeley University Press.

Mayer, Peter, 1993, 'Inventing Village Trading: The Late 19th Century Origin of North Indian Jajmani System.' *Modern Asian Studies* 27, no. 2: 378–386.

Mintz, W., 1986, *Sweetness and Power: The Place of Sugar in Modern History*. Harmondsworth: Penguin.

Mir, Moin, 2018, *Surat: Fall of a Port, Rise of a Prince: Defeat of the East India Company in the House of Commons*. New Delhi: Roli Books.

Mishra, B. B., 1965, *The Indian Middle Class*. London: Oxford University Press.

Misra, S. C., 1964, *Muslim Communities of Gujarat*. Bombay: Vikas Publishing House.

———, 1991, 'Urban History in India: Possibilities and Perspectives.' In *The City in Indian History*, edited by Indu Banga, 1–9. New Delhi: Manohar Publishers.

Mohan, Rakesh, 1992, 'Industrial Policy and Control.' In *The Indian Economy: Problems and Prospects*, edited by Bimal Jalan, 85–115. New Delhi: Viking.

Mokyr, Joel, 2009, *The Enlightened Economy: Britain and the Industrial Revolution 1700–1850*. London: Penguin Books.

Mommsen, W. J., and J. A. de Moor, eds., 1992, *European Expansion and Law: The Encounter of European and Indigenous Law in 19th- and 20th-century Africa and Asia*. New York, NY: Oxford University Press.

Moreland, W. H., 1923, *From Akbar to Aurangzeb*. London: Macmillan.

———, 1962, *India at the Death of Akbar: An Economic Study*. New Delhi: Atma Ram & Sons.

———, 1998, 'Ranks (Mansab) in Mughal State Service.' In *The Mughal State 1526–1750*, edited by Muzaffar Alam and Sanjay Subrahmanyam. New Delhi: Oxford University Press.

Moosavi, Shireen, 1987. *The Economy of the Mughal Empire c. 1595: A Statistical Study.* New Delhi: Oxford University Press.

Morris, Morris David, 1982, 'Growth of Large-scale Industry in India to 1947.' In *The Cambridge Economic History of India*, Vol. II, c. 1757–c. 1970, edited by Dharma Kumar, 553–676. Cambridge, UK: Cambridge University Press.

————, 1987 'Indian Industry and Business in the Age of Laissez Faire.' In *State and Business in India: A Historical Perspective*, edited by Dwijendra Tripathi, 123–156. New Delhi: Manohar Publishers.

————, 1968, 'Towards a Reinterpretation of Nineteenth-century Indian Economic History.' *The Indian Economic and Social History Review* 5, no. 1: 3–39.

Morris, Morris David, and Clyde B. Dudley, 1975, 'Selected Railway Statistics for the Indian Subcontinent (India, Pakistan, Bangladesh) 1853–1946/7.' *Artha Vijnana* 17, no. 3: 185–298.

Morris, Ian, and Richard P. Saller, eds., 2007, *The Cambridge Economic History of Greece and Roman World.* Cambridge, UK: Cambridge University Press.

Mourad, Kenize, 2012, *In the City of Gold and Silver: The Story of Begum Hazrat Mahal.* New Delhi: Full Circle Publishing.

Mukherjee, Mithi, 2010, *India in the Shadow of Empire: A Legal and Political History, 1774–1950.* New Delhi: Oxford University Press.

Mukherjee, Ramakrishna, 1974, *The Rise and Fall of the East India Company.* New York, NY: Monthly Review Press.

Mukherjee, Rundrangshu, February 1982, 'Trade and Empire in Awadh 1765–1804.' *Past and Present* 92: 85–102.

————, 1998 (2007), *Spectre of Violence: The 1857 Kanpur Massacres.* New Delhi: Penguin India.

————, 2008, *A Century of Trust: A Story of Tata Steel.* New Delhi: Penguin India.

Mukhia, Harbans, 2004, *The Mughals of India.* Oxford, UK: Blackwell Publishing.

————, ed., 2012, *History of Technology in India*, Vol. II. New Delhi: Indian National Science Academy.

Mukund, Kanakalatha, 1992, 'Indian Textile Industry in the 17th and 18th Centuries: Structures, Organisation and Responses.' *Economic & Political Weekly* 19, no. 38 (September): 2057–2065.

Mumford, Lewis, 1961, *The City in History: Its Origins, Its Transformation, and Its Perspective.* London: Secker & Warburg.

Mun, Thomas, 1664 (1928), *England's Treasure by Foreign Trade.* Oxford, UK: Basil Blackwell.

————, 1621 (1930), *A Discourse of Trade from England unto the East Indies.* Oxford, UK, and New York, NY: Basil Blackwell and Facsimile Text Society.

Nadri, Ghulam A., 2012, *Eighteenth-century Gujarat: The Dynamics of Its Political Economy, 1750–1800.* Leiden and Boston: Brill.

Naqvi, Hamida Khatoon, 1986, *Agriculture, Industrial and Urban Dynamics Under Sultans of Delhi.* New Delhi: Munshiram Manoharlal Publishers.

Naqvi, Hamida Khatoon, 2012, 'Dyeing Agents in India (AD 1200–1600).' In *History of Technology in India*, Vol. II, edited by Harbans Mukhia, 381–402. New Delhi: National Science Academy.

Naoroji, Dadabhai, 1901 (1962), *Poverty and Un-British Rule of India*. Reprint. New Delhi: Publications Division, Government of India.

Neff, J. U., 1943, 'Industrial Revolution Reconsidered.' *The Journal of Economic History* 3, no. 3: 2–29.

Nehru, Jawaharlal, 1947, *The Discovery of India*. London: Meridian Books.

Nigam, R. K., 1957, *The Managing Agency in India*. New Delhi: Ministry of Commerce, Government of India.

Nightingale, Pamela, 1970, *Trade and Empire in Western India 1784–1806*. New York, NY: Cambridge University Press.

Nockolds, Harold, 1959, *The Magic of a Name*. London: G. T. Foulis.

Noel, Dear, 1949/1958, *The History of Sugar*. London: Chapman & Hall.

Evenson, Norma, 1989, *The Indian Metropolis: A View Towards West*. New Delhi: Oxford University Press.

North, Douglas C., 1990, *Institutions Institutional Change and Economic Performance*, Cambridge, MA: Cambridge University Press.

———, 2006, *Understanding the Process of Economic Change*. New Delhi: Academic Foundation.

Ogilvie, Sheilagh C., and Marcus Cerman, eds., 1996, *European Proto-industrialization*. Cambridge, UK: Cambridge University Press.

Olson, M., 1965, *Logic of Collective Action: Public Goods and Theory of Group*. Cambridge, MA: Harvard University Press.

———, 1982, *The Rise and Decline of Nations: Economic Growth, Stagflation and Social Regulation*. New Haven, CT: Yale University Press.

Om Prakash, 1985, *The Dutch East India Company and Economy of Bengal 1630–1770*. Princeton, NJ: Princeton University Press.

———, 1998, 'Trade and Politics in Eighteenth Century Bengal.' In *On the Eighteenth Century as a Category of Asian History: Van Leur in Retrospect*, edited by Leonard Blusse and Femme S. Gaastra. Aldershot: Ashgate Publishing.

———, 2007, 'From Negotiation to Coercion: Textile Manufacturing in the Eighteenth Century.' *Modern Asian Studies* 41, no. 6: 1331–1368.

———, 1998, *European Commercial Enterprises in Precolonial India*. Cambridge, UK: Cambridge University Press.

O'Rourke, Kevin H., and Jeffrey G. Williamson, 2002, 'After Columbus: Explaining the Global Trade Boom 1500–1800.' *The Journal of Economic History* 62, no. 3: 417–456.

Ovington, J., 1689 (1929), *A Vovage to Surat in the year 1689*. Edited by H. G. Rawlinson. London: Hakluyt Society.

Palsetia, Jesse S., 2001, *The Parsis of India: Preservation of Identity in Bombay City*. Leiden: Brill.

Parker, W. N., 1982, 'European Development in Millennial Perspective.' In *Economics in Long View*, Vol. II, edited by C. P. Kingleberger and G. di Fella. London: Macmillan.

Parthasarathi, Prasannan, 2001, *The Transition to a Colonial Economy Weavers, Merchants and Kings in South India, 1720–1800*. Cambridge, UK: Cambridge University Press.

———, 2009, 'Cotton Textiles in Indian Subcontinent, 1200–1800.' In *The Spinning World: A Global History of Cotton Textiles, 1200–1850*, edited by Giorgio Riello and Prasannan Parthasarathi, 17–42. New York, NY: Oxford University Press.

———, 2011, *Why Europe Grew Rich and Asia Did Not: Global Divergence 1600–1850*. Cambridge, UK: Cambridge University Press.

Patel, S. J., 1952, *Agriculture Labourers in Modern India and Pakistan*. New Delhi: Asia Publishing House.

Pavlov, V. I., 1964, *The Indian Capitalist Class*. Moscow: PPH.

———, 1976, *Historical Premises for India's Transition to Capitalism*. Moscow: Nauka Publishing House.

Pearson, Michael N., 1994, *Pious Passengers: The Hajj in Earlier Times*. London: Hurst Publishers.

———, 2007, 'Markets and Merchants in the Indian Ocean.' In *Portuguese Oceanic Expansion, 1400–1800*, edited by Francisco Bethancourt and Diogo Ramada Curto, 88–108. New York, NY: Cambridge University Press.

Pederson, Olaf, 1997, *The First Universities: Studium Generale and the Origins of University Education in Europe*. Cambridge, UK: Cambridge, University Press.

Pelsaert, Francisco, 1925, *Jahangir's India: The Remonstrantie of Francisco Pelsaert*. Translated from Dutch by W. H. Moreland and P. Geyl. Cambridge, UK: W. Heffer & Sons.

Perlin, Frank, 1983, 'Proto-industrialization and Pre-colonial South Asia.' *Past and Present* 98, no. 1: 30–95.

Pichon, Alain Le, 2006, *China Trade and Empire: Jardine Matheson and Company and Origin British Rule in Hong Kong, 1827–1843*. London: Oxford University Press.

Pillai, A. S., 1930, 'Monograph on Nattukottai Chettis' Banking Business.' In *Madras Provincial Banking Enquiry Committee, Vol. III, Written Evidence*, 1170. Madras.

Piore, M. J., and C. F. Sabel, 1984, *The Second Industrial Divide*. New York, NY: Basic Books.

Piramal, Geeta, and Margaret Herdeck, 1986, *India's Industrialist*. Bombay: India Book House Distributors.

Piramal, Geeta, 1998, *Business Legends: Indepth Profiles of India's Most Daring and Innovative Entrepreneurs*. New Delhi: Penguin India.

Pollard, Sidney, 1968, *The Genesis of Modern Management*. London: Penguin.

Parthasarathi, Prasannan, and Giorgio Riello, 2012, 'From India to the World: Cotton and Fashionability.' In *The Oxford Handbook of the History of Consumption*, edited by Frank Trentmann, 145–172. Oxford, UK: Oxford University Press.

Prescott, William H., 1947, *History of the Conquest of Mexico* and *History of the Conquest of Peru*. New York, NY: Random House.

Pugh, Peter, 2000, *The Magic of a Name: The Rolls-Royce Story: The First Forty Years*. London and Flint, MI: Icon Books and Totem Books.

Putnam, R., 2000, *Bowling Action: The Collapse and Revival of American Community*. New York, NY: Simon & Schuster.

Ramaswamy, Sumathi, 2011, *The Goddess and the Nation: Mapping Mother India*. New Delhi: Zubaan.

Ramaswamy, Vijaya, 1980, 'Notes on Textile Technology in Medieval India with Special Reference to South.' *The Indian Economic and Social History Review* 17: 227–241.

———, 2008, 'Traditional Crafts, Technology and Society in Pre-colonial Peninsular India. In *Rethinking a Millennium: Perspectives on Indian History from the Eighth to the Eighteenth Century: Essays for Harbans Mukhia*, edited by Rajat Datta, 27. New Delhi: Aakar Books.

———, 2012, 'Textile Technology in Medieval India with Special Reference to the Peninsula: A Note.' In *History of Technology in India*, Vol. II, edited by Harbans Mukhia, 295–318. New Delhi: Indian National Science Academy.

Ray, Himanshu Prabha, 2016, *Ganga to Mekong: A Cultural Voyage Through Textiles*. New Delhi: Manohar Publishers.

Ray, Indrajit, 2005, 'The Silk Industry in Bengal During Colonial Rule: The De-industrialization Thesis Revisited.' *The Indian Economic and Social History Review* 42, no. 3: 339–375.

Ray, Rajat Kanta, 1982, 'Pedhis and Mills: The Historical Integration of Formal and Informal Sectors of the Economy in Ahmedabad.' *Indian Economic and Social History Review* 19, no. 3–4: 239–265.

———, ed., 1992, *Entrepreneurship and Industry in India 1800–1947*. New Delhi: Oxford University Press.

———, 1998, 'India, Its Society and British Supremacy.' In *The Oxford History of the British Empire*, Volume II: *The Eighteenth Century*, edited by Peter J. Marshall, 495–530. Oxford, UK: Oxford University Press.

———, 2002, 'Indigenous Banking and Commission Agency in India's Colonial Economy.' In *Money and Credit in Indian History*, edited by Amiya Kumar Bagchi. New Delhi: Tulika Books.

Roy, Tirthankar, 1993, *Artisans and Industrialization: Indian Weaving in the Twentieth Century*. New Delhi: Oxford University Press.

———, 1999, *Traditional Industry in the Economy of Colonial India*. Cambridge, UK: Cambridge University Press.

———, 2000, *The Economic History of India 1857–1947*. New Delhi: Oxford University Press.

———, 2006, *The Economic History of India 1857–1947*. New Delhi: Oxford University Press.

———, 2008, *Rethinking Change in India: Labour and Livelihood*. London and New York, NY: Routledge.

———, 2010, *Company of Kinsmen: Enterprise and Community in South Asian History 1700–1940*. New York, NY: Oxford University Press.

Roy, Tirthankar, 2013, *An Economic History of Early Modern India*. London and New York, NY: Routledge.

Raychaudhuri, Tapan, 1982, 'Non-agricultural Production in Mughal India.' In *The Cambridge Economic History of India*, Vol. 1, c. 1200–c. 1750, edited by Tapan Raychaudhuri and Irfan Habib, 261–307. Cambridge, UK: Cambridge University Press.

Reid, Anthony, 1993, *Southeast Asia in the Age of Commerce 1450–1680: Expansion and Crisis*, Vol. II. New Haven, CT: Yale University Press.

Riello, Giorgio, and Prasannan Parthasarathi, eds., 2011, *The Spinning of the World: Global History of Cotton Textiles, 1200–1850*. New York, NY: Oxford University Press.

Riello, Giorgio, and Tirthankar Roy, eds., 2009, *How India Clothed the World: Cotton Textiles and the Indian Ocean, 1500–1850*. Leiden: Brill.

Rich, E. E., 1952, *The Cambridge Economic History of Europe*, Vol. II. Cambridge, UK: Cambridge University Press.

Richard, D. S., ed., 1970, *Islam and Trade in Asia*. Oxford, UK: Oxford University Press.

Richards, John F., 1975, *Mughal Administration in Golconda*. New Delhi: Oxford University Press.

———, ed., 1978, *Kingship and Authority in South Asia*. Madison, WI: Centre of South Asian Studies, University of Wisconsin.

———, 1983, *Precious Metals in the Later Medieval and Early Modern World*. Durham: Carolina Academic Press.

———, ed., 1987, *The Imperial Monetary System of Mughal India*. London: Oxford University Press.

Richard, Robert, 1996, 'West Africa and Pondicherry Textile Industry.' In *Cloth and Commerce: Textiles in Colonial India*, edited by Tirthankar Roy. New Delhi: SAGE.

Richards, J. F., and V. Narayana Rao, 1998, 'Banditry in Mughal India: Historical and Folk Perception.' In *The Mughal State 1526–1757*, edited by Muzaffar Alam and Sanjay Subrahmanyam, 491–519. New Delhi: Oxford University Press.

Ridder-Symoens, Hilde de, 1993, *A History of the University in Europe*. Cambridge, UK: Cambridge University Press.

Rider, Christine, ed., 2007, *Encylopaedia of the Age of the Industrial Revolution, 1700–1920*, Vols. I–II. London: Greenwood Press.

Riello, Giorgio, and Tirthankar Roy, eds., 2009, *How India Clothed the World: The World of South Asian Textiles 1500–1850*. Leiden: Brill.

Riello, Giorgio, 2009, 'The Globalization of Cotton Textiles: Indian Cottons, Europe and the Atlantic World, 1600–1850. In *The Spinning World: A Global History of Textiles, 1200*–1850, edited by Giorgio Riello and Prasannan Parthasarathi, 261–290. New York, NY: Oxford University Press.

Riello, Giorgio, and Prasannan Parthasarathi, eds., 2009, *The Spinning World: A Global History of Textiles, 1200–1850*. New York, NY: Oxford University Press.

Rizvi, S. A. A., 1982 (2005), *The Wonder That Was India*, Vol. II (1200–1700). London: Picador.

Robbins, Lionel, 1998, *A History of Economic Thought: The LSE Lectures*. Edited by Steven G. Medema and Warren J. Samuels. Oxford, UK: Oxford University Press.

Robins, Nick, 2006, *The Corporation That Changed the World: How the East India Company Shaped Modern Multinationals*. Hyderabad: Orient Longman.

Robinson, F. P., 1912, *The Trade of the East India Company from c. 1709–c. 1813*. Cambridge, UK: Cambridge University Press.

Rosen, George, 1958, *Industrial Change in India*. Glencoe, IL: The Free Press.

Rosenberg, Nathan, 1976, *Perspectives on Technology*. Cambridge, MA: Cambridge University Press.

————, 2000, 'Charles Babbage in the Complex Word.' In *Complexity in History of Economic Thought*, edited by David Colander, 37–59. London and New York, NY: Routledge.

Rostow, W. W., 1957, *Stages of Economic Growth: A Non Communist Manifesto*. Cambridge, MA: Cambridge University Press.

————, 1963, *The Take-off into Self-sustained Growth*. London: Macmillan.

Rothermund, Dietmar, 1992, *India in the Great Depression, 1929–1939*. New Delhi: Manohar Publishers.

Rubin, Isaak Illich, 1979, *A History of Economic Thought*. London: Ink Links.

Ruderner, David, 1994, *Caste and Capitalism in Colonial India: The Nattukottai Chettiers*. Berkeley, CA: University of California Press.

Rungta, Radhey Shyam, 1970, *The Rise of Business Corporation in India, 1851–1900*. Cambridge, MA: Cambridge University Press.

Sampson, Anthony, 1996, *Company Man: The Rise and Fall of Corporate Life*. London: HarperCollins.

Sangar, S. P., 1974, 'Export of Indian Textiles to Middle East and Africa in the Seventeenth Century.' *Journal of Historical Research* 17, no. 1: 1–28.

Sanyal, H. R., 1968, 'The Indigenous Iron Industry of Birnbaum.' *The Indian Economic and Social History Review* 5, no. 1: 102–125.

Sarkar, Jadunath, 1973, *Shivaji and His Times*. New Delhi: Orient Longman.

Sarkar, S., 1983, *Modern India 1885–1947*. New Delhi: Macmillan.

Sarwani, Abbas Khan, 1974, *Tarikh-i-Shershahi*. Translated into English by B. P. Ambashthya. Patna: K.P. Jayaswal Research Institute.

Schmoller, Gustav von, 1902, *The Mercantile System and Its Historical Significance: Illustrated Chiefly from Prussian History*. New York, NY: Macmillan.

Schumpeter, J. A., 1934, *The Theory of Economic Development*. Cambridge, MA: Harvard University Press.

————, 1947, *Capitalism, Socialism and Democracy*. New York, NY: Harper & Brothers.

————, 1954, *History of Economic Analysis*. London: Oxford University Press.

Schwab, Raymond, 1984, *The Oriental Renaissance: Europe's Rediscovery of India and the East 1680–1880*. New York, NY: Columbia University Press.

Scott, William R., 1909–1912, *The Constitution and Finance of the English and Irish Joint-Stock Companies to 1720*, Vols. I–III. Cambridge, UK: Cambridge University Press.

Seabrook, Jeremy, 2014, *The Song of The Shirt: Cheap Cloth Across Continents and Centuries*. New Delhi: Nayana.

Sen, Sudipta, 1998, *Empire of Free Trade: East India Company and the Making of Colonial Market Place*. Philadelphia, PA: University of Philadelphia Press.

Sen, Sunil Kumar, 1972, *Studies in Economic Policy and Development of India 1848–1939*, Chapter II. New Delhi: Progressive Publishers.

Seth, Vijay K., 1987, *Industrialization in India: A Spatial Perspective*. New Delhi: Commonwealth Publications.

———, 1994, 'Labour Market Restructuring and Structural Adjustment Programme in India.' *Indian Journal of Labour Economics* 37, no. 4: 523–534.

———, 1998, 'Economic Reforms and Capacity Utilization in Indian Industry.' *Productivity* 39, no. 3: 391–398.

———, 1999, *Capacity Utilisation in Industry: Theory and Evidence*. New Delhi: Deep and Deep Publications.

———, 2002, 'Primitive Flexible to Modern Flexible Manufacturing and the Process of Skilling and Deskilling of Labor.' *Indian Journal of Labor Economics* 45, no. 4: 1175–1194.

———, 2003, 'The Beginning and the End of Primitive Flexible Manufacturing System.' *Journal of Management Research* 3, no. 2: 73–86.

———, 2006, *Economics of Services: A Story of Transformation of Cinderella into the Queen of Hearts*. New Delhi: Ane Books.

———, 2008, 'Primitive Flexible Manufacturing and Mughal Empire.' *Journal of Management Research* 8, no. 2: 76–95.

———, 2012, 'The East India Company: A Case Study in Corporate Governance.' *Global Business Review* 13, no. 2: 221–238.

———, 2014, 'Debate on De-industrialization Revisited: The Process of Decline of Traditional Flexible Manufacturing.' *Global Business Review* 15, no. 3: 597–610.

———, 2017, 'Tale of Two Cities of South Asia: Consequence of Changes in the Nature of Manufacturing on Dhaka and Kolkata.' *Global Business Review* 18, no. 6: 1613–1633.

———, 2018, *The Theory of Indian Manufacturing: Encounters with the Mughal and British Empire (1498–1947)*. Singapore: Palgrave Macmillan.

Sethia, Tara, 1996, 'The Rise of Jute Manufacturing Industry in Colonial India: A Global Perspective.' *Journal of World History* 7, no. 1: 35–56.

Shavell, S., 1979, 'Risk Sharing and Incentives in the Principal and Agent Relationship.' *Bell Journal of Economics* 10, no. 1: 53–73.

Shelvankar, K. S., 1940, *The Problem of India*. London: Penguin.

Shrikov, G. K., 1973, *Industrialization in India*. Moscow: Progress Publishing House.

Siddiqi, Asiya, 1982, 'The Business World of Jamsetjee Jeejeebhoy.' *The Indian Economic and Social History Review* 19, no. 3–4: 328–345.

———, 1995, 'The Business World of Jamsetjee Jeejeebhoy.' In *Trade and Finance in Colonial India 1750–1860*, edited by Asiya Siddiqi, 186–217. New Delhi: Oxford University Press.

———, 1995, *Trade and Finance in Colonial India 1750–1860*, edited by Asiya Siddiqi, 250–264. New Delhi: Oxford University Press.

Simmons, C., 1985, 'De-industrialization, Industrialization and the Indian Economy, c. 1850–1947.' *Modern Asian Studies* 19, no. 3: 593–672.

Singer, Chargles, E. J. Holmyard, A. R. Hall, and Trevor I. Williams, eds., 1958, *A History of Technology*, Vols. II–IV. Oxford, UK: Clarendon Press.

Singh, B., 1966, *European Agency Houses in Bengal*. Calcutta: Firma K. Mukhopadhyaya.

Singh, Chetan, 1991, *Region and Empire: Punjab in the Seventeenth Century*. New Delhi: Oxford University Press.

Singh, Khushwant, 1956, *A History of the Sikhs*, Vol. I. Oxford, UK: Oxford University Press.

Singh, M. P., 1977, 'Mulla Muhammad Ali: The Merchant Prince of Surat.' *Proceedings of the India History Congress*, 38. Held at Utkal University, Bhubaneswar on 28 December 1977.

Sinha, N. K., ed., 1968, *The Economic History of Bengal*. Calcutta: Firma K. Mukhopadhyaya.

———, 1992, 'Indian Business Enterprises Its Failure in Calcutta.' In *Entrepreneurship and Industry in India: 1800–1947*, edited by Rajat Kanta Ray, 70–82. New Delhi: Oxford University Press.

Sinha, P., 1990, 'Calcutta and Current History 1690–1912.' In *Calcutta: The Living City*, edited by S. Chaudhuri, Vol. 1, 33–44. New Delhi: Oxford University Press.

Smith, Adam, 1776 (2003), *The Wealth of Nations*. Introduction by Alan B. Krueger. New York, NY: Bantam Classics.

Smith, B. M. D., 1967, 'The Galtons of Birmingham: Quacker Gun Merchants and Bankers.' *Business History* 9, no. 2: 135–148.

Solymar, Laszlo, 1999, *Getting the Message: A History of Communication*. Oxford UK: Oxford University Press.

Spiro, K., 1992, *The City Assembled: Elements of Urban Form Through History*. London: Thames & Hudson.

Stein, Burton, 1985, 'State Formation and Economy Reconsidered.' *Modern Asian Studies* 19, no. 3: 387–413.

———, 1998, *A History of India*. New Delhi: Oxford University Press.

Stern, Philips, 2004, 'One Body Corporate and Politic: The Growth of East India Company State in the Late Seventeenth Century.' Unpublished PhD thesis, Columbia University, New York City.

Storper, Michael, 2008, 'Community and Economics.' In *Community, Creativity and Organization*, edited by Ash Amin and Joanne Roberts, 37–68. New York, NY: Oxford University Press.

Storper, M., and S. Christopherson, 1987, 'Flexible Specialization and Regional Agglomeration.' *Annal of the Association of American Geographers* 77, no. 1: 25–48.

Subramanian, Lakshmi, 1987, 'Banias and Business: The Role of Indigenous Credit in the Process of Imperial Expansion in Western India in the Second Half of the Eighteenth Century.' *Modern Asian Studies* 21, no. 3: 455–520.

———, 1987, 'The Castle Revolution of 1759 and the Banias of Surat; Changing British India Relations in Western India.' In *State and Business in India: A Historical Perspective*, edited by Dwijendra Tripathi, 91–122. New Delhi: Manohar Publishers.

———, 1996, *Indigenous Capital and Imperial Expansion: Bombay, Surat and the West Coast*. New Delhi: Oxford University Press.

———, 2010, *History of India 1707–1857*. New Delhi: Orient Blackswan.

———, 2014, *Three Merchants of Bombay: Doing Business in Times of Change*. New Delhi: Penguin India.

Subrahmanyam, Sanjay, 1990, *Improvising Empires: Portuguese Trade and Settlements in the Bay of Bengal 1500–1700*. Oxford, UK: Oxford University Press.

———, 1993, 'Of "Imarat and Tijarat": Asian Merchants and State Power in Western Indian Oceans 1400–1730.' *Comparative Studies in Society and History* 37, no. 4: 225–247.

———, 1993, *Portuguese Empire in Asia 1500–1700: A Political Economic History*. Oxford, UK: Oxford University Press.

Sullivan, Raymond, 1937, *One Hundred Years of Bombay*. Bombay: The Times of India Press.

Sutherland, Lucy, 1952, *The East India Company in the Eighteenth Century Politics*. Oxford, UK: Clarendon Press.

Taylor, F. W., 1947, *Scientific Management*. New York, NY: Harper & Row.

———, 1885 (1919), *Two Papers on Scientific Management*. London: Routledge.

Tchitchirov, Alexander L., 1998, *India: Changing Economic Structure in the Sixteenth–Eighteenth Centuries: Outline History of Crafts and Trade*. New Delhi: Manohar Publishers.

Thapar, Romila, 2002, *The Penguin History of Early India: From the Origins to AD 1300*. London: Penguin.

The Economist, 2006, 'Genghis Khan's Legacy: Battle for Mongolia's Soul.' 19 December.

Thevenot, Jean de, 1687 (1949), *Indian Travels of Thevenot and Careri*. Edited by Surendranath Sen. New Delhi: National Archives of India.

Thirsk, Joan, 1994, 'Industries in Countryside.' In *Pre-industrial Britain*, edited by J. A. Chartres. London: Blackwell Publishing.

Thomas Issac, T. M., 1984, 'Class Struggle and Industrial Structure: A Study of Coir Weaving Industry in Kerala 1859–1980.' PhD thesis, Centre for Development Studies, Thiruvananthapuram, Kerala.

Thorner, Daniel, 1950, *Investment in Empire, British Railways and Steam Shipping Enterprise 1825–1849*. Philadelphia, PA: University of Pennsylvania Press.

——, 1951, 'Great Britain and the Development of Indian Railways.' *The Journal of Economic History* XI, no. 4: 64–65.

Thorner, Daniel, and Alice Thorner, 1962, '"De-industrialization" in India 1881–1931.' In *Land and Labour in India*, edited by Daniel Thorner and Alice Thorner. New York, NY: Asia Publishing House.

Thorner, Daniel, 1980, *Shaping of Modern India*. Bombay: Sameeksha Trust.

Tilly, C., and Tilly, R., 1972, 'Agenda for European Economic History in 1970s.' *The Journal of Economic History* 31, no. 1: 176–196.

Tinberg, T. A., 1971, 'A Study of Great Marwari Firm: 1860–1914.' *The Indian Economic and Social History Review* 8, no. 3: 267–280.

Tirmizi, S. A. I., 1984, 'Muslim Merchant of Medieval Gujarat.' In *Business Communities of India: A Historical Perspective*, edited by Dwijendra Tripathi, 59–67. New Delhi: Manohar Publishers.

Tod, J., 1829 (1993), *Annals and Antiquities of Rajasthan*, Vols. I–III. Edited by W. Crooke. Reprint Bibliotheque.

Tomilson, Brian P., 1978, 'Foreign Private Investment in India 1920–1960.' *Modern Asian Studies* 12, no. 4, 655–677.

——, 1979, *Political Economy of the Raj*. London: Oxford University Press.

——, 1981, 'Colonial Firms and Decline of Colonialism in Eastern India 1914–1947.' *Modern Asian Studies* 15, no. 3: 455–486.

——, 1993, *The Economy of Modern India 1860–1970*. Cambridge, UK: Cambridge University Press.

Torri, Michelguglielmo, 1987, 'Surat During the Second Half of the Eighteenth Century: What Kind of Social Order?' *Modern Asian Studies* 21, no. 4: 679–710.

Torri, Michelguglielmo, 1991, 'Trapped Inside the Colonial Order: The Hindu Bankers of Surat and Their Business World in the Second Half of the Eighteenth Century.' *Modern Asian Studies* 25, no. 2: 280–325.

Toynbee, A., 1958, *Industrial Revolution*. Boston, MA: Beacon Press.

Travers, Robert, 2007, *Ideology and Empire in Eighteenth-century India: The British in Bengal*. Cambridge, UK: Cambridge University Press.

Trebilcock, C., 1969, '"Spin-Off" in British Economic History: Armaments and Industry 1760–1914.' *Economic History Review*, 2nd Session, 22, no. 3: 479–490.

Trentman, Frank, ed., 2012, *The Oxford Handbook of the History of Consumption*. Oxford, UK: Oxford University Press.

Tripathi, D., and M. Mehta, 1990, 'The Nagarsheth of Ahmedabad: The History of Urban Institutions in a Gujarat City.' In *Essays in Medieval Indian Economic History*, edited by Satish Chandra. New Delhi: Munshiram Manoharlal Publishers.

Tripathi, Dwijendra, 1981, *The Dynamics of Tradition: Kasturbhai Lalbhai and His Entrepreneurship*. New Delhi: Manohar Publishers.

Tripathi, Dwijendra, 2004, *The Oxford History of Indian Business*. New Delhi: Oxford University Press.

———, 2011, 'From Community to Class: The Marwaris in a Historical Perspective.' In *The Oxford India Anthology of Business History*, edited by Medha M. Kudaisya, 133–142. New Delhi: Oxford University Press.

———, ed., 1991, *Business and Politics in India: A Historical Perspective*. New Delhi: Manohar Publishers.

Tripathi, Dwijendra, 1991, 'Business and Princely States: The Case of Baroda.' In *State and Business in India: A Historical Perspective*, edited by D. Tripathi, 274–301. New Delhi: Manohar Publishers.

Tripathi, Dwijendra, and Makrand Mehta, 1990, *Business Houses in Western India: A Study in Entrepreneurial Response, 1850–1956*. New Delhi: Manohar Publishers.

Trivedi, K. K., 1998, *Agra: Economic and Political Profile of a Mughal Suba: 1580–1707*. Pune: Ravish Publishers.

Tucker, Josiah, 1763, *The Case of Going to War: For the Sake of Procuring, Enlarging, or Securing of Trade, Considered in a New Light*. London: R. and J. Dodsley.

Tucker, Robert, and David Hendrickson, 1982, *The Fall of the first British Empire Origins of the war of American Independence*. University of Baltimore Press.

Ucko, Peter, and G. W. Dimbleby, eds., 1969, *The Domestication and Explanation of Plants and Animals*. Chicago, IL: Aldine Publishing Company.

Vanina, Eugenia, 2004, *Urban Crafts and Craftsmen in Medieval India: Thirteenth–Eighteenth Centuries*. New Delhi: Munshiram Manoharlal Publishers.

Vansanten, H. W., 1991, 'Trade Between Mughal India and Middle East and Mughal Monetary Policy.' In *Asian Trade Routes: Continental and Maritime*, edited by Karl Reinhold Haellquist. London: Routledge, Scandinavian Institute of Asian Studies.

Varadarajan, Lotika, 2012, 'Pre-industrial Indian Textile Technology and Central Asian Influence.' In *History of Technology in India*, Vol. II, edited by Harbans Mukhia, 276–294. New Delhi: Indian National Science Academy.

———, 1999, 'Syncretic Symbolism and Textiles: Indo-Thai Expression.' In *Commerce and Culture in Bay of Bengal 1500–1800*, edited by Om Prakash and Denys Lombard, 361–382. New Delhi: Oxford University Press.

Varshney, Ashutosh, 1999, *Democracy, Development, and the Countryside: Urban–Rural Struggles in India*. New York, NY: Cambridge University Press.

Verdier, Daniel, 2002, *Moving Money: Banking and Finance in the Industrialized World*. New York, NY: Cambridge University Press.

Verelst, Harry, 1776, *A View of the Rise, Progress, and Present State of the English Government in Bengal*. London: J. Nourse.

Verma, Tripta, 1994, *Karkhanas Under the Mughals*. New Delhi: Pragati Publications.

Victor, Hehn, 1885, *Wanderings of Plants and Animals from Their First Home*. Edited by James S. Stallybrass. London: Swan Sonnenshein.

Vijay Bhaskar, M., 2001, 'Industrial Formation Under Conditions of Flexible Accumulation: The Case of Global Knitwear Node in Southern

India.' Unpublished PhD thesis, Centre for Development Studies, Thiruvananthapuram, Kerala (Mimio).

Vogt, John, 1975, 'Notes on Portuguese Trade in West Africa 1480–1540.' *International Journal of African Historical Studies* 8, no. 4: 625–648.

Wacha, D. E., 1910, *A Financial Chapter in the History of Bombay City.* Bombay: A. J. Combridge & Co.

Walker, B., 1968, *Hindu World: An Encyclopedic Survey Hinduism.* London: Allen & Unwin.

Wallace, D. R., 1928, *Romance of Jute: A Short History of the Calcutta Jute Mill Industry 1855–1927.* London: W. Thacker & Co.

Watson, J. Fabes, 1879, *Report on Cotton Gins and Cleaning Quality Indian Cotton.* London: Indian Office Library.

———, 1887, *The Textile Manufactures and Costumes of the People of India.* London: Indian Office Library.

Watson, Peter, 2006, *Ideas in History of Thoughts and Invention from Fire to Freud.* New York, NY: Harper Perennial.

Weatherford, Jack, 2004, *Genghis Khan and Making of the Modern World.* New York, NY: Crown Publishers.

Weber, Alfred, 1929, *Theory of Location of Industry.* Translated by C. J. Friedrich from German) Chicago, IL: Chicago University Press.

Weber, Max, 1927, *General Economic History.* Translated from German by Frank H. Knight. New York, NY: Greenberg.

———, 1958, *Religion of India: The Sociology of Hinduism and Buddhism.* Translated and edited by Hans H. Gerth and Don Martindale. New York, NY: Free Press.

———, 1958, *The Protestant Ethic and the Spirit of Capitalism.* New York, NY: Charles Scribner's Sons.

Weiss, A., 1990, *Efficiency Wages: A Model of Unemployment Lay-offs and Wage Dispersion.* Oxford, UK: Clarendon Press.

Wenger, E. C., 1998, *Community of Practice: Learning, Meaning and Identity.* Cambridge, UK: Cambridge University Press.

West, E. J., 1976, *Adam Smith: The Man and His Work.* Indianapolis, IN: Liberty Press.

White, David L., 1979, *Parsis as Entrepreneurs in the 18th Century Western India: The Rustom Manok Family and Parsi Community of Surat and Bombay.* PhD dissertation, University of Virginia.

Whiteway, R. S., 1889, *The Rise of Portuguese Power in India: 1497–1550.* Westminster: Archibald Constable & Co.

Wild, Anthony, 1999, *The East India Company: Trade and Conquest from 1600.* London: Harper Collins.

Willams, K., T. Cutler, J. Williams, and C. Hasham, 1987, 'The End of Mass Production?' *Economy and Society* 16, no. 3: 405–439.

Williams, Neville, 1965, *Chronology of the Modern World.* London: Penguin Books.

Wilson, Charles, 1965, *England's Apprenticeship 1603–1963.* London: Longman.

Wilson, Charles, 1994, 'Entrepreneurship in Industrial Revolution.' In *The Industrial Revolution in Britain*, edited by John Happit and E. A. Wrigley, 305–328. Oxford, UK: Blackwell.

Winch, Donald, 1978, *Adam Smith's Politics: An Essay in Historiographic Revision*. Cambridge, UK: Cambridge University Press.

Wink, Andre, 1986, *Land and Sovereignty in India: Agrarian Society and Politics Under the Eighteen Century Maratha Swarajya*. Cambridge, UK: Cambridge University Press.

Wiser, William Hendrick, 1969, *The Hindu Jajmani System*. Lucknow: Lucknow Publishing House.

Womack, J. P., and D. T. Jones, 1996, *Lean Thinking Banish Waste and Create Wealth in Your Corporation*. New York, NY: Simon and Schuster.

Womack, J. P., D. T. Jones, and D. Ross, 1990, *The Machine That Changed the World: The Story of Lean Production*. New York, NY: Rawson Associates.

Wright, Rita, 2010, *The Ancient Indus Urbanism Economy and Society*. Cambridge, UK: Cambridge University Press.

Wright, Ronald, 2000, *Stolen Continents: A Conquest and Resistance in the America*. London: Phoenix Press.

Wrigley, E. A., 1988, *Continuity Chance and Change: The Character of Industrial Revolution in England*. Cambridge, UK: Cambridge University Press.

Wrigley, E. A., and Schofield Roger, 1981, *The Population History of England 1541–1871: A Reconstruction*. Oxford, UK: Oxford University Press.

Zeitlin, Jonathan, 1995, 'Flexibility and Mass Production at War: Aircraft Manufacturing in Britain United States, and Germany, 1939–1945.' *Technology and Culture* 36, no. 1: 46–49.

INDEX

ABOUT THE AUTHOR

Vijay K. Seth, PhD (Delhi School of Economics), is former Professor at International Management Institute, New Delhi, and Faculty of Management Studies, University of Delhi. He has authored seven books, including *The Story of Indian Manufacturing: Encounters with the Mughal and British Empires (1498–1947)*, published in 2018. He has also published around one hundred research papers, chapters in edited books, review articles and book reviews which have appeared in a number of Indian and foreign journals. He has presented several research papers in India and abroad. Dr Seth is the founding editor of *Emerging Economy Studies*, a journal published by SAGE India. Dr Seth has travelled widely across Europe and trekked in various parts of the Himalayas and the Eastern and Western Ghats of India.